Architecture and Waste

A (Re)Planned Obsolescence

Hanif Kara
Leire Asensio Villoria
Andreas Georgoulias

Harvard University
Graduate School of Design

ARCHITECTURE AND WASTE:
A (RE)PLANNED OBSOLESCENCE

Published by
Actar Publishers
Harvard University Graduate School of Design

Distributed by
Actar D USA
440 Park Avenue South, 17th Floor
New York, NY 10016
T +1 212 966 2207
F +1 212 966 2214
salesnewyork@actar-d.com

Actar D Europe
Roca i Batlle 2
E-08023 Barcelona
T +34 93 417 49 93
F +34 93 418 67 07
office@actar-d.com
www.actar-d.com

IMPRINT

ISBN 978-1-945150-05-0
Library of Congress Control Number: 2016958863

The idea presented here—that it is possible to use the most advanced waste management processes to promote interdisciplinary cooperation in which the architectural, structural, and thermodynamic aspects, suitably combined, would generate urban units with new political and social contents—suggests a way of understanding technical, cultural, and social interactions that lie at the heart of a large number of professionals in charge of considering future scenarios of global cities and metropolitan areas.

Foreword

IÑAKI ÁBALOS

Professor in Residence and Chair of the Department of Architecture,
Harvard University Graduate School of Design

Architecture and Waste: A (Re)Planned Obsolescence is undoubtedly a magnificent manual for rethinking the method in which we manage resources and the ways in which industrial architecture can be considered today with renewed vigour. But it is not just that. This book conceals, in a sophisticated manual, the ambition of a real treatise on the relations between technology, culture, and society. In other words, by choosing a precise type of waste recycling plant and analyzing its whole potential on different scales, this book gives rise to a considerable list of questions regarding architecture and its kindred spirit, engineering, pointing to the new environmental technological developments as triggering factors of new prototypes with forceful urban and disciplinary repercussions. The initiative that gives rise to this project, resulting from specialized investigations carried out in Scandinavia and which comes to the Harvard University Graduate School of Design in search of experimental answers in architecture, could not be more exemplary.

The idea presented here—that it is possible to use the most advanced waste management processes to promote interdisciplinary cooperation in which the architectural, structural, and thermodynamic aspects, suitably combined, would generate urban units with new political and social contents—suggests a way of understanding technical, cultural, and social interactions that lie at the heart of the interests of the Department of Architecture at the Harvard University Graduate School of Design (GSD) and, of course, of a large number of professionals in charge of considering future scenarios of global cities and metropolitan areas.

The splendid work led by Hanif Kara, Leire Asensio Villoria, and Andreas Georgoulias and developed by the students of the Harvard GSD, combines a series of research seminars and option studios to shape a book for considering architecture, its types, and its urban, social, technological, and formal interactions, much like an open door to the most advanced architectural research to arise after the agonizing death of the postmodern episode and its iconic and banal imitators. This open door is based on a precise genealogy in which the ideas of Joseph Paxton (Crystal Palace), Cedric Price (Fun Palace), and Buckminster Fuller (Montreal Biosphere) harmonize with the great palaces of the past (Baths of Caracalla and Hagia Sophia, for example), dealing in its way with collective needs from new formulations of the form/matter/energy equation, which make architecture a science and an art that is always the same, yet always changing.

This book is also a methodological model for rethinking other disciplinary aspects that are of concern to both industry and the academic world, such as housing, data centers, heating and cooling systems, large intermodal transport infrastructures, and more.

On a personal note, I can add that my early experience with industrial architecture (water purification and waste recycling plants) was a true revelation, not only regarding how the excess could and should be disposed of in nonindustrial architecture, but also, and in a more in-depth fashion, about the relationship between the different scales of matter, from the molecular structure of various materials to urban planning methods, and the essentially reactionary viewpoint that understood the architect's work as a cosmetic treatment of outsides or facades. Applying those lessons to works and projects with very small programs or urban and regional scales helps further a better understanding of the interaction and connectivity of the social, environmental, and material processes that give our work meaning.

Architecture and Waste engages these issues and it is for this reason that we can hail its publication with the emotion that accompanies the presence of good architecture. And it is extraordinary to find how teachings that combine research and design, when they are approached strictly and with knowledge, can extend in the academic field where they were devised and so become a real laboratory of the future to be built.

7

Acknowledgments

The Waste-to-Energy Design Lab and this publication would not have been possible without many activities and multiple collaborations, especially the support of Mohsen Mostafavi, Patricia Roberts, Iñaki Ábalos, and Anne Matthews at the Harvard University Graduate School of Design. The three authors wrote the book's content, created diagrams, and developed charts. Our research associate, Laura Smead, took a lead in editing the manuscript, drafting text and graphics, producing layout, and working out numerous details. Our tireless research assistants played important roles related to research assistance, writing, and graphics production. They included Georgios Athanasopoulos, Michael Clapp, Alberto Embriz de Salvatierra, Carlos Felix Raspall Galli, Nikos Georgoulias, Yinjia Gong, Daniel Hemmendinger, Kyriaki Kasabalis, Elaine Kwong, Ethan Levine, Katie MacDonald, Jana Masset, Alkistis Mavroeidi, Olga Mesa, Felipe Oropeza Jr., Zach Seibold, Aman Singhvi, Ling Li Tseng, and Nélida Escobedo. Interactions with architects Iñaki Ábalos, Peter Rowe, Jean Mazaud, and Bjarke Ingels provided extremely useful input.

The Sven Tyréns Trust provided funding for the overall Waste-to-Energy (WtE) Design Lab project. We particularly thank Chief Executive Officer Ulrika Francke and Executive Vice President Birgitta Olofsson of Tyréns, and their representatives Elisabet Hoglund, Anna Sjostrom, Karl Graah-Hagelbäck, Håkan Rosqvist, and Christer Andersson for providing background material and reviewing our research, proposals, and designs. We also thank the plant managers, planners, operators, and designers at the numerous WtE facilities we visited across Europe and in the United States, including John Vinson, Barbara Vars-Breton, Monica Jackson, Niklas Svensson, Johan Alsparr, Tomas Nilsson, Tomas Hago, Niclas Åkerlund, Jan Andhagen, Jesper Baaring, Per Kind, and Claus Hermansen.

At the Harvard University Graduate School of Design, Publications Editor-in-Chief Jennifer Sigler and writer/editor Krista Sykes provided helpful comments and advice. ACTAR Director Ramon Prat created the elegant layout templates. Anita Kan photographed the work of the WtE Design Lab seminar and options studio, as well as related events.

We also thank the following individuals for their contributions:

Anders Agebro, Mounir Ainholm, Tomas Alsmarker, Jesper Baaring, Larry Barth, Martin Bechthold, Jennifer Bonner, Eric Carlsson, Salvardor Cejudo Ramos, Salmaan Craig, Petter Eklund, Ulrica Ericsson, Andreas Eriksson, Sofi Erselius, Stellan Fryxell, Camilo Galletti, Max Goldstein, James Grant, Terence Hales, Ari Halinoja, Malin Harders, Patrick Heddini, Cristoffer Högberg, Andrew Holder, Bjarni Ingvason, El Hadi Jazairy, Anton Johansson, Britt-Marie Josefsson, Mårten Juvander, Iro Kalogeropoulou, Bettina Kamuk, Pernilla Knutsson, Dorthe Lærke, Grace La, Fredrik Lange, Elerin Laud, Chris Lee, Mårten Leringe, Hans Linnman, David Mah, Aleksandra Masalska-Skwira, Marcus Mattson, Matan Mayer, Fredrik Moberg, Kiel Moe, Anders Ohlin, Richard Pålsson, Tom Phelps, Nina Rappaport, Nathalie Rasti, Åsa Rodin, Therese Rowland, Petra Sörme, Jakob Sahlén, Jennita Schaaphot, Alexander Ståhl, Frida Stockhaus, Lovisa Strandlund, Geert Stryg, Belinda Tato, Jeremy Thompson, Lena Tomani, Fanny Wahlqvist, Lotta Werner, Tina Wik, and Maja Zachrisson.

A Mill Street, 1907

Introduction

As the world's population rapidly expands, the need for architects' engagement in the industrial and infrastructural realm becomes increasingly urgent. Yet, with the exception of a few cases, architects remain conspicuously absent from the conception, design, and implementation of such projects.

With the knowledge collected in *Architecture and Waste,* derived from two years of intense design research, we investigate, explore, and challenge the roots of this divide, seeking opportunities to reverse it by focusing on the Waste-to-Energy (WtE) facility. In the context of this subject, WtE facility buildings bridge (in scale, function, and output) the gap between conventional industrial buildings (factories) and large-scale infrastructural facilities (such as airports and power stations). Using WtE infrastructure as a manageable vehicle, we demonstrate that, when approached from an architectural perspective, building types associated with WtE offer tremendous opportunities for innovation, creativity, and community enrichment.

We therefore offer *Architecture and Waste* as a manual on two fronts. First, we envision the book as a guide for architects as they engage in the design of buildings in the industrial and infrastructural field. Initiated as a design research effort at the Harvard University Graduate School of Design (GSD) and sponsored by the Sven Tyréns Trust, this material embodies a precise and replicable methodology to assist architects as they approach these project types, since often viewed as existing outside the purview of contemporary practice. Second, the book functions as a detailed resource for architects and others involved with WtE facility design. It contains an inventory of WtE components and their requirements, as well as an illustrative catalog of WtE plant design strategies, tactics, and spatial configurations. As both a general and targeted guide, and as the subtitle *(Re)Planned Obsolescence* suggests, this body of work also questions the concept of architectural waste and investigates opportunities for buildings to remain in use, even after their initial functions become obsolete.

Architects, Waste, and Design Research

HANIF KARA

Baltimore from Federal Hill, 1903

13

Thomas Pritchard, Iron Bridge,
Coalbrookdale, England, 1779

Walter Gropius and Adolf Meyer, Faguswerke
Factory, Alfeld (Leine), Germany, 1912

Albert Kahn, Packard Motor Company,
Detroit, Michigan, United States, 1911

WHY ARCHITECTS?

Today architects play a minor role in the design of industrial and infrastructural projects. Yet this was not always the case. The history of modern architecture, intricately tied to the rise of industrialization from the mid-18th century on, is rife with architects' contributions to the industrial realm. Innovative creations such as Thomas Pritchard's Iron Bridge at Coalbrookdale, England (1775–1779)—often cited as the first single-span cast-iron structure—purportedly set the stage for later developments, including Walter Gropius and Adolf Meyer's seemingly weightless Faguswerke factory in Alfeld on Leine, Germany (1911–1912), which is hailed as an embodiment of an early 20th-century industrial aesthetic.[1] Likewise, across the Atlantic Ocean, Albert Kahn utilized reinforced concrete to design a series of wide-span automotive plants, ideal environments for the efficient assembly-line production, or Taylorization, for which Henry Ford's factories became known. These are but a few of the many architects who worked on industrial architecture alongside businessmen and engineers in the early 20th century.

In the years following World War II and as the global economy moved toward recovery in the 1950s and 1960s, architects continued their involvement with industrial projects. The United States saw architects such as Eero Saarinen and the firm Skidmore, Ownings & Merrill engaged in industrial work, notably with their contributions to the burgeoning industrial campus complex type. In Europe, architects such as Angelo Mangiarotti in Italy, Fritz Haller in Switzerland, and Norman Foster in England began enlisting prefabricated modular building systems, which allowed vast, flexible, open-span factories to accommodate a variety of manufacturing setups. These prefab systems, which could be erected more quickly and more economically than previous industrial buildings, became a widespread alternative to individually designed factories.

Not surprisingly, the building owners' desire to cut costs coupled with the efficiency of prefabricated modular systems to steadily eclipse the architect's role in industrial building design. Mass production and "industrialized systems" hastened the rapid construction of many different building types during this period. Simultaneously, seeing fewer opportunities for creativity in such "mundane" or "ugly" work, architects turned their attention away from industrial and infrastructural projects. Additionally, the growth of other disciplines gave

Angelo Mangiarotti, FM Constructive System Factory Building, Lissone, Monza, Italy, 1964

Foster and Associates, Reliance Controls Electronics, London, England, 1967 rise to engineers and project managers, who legitimately claimed to be able to produce buildings rather than "design" them, further undermining the role of the architect.

Despite the shift to service- and knowledge-oriented industries in the latter 20th and early 21st centuries, a time marked by the emergence of widespread economic and ecological changes, architects' contributions to these building types have remained conspicuously absent. Yet this need not be the case. Architects bring much to the conception and creation of such projects, beginning with a holistic approach that extends beyond functionality to embrace the physical, social, and environmental issues that affect each project. By virtue of education and experience, architects hone the ability to devise creative spatial configurations to address real-world problems. Furthermore, architects are trained to design not just for the present, but for the future ways in which buildings may be used. This skill in particular figures prominently into our contemporary landscape, where in many cases a building's physical presence may long outlive its initial purpose. And, as numerous examples in our past and present demonstrate, such industrial buildings do not have to be ugly.

The past few decades saw a minor eruption in the adaptation of redundant existing industrial buildings and large-scale infrastructures for public use. Projects like the Tate Modern (England, Herzog & de Meuron) and the Hamburg Philharmonic (Germany, Herzog & de Meuron); the Rosario Museum of Contemporary Art (Argentina, Ermete de Lorenzi); the Zollverein Power Station (Germany, Rem Koolhaas's Office for Metropolitan Architecture, Böll and Krabel); the High Line (United States, Diller Scofido + Renfro); the Contemporary Jewish Museum (United States, Studio Libeskind); and the Modern Museum of Malmö (Sweden, Tham & Videgård Arkitekter) have captured the public imagination and become new architectural touchstones. Note that many of these readapted structures exist in developed areas that have transformed from industrial to service societies (a cycle likely to repeat in the future). In addition, these projects involve not only the reuse of materials, but also a respect for the old while infusing the new. They are complex projects that encourage cultural interactions and multiple programs in spaces previously conceived for singular functions and occupied by only a few individuals.

Architects bring much to the conception and creation of such projects, beginning with a holistic approach that extends beyond functionality to embrace the physical, social, and environmental issues that affect each project.

Herzog & de Meuron, Hamburg Philharmonic, Hamburg, Germany, 2017

Ermete de Lorenzi, Rosario Museum of Contemporary Art, Rosario, Argentina, 2004

Fritz Schupp and Martin Kremmer, Zollverein Power Station, Essen, Germany, 1932

Diller Scofidio + Renfro, Field Operations, and Piet Oudolf, High Line, New York, United States, 2009

Studio Libeskind, Contemporary Jewish Museum, San Francisco, United States, 2005

Tham & Videgård Arkitekter, Modern Museum of Malmö, Malmö, 2009

These buildings and structures were initially created to serve a specific use; yet through architectural interventions, they have been successfully repurposed as cultural icons. Architects introduced unique skills and perspectives to these transformational projects, all largely well received. In turn, these adaptations have bolstered their architects' reputations. We believe that architects can add similar value to, and likewise benefit from, the design of industrial and infrastructural projects. In particular, we are focused on WtE facilities, which are much needed in both developing and developed societies.

Along with global population growth and increased urbanization comes an exponential rise in the production of solid waste. In 2012, urban populations generated roughly 1.3 billion tons of solid waste. By 2025, the World Bank estimates that this number will likely increase to 2.2 billion tons.[2] How do we address this mounting volume of waste? This question becomes all the more pressing when we consider that landfills—currently (and historically) the most prevalent means of waste disposal—are quickly becoming less plausible due to space restrictions, environmental concerns, mandates to close existing sites, and legislation that prevents the creation of new landfills.

Waste-to-Energy facilities offer a proven and increasingly attractive solution for dealing with solid waste. Indeed, far from the pollution-spewing industrial behemoths of yore, WtE plants are an environmentally conscious option for coping with garbage. Strategically placed near or within urban areas, WtE plants can generate alternative energy for local use and eliminate the need to transport waste to rural areas or across state lines, thus reducing travel-related emissions. And as we will later discuss in detail, WtE infrastructure offers a range of beneficial possibilities for future development, including opportunities to develop hybrid programs that positively impact their communities. Such innovative arrangements are already in operation in Sweden, recognized as a leader in WtE use, as well as other countries.

WHY WASTE-TO-ENERGY?

There is little doubt that, as the world's population grows, local WtE infrastructure will be increasingly needed in cities. As densities increase and consumption patterns change, WtE will continue to emerge as an acceptable and affordable source of renewable energy alongside a portfolio of other sources, such as solar, wind, and biomass. As additional WtE infrastructure is conceived and constructed, architects' involvement will help ensure the best functional, social, and aesthetic results. Indeed, a handful of high-profile architects, including Bjarke Ingels and Zaha Hadid, have recently engaged in WtE projects, signaling a shift in thought regarding the desirability of and value generated by architects' involvement in such projects.

With these ideas in mind, we selected WtE facilities as a means to reengage architects and interdisciplinary design with industrial buildings and infrastructure. We conducted design research on novel and effective ways to rethink the relationship of architecture and waste—a (re)planned obsolescence.

THE WASTE MANAGEMENT HIERARCHY

The Waste Management Hierarchy is an internationally recognized ranking of the various waste management practices in the order from most to least preferred with respect to greenhouse gas emissions. Priority is given towards the prevention and reuse of waste followed by recycling, energy recovery, and disposal. Energy recovery from the combustion of Municipal Solid Waste (MSW) is a critical component to this hierarchy because it diverts and ultimately decreases the total volume of waste that would have otherwise been destined for landfills. The WtE Design Lab chose to narrow the focus of design speculation around the method combustion—as opposed to pyrolysis and gasification—because it is the most widely implemented. Ranked a tier above natural gas but just below solar photo voltaic, the energy produced by this renewable energy source has a reduced carbon emission record—as compared to petroleum and coal—by offsetting the need for energy from fossil fuel sources and reducing methane generation from landfills.

Ábalos & Herreros, Northeast Coastal Park, Barcelona, Spain, 2004

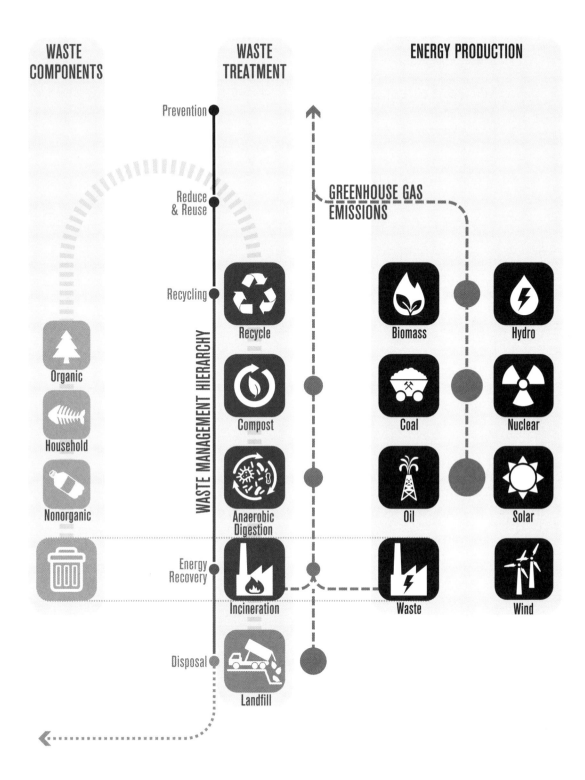

WASTE COMPONENTS

WASTE TREATMENT

ENERGY PRODUCTION

Prevention

Reduce & Reuse

GREENHOUSE GAS EMISSIONS

Recycling

Organic

Recycle

Biomass

Hydro

WASTE MANAGEMENT HIERARCHY

Household

Compost

Coal

Nuclear

Nonorganic

Anaerobic Digestion

Oil

Solar

Energy Recovery

Incineration

Waste

Wind

Disposal

Landfill

NOTES

1. William J. R. Curtis, *Modern Architecture Since 1900*, 3rd ed. (Phaidon: London, 1996), 104.

2. Daniel Hoornweg and Perinaz Bhada-Tata, *What a Waste: A Global Review of Solid Waste Management*, Urban Development Series, Knowledge Papers no.15 (Washington, DC: World Bank, 2012), https://openknowledge .worldbankorg/handle/10986/17388.

Comparison of WtE facilities' greenhouse gas emissions to those of other energy generation technologies; the waste hierarchy including WtE energy recovery process; and landfill disposal practices ranked by greenhouse gas emissions

The history of industrial architecture is deeply rooted in the history of modern architecture. Looking back at modern architecture's origins, we see that it corresponds to and is contiguous with industrial architecture from the Industrial Revolution through the 1900s. As industry grew and diversified through the 19th and 20th centuries, architectural and engineering systems reacted with new materials, such as iron, steel, glass, aluminum, and reinforced concrete, and new forms that corresponded to these materials. Indeed, the architecture of industry and the machine aesthetic directly influenced architects central to the modern movement, including Karl Friedrich Schinkel, Auguste Perret, Le Corbusier, and Mies van der Rohe. Yet the emergence of technology, computation, and telecommunication at the turn of the 21st century has changed this equation, prompting new modes of design, materials, and production.

While industrial architecture and, to a certain extent, the infrastructure for modern urbanism share a common set of materials, methods, and techniques, only recently can we begin to separate the dynamics of industrial architecture from the currents of modern architecture. One reason for this clarification is that the transformation wrought by the information age has generated its own architecture with concomitant effects on industry and industrial architecture. These recent changes have precipitated a different type of industry and consequently a new, different architecture. This cleavage allows us to outline a history of industrial architecture that is distinct from modern architecture's stylistic and social concerns. Furthermore, we can revisit the industry's history and transformations with the understanding that, in the future, industry as we know it today may change drastically. Technological innovation in the 19th and early 20th centuries fundamentally altered architecture by producing materials that made construction more effective, robust, and flexible. Today a similar transformation may occur through 21st-century technology, producing equally dramatic results.

Industrial Buildings Don't Have To Be Ugly

HANIF KARA

John McAslan + Partners, Olympic Energy Centres, London, England, 2012

Thinking about a possible "end of industry" and its historic continuum allows us to articulate the history of industrial architecture more clearly. Since its inception in the mid-1700s, industrial architecture had reacted to and motivated by the industry it served, rising on the social and economic foundation provided by industrialization and industrial capitalism. Now with the possibility of major disruption to industry as it has been practiced for 200 years, we have a new perspective to understand these longstanding alignments between industry, modernity, architecture, and engineering within the context of contemporary business developments and corporate capitalism. With this in mind, let us rehearse a brief history of industrial architecture, drawing primarily from Western European and North American examples. Our goal is to highlight important milestones and benchmarks that provide a foundation for the work we set forth in here in *Architecture and Waste*.

18TH AND 19TH CENTURIES

The early iron factories and bridges of England stand as the origins of today's industrial architecture. The first dramatic icon of the Industrial Revolution, Abraham Darby III and architect Thomas Pritchard's Iron Bridge at Coalbrookdale (1775–1779), took advantage of the new technique of smelting iron using coke to produce cast iron. A part of the era's new and growing railway-based distribution network, the Iron Bridge and its contemporaries planted the seed for industrial building and architecture as we know it.

Throughout the late 18th and early 19th centuries, cast iron became an increasingly popular material for bridges, railway stations, warehouses, and factories—all structures integral to the development and growth of the Industrial Revolution. Indeed, factories were not only settings for the manufacture of the Industrial Revolution's new products; they were themselves produced by these new construction methods. This was particularly evident in mills in northern England such as Charles Bage's Shrewsbury Mill (1796–1797), which was the first iron-frame building to use cast-iron columns and beams. Bage's design was inspired by engineer William Strutt's use of iron for industrial architecture. Bage was also an associate of steam-engine producers Matthew Boulton and James Watt, who provided engines to power this mill as well as the Twist Mill in Salford, Manchester (1799–1801), which utilized the same combination of structural

Jules Saulnier, Menier Chocolate Factory,
Noisiel-sur-Marne, France, 1873

22

cast-iron beams supported by round columns integrated into a brick wall. The amalgamation of architecture, engineering, and industry seen in these mills is indicative of the close relations these disciplines would maintain for the following two hundred years.

The second half of the 19th century in England and Europe saw a number of industrial buildings constructed in iron, similar to Joseph Paxton's Crystal Palace in London (1851), that attempted to adapt iron construction to existing architectural styles. The Menier Chocolate Factory in Noisiel-sur-Marne, France (1871–1873), by architect Jules Saulnier, is typical of industrial architecture that radically employed, for the first time, an iron skeleton visible on the exterior but subsumed within an envelope of decorative brickwork.

The most important cast-iron system from the early 19th century, preceding the later combinations of iron and steel, appears in the Sheerness Boat Store in Kent, England (1856–1860). Designed by engineer Colonel Godfrey Greene, the multistoried warehouse has a cast-iron frame clad in lightweight sheet-metal panels with large windows. This structure was the first of is kind to employ manufactured beams, columns, panels, and glass plates, foreshadowing the steel-framed, steel-paneled sheds of the 20th century. Built around the same time as the Crystal Palace, the Boat Store's stark and simple cast-iron design, hidden largely from public view in its industrial riverside location, contrasted with the decoratively embellished cast-iron architecture employed by Paxton. Greene proposed no aesthetic for his design, relying instead on the formal properties of the structure and its materials as an engineering solution, a strategy that would be repeated frequently across the globe throughout the 20th century.

EARLY 20TH CENTURY

Throughout the 20th century, the demands of industry—in particular the pressing need to develop building systems to accommodate the speed and scale of fast-growing industries—dictated the nature of industrial architecture. This especially can be seen in the development of reinforced-concrete construction technology by figures such as Ernest Ransome and Robert Maillart in the early part of the 20th century, which went on to play a key role in the rapid growth of industrial architecture in factory buildings. Examples, such as Ransome's Pacific Coast Borax Factory in Bayonne, New Jersey (1895), and later Maillart's Pirelli Cable Factory in Villanueva, Barcelona (1901–1902), utilized reinforced concrete to build a modular system of columns supporting glazed roofs.

This was the beginning of the iconic saw-tooth form, which would be associated with factory buildings for many years and arose from the need to introduce daylight into the shed structures to support workflow while preventing additional heat buildup. Concurrent innovations in reinforced concrete and glass allowed for the rapid construction of large shed structures throughout the industrial world. Yet, in architectural terms, they generated only a few buildings of distinction. One of these factories was Giacomo Mattè-Trucco's Fiat Lingotto Factory in Turin, Italy (1922), with its rooftop test track making it one of the most original of the period. There was also Erich Mendelsohn's angular crystal form comprised of brick with a reinforced-concrete skeleton, the Hat Factory in Luckenwalde, Germany (1921). Nevertheless, for many of the industrial buildings of this era, architecture was second in priority to technical advancements in reinforced concrete, steel structures, fire insulation, ventilation, and lighting. On the whole, economic interests led industrial architecture.

Earlier in the century, Germany was responsible for what is considered the genesis of modern industrial architecture; this is the first time we can identify a meaningful union of industry and architecture in the context of new architectural theory and education, pointing toward a modern architecture based on the ideals of industry and industrial architecture. The establishment of the Deutscher Werkbund (1907) and the Bauhaus in Weimar (1919) are two examples of an alignment between the German economy and German architecture. This modern architecture sought to harmonize aesthetics and engineering, relying heavily on a century's worth of architectural theory by the likes of

J. A. Brinkman & L. C. van der Vlugt, Van Nelle Factory, Rotterdam, the Netherlands, 1929

Marc-Antoine Laugier, Eugène Violet-le-Duc, Henri Labrouste, Gottfried Semper, Auguste Choisy, Auguste Perret, and Charles Garnier. In particular, Garnier's ideas, outlined in his Cité Industrielle, introduced the idea of industrial buildings as important parts of the modern city, situated next to areas of habitation.

The evolution of German industrial architecture can be shown by two important industrial buildings of the early 20th century, the AEG Turbine Hall in Berlin (1909) by Peter Behrens, and the Faguswerke Factory in Alfeld (Leine, 1911–1914) by Walter Gropius and Adolf Meyer. While the AEG Turbine Hall retains some symbolic neoclassical character to its architecture, the Faguswerke Factory abandons all but a latent symmetry, shifting to a complete commitment to rational and scientific architecture in a factory building that emphasizes structure, glass, and light. The Faguswerke's transparent architecture was a response to the client, entrepreneur Carl Benscheidt, who demanded that the factory be well lit and make a break from architecture of the past. Gropius's design successfully navigates this combination of functional and symbolic requirements to create a factory typology that had many successors in the 20th century.

The major transformation that the architecture of the Faguswerke factory represents is seen more clearly when compared to Albert Kahn's Packard Motor Company factory in Detroit, Michigan (1905), which employed steel-reinforced concrete as the primary building material (for the first time in an automobile factory), but hid this structural skeleton behind a conventional facade. Kahn is sometimes considered the first industrial architect, though he was not necessarily a modernist. His projects, such as the Pierce Arrow Motor Car Company in Buffalo, New York (1906), the Ford Highland Park Plant in Highland, Michigan (1910), and the massive Ford River Rouge Complex in Dearborn, Michigan (1917), were landmark "generic" factory buildings for their time, driven by the rapid growth of the automotive industry in the United States and the development of the assembly line. They utilized decorative envelopes of brick or stone to conceal a concrete and steel structural framework, eschewing the aesthetic of industrial architecture then favored in Germany. Instead, Kahn's architecture was guided by his industrialist clients' business needs, with his own offices organized into a quasi production line, focusing on the managerial aspects of the construction process.

Peter Behrens, AEG Turbine Hall, Berlin, Germany, 1909

1930s AND 1940s

The outbreak of World War II in 1939 meant a temporary break in the development of industrial architecture, which was eclipsed by the war industry's need for the construction of a large number of generic steel and reinforced-concrete factories.

Prior to this, modern architecture had been emerging as a distinct style, with industrial architecture starting to appropriate some of its design features. This can be seen clearly in J. A. Brinkman & L. C. van der Vlugt's Van Nelle Factory in Rotterdam, the Netherlands (1929), with its wide, sweeping glass curtain wall subsumed within a carefully organized geometry of reinforced concrete that reflected the International Style of the time. The mushroom columns hidden behind the glass facade later emerged as an important visual feature of industrial architecture in Sir Owen Williams's Boots Pure Drug Factory in Nottingham, England (1932). In this multistory building, which housed different functions on each of the open floors, the prominent all-glass facade is supported awkwardly at its base by exposed reinforced-concrete mushroom columns. More typical of the 1930s were buildings such as the Borgward Automotive Factory in Bremen, Germany (1935–1937), by Rudolf Lodders, or Kahn's Chrysler Half-Ton Truck Plant in Warren, Michigan (1938), that used all-steel structures to create larger, more expansive factory floors with fewer columns to impede the manufacturing of large trucks and planes.

Erich Mendelsohn, Hat Factory,
Luckenwalde, Germany, 1921

1950s

The 1950s saw the emergence of a broad range of industrial architecture that took into account the more diversified nature of the global economy and industrial manufacturing, yet still fell under the influence of modern architecture's aesthetic. This period also saw the emergence of industry directed toward the consumer economy, made possible by large-scale modern infrastructure. In buildings for the production of raw materials, such as Alvar Aalto's A. Ahlström Company Sawmill in Varkaus, Finland (1944–1946), and Fritz Schupp's Germania Colliery in Dortmund, Germany (1952), we see how the architects clearly employed the clean geometries of modern architecture to organize the disparate industrial functions and structural elements into a unified design. In a similar modernist fashion, the Textile Mill in Blumberg, Germany (1950), by Egon Eiermann, subsumes the reinforced-concrete structure that holds up an expansive steel-trussed roof in the style of postwar modern architecture, achieving structural clarity in a building that was the first industrial building constructed in Germany after World War II.

In a comparable gesture to structural logic and visual clarity, the Cilag Chemical Factory in Milan, Italy (1952), by Giordano Forti, uses materials and techniques such as prefabricated concrete floors, reinforced-concrete columns, and steel-and-glass facades, embodying a constructivist style and a consistent design language that gives each building its individual character.

Reconstruction in postwar Europe often entailed the construction of industrial buildings in existing urban sites, limiting their size, while still allowing for the advancement of features specific to industrial architecture. One of the best examples of this is the Engineering Plant for Siemens & Halske in Braunschweig, Germany (1957), by Walter Henn, where we see clear attention to the aesthetics of the building in its urban context, along with the detailed optimization of construction and workplace qualities, such as light and ventilation in a large shed structure.

Alvar Aalto, A. Ahlström Company Sawmill, Varkhaus, Finland, 1946

Egon Eiermann, Textile Mill, Blumberg, Germany, 1950

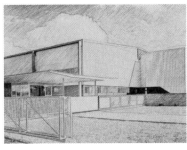

These trends were also reflected in the countries of Eastern Europe and the Sovietic bloc, which, since the 1930s, had applied long-range industry planning that included within its scope the construction of factories and infrastructure such as dams. Architecture in the Soviet states followed and mirrored developments in the West; Kahn had designed buildings in Russia in the 1930s, and in a few buildings of note, such as the Runotex Mill in Kalisz, Poland (1957–1962), by Stanisław Sikorski and Jerzy Główczewski, the application of suspended post-tensioned concrete panels created an innovative saw-tooth roof, showing an aspect of the creative design in Eastern Europe in this period.

In the United States, postwar reconstruction meant the expansion of corporate America, building factories in newly developing industrial parks or in large industrial/administrative campus-type complexes outside major cities. Examples by Kahn and Skidmore, Owings & Merrill were prominent, but the most important of these postwar industrial buildings is undoubtedly Eero Saarinen's General Motors Technical Center in Warren, Michigan (1946–1956); this series of low buildings, set around a reflecting pool, recalls the Illinois Institute of Technology campus designed by Mies van der Rohe in the 1940s. At the General Motors Technical Center Saarinen goes further, incorporating the technical aspects of the building into a futuristic vision of American corporate business strength that would, later in the century, expand throughout the United States and the rest of the world.

Eero Saarinen, General Motors Technical Center,
Warren, Michigan, United States, 1956

1960s

As a consequence of the worldwide economic boom, the 1960s can be seen as a golden age for industrial architecture. There were marked increases in the number of new factories, and infrastructural projects expanded in size and scale as part of this postwar period of high-productivity growth. Automation technologies aided the global expansion of manufacturing, while wholesale and retail trade advanced as a result of new highway systems, distribution warehouses, and material handling equipment such as forklifts. While the United States flexed the scale of its corporate muscle and industrial capacity, industrial architecture as a structural art and social-minded discipline found new avenues of expression in Europe and the rest of the world. In this period, structural innovation such as modular steel systems, prefabricated concrete elements, and concrete shells joined new developments in buildings that displayed sensitivity to workplace conditions as well as to the urban and natural environment.

The general increase in manufacturing also had an effect on the construction sector, with the growth of construction as an industry marked by new manufactured elements for construction. In the same way that cast-iron and steel construction in the mid-19th century led to the advancement in the industry of the period, the design and development of prefabricated and manufactured steel and concrete products spurred growth in the construction industry. Architects and designers, such as Angelo Mangiarotti in Italy and Fritz Haller in Germany, developed advanced, technically precise structural systems with general applicability—the primary objective was for these systems to be labor-saving, fast, and very economical in construction and assembly. Bruno and Fritz Haller's Office Furniture Factory in Münsingen, Switzerland (1965), and Mangiarotti's FM Constructive System Factory Building in Lissone, Italy (1964), were the most important buildings of this initial period of industrialized architecture, in which prefabricated systems' orientation toward specific programmatic requirements became secondary to the need to optimize the manufacturing process of the building elements. Of course the ubiquity of these systems did result in the repetition of standardized design tropes, which led to many simple, cheap versions of the boxy sheds, reducing the impact of architectural creativity on industrial architecture. Nevertheless, the leap made by likes of Mangiarotti and Haller was to be long lasting.

Foster Associates, Renault Distribution Centre, Swindon, England, 1982

Industrial architecture in the 1960s also continued to be influenced by modern architecture, but now in buildings at a much larger scale and size than their predecessors. The need to quickly develop vast production facilities for multinational companies, such as Olivetti, Volkswagen, and Cummins, prompted the development of modern-style prefabricated building systems and modular systems that provided envelopes for open-floor factories that assured maximum flexibility. The Cummins Engine Component Factory in Darlington, England (1966), by Kevin Roche, John Dinkeloo and Associates, is a typical Miesian shed with a prominent exposed structure of CorTen steel beams and columns. Foster and Associates' Reliance Controls Electronics Factory in Swindon, England (1967; developed in 1983 into the Renault Distribution Center), takes this Miesian approach one step further with a series of I-beams and columns braced by diagonal tubes.

This was also the age of innovation with structural engineering, in steel trusses and space frame structures that provided flexibility in layout, plan, and future expansion to accommodate a variety of manufacturing processes. To optimize construction and performance, mechanical and electrical systems were integrated into these structures, as can be seen in Kenzo Tange's Tosho Printing Plant in Haramachi, Japan (1961), where a central concrete box girder supports lateral steel trusses that simultaneously act as the primary conduit for the air-conditioning system. The expressive and functional aspects of concrete also featured prominently in projects such as Henn's High-Voltage Test Laboratory in Siemens, Berlin (1960), which employed concrete vaults as roof shells to create large spans for production and technical facilities, and Pier Luigi Nervi's Paper Factory in Mantua, Italy (1961–1962), which used bridge-like concrete pylons to hold up the building's roof and curtain wall.

Lastly, environmental and workplace aspects figured into a number of projects, especially in northern European countries. For example, the use of modernist and plastic architectural effects in Matti Mäkinen's Turku Dairy, in Turku, Finland (1965–1966), and Geir Grung and Georg Greve's Wholesale Bakery in Bergen, Norway (1965), carefully integrated the buildings into their natural and urban Scandinavian environments while optimizing interior air ventilation and lighting.

Herman Hertzberger, Textile Workshop, Amsterdam, the Netherlands, 1964

Matti Makinen, Turku Dairy, Turku, Finland, 1966

Angelo Mangiarotti, FM Constructive System Factory Building, Lissone, 1964

1970s

In the 1970s, the popularity of flexible, multifunctional spatial envelopes increased worldwide, responding to advances in assembly and production technologies. The economic uncertainties of the time, marked by oil crises and the disintegration of aging heavy industry dating from the late 19th and early 20th centuries, were partly counterbalanced by new developments in electronics and computers. The need for change determined the architecture of factory buildings, with the majority adhering to the trend for modular grids and prefabrication. Most of these were fairly undistinguished in design, but they were often built at increasingly larger scales, resembling small towns.

At this time, prefabricated and modular systems were becoming increasingly sophisticated, particularly in Italy, with leading figures such as Angelo Mangiarotti and Marco Zanuso, and in the United Kingdom, with Richard Rogers and Derek Walker. Zanuso, who had designed factories for Olivetti in the 1960s in Italy and South America, completed the Olivetti Factory in Scarmango, Italy (1970), using a prefabricated system of fitted reinforced-concrete bases, columns, and beams based on a 12-by-18-meter grid, spread over a wide area in a series of open and closed modules that could be extended infinitely. Zanuso's work as a designer gave him insight into the industrial process, and he was able to articulate a building as a system that coordinated architectural elements, technological circuitry, mechanical production, and a qualitative organization of the workplace. This resulted in aspects of production being organized into different modular components specific to their tasks, set in a groundbreaking factory typology.

Olivetti commissioned numerous leading architects of the day to create factory buildings, including Louis Kahn for the Olivetti Underwood Factory in Harrisburg, Pennsylvania (1970), which presented another progressive design in structural engineering and architecture, utilizing pre-stressed hexagonal shells to create a column-free open-plan factory floor for this typewriter factory.

Other important work in prefabrication and modular systems included Derek Walker's lightweight steel-truss system for the Industrial and Commercial Prototypes in Milton Keynes, England (1971); Richard Rogers and Renzo Piano's steel and sandwich panel

Angelo Mangiarotti, Snaidero Factory, Majano, Italy, 1978

system for the PA Technology Centre in Cambridge, England (1976); and Mangiarotti's massive triangular steel-truss frames on concrete piers that support the steel and glass roof of the Snaidero Factory in Majano, Italy (1978).

Urban infrastructure also played a key role in this period as cities expanded into suburban areas, creating fewer divisions between industrial and residential zones. The buildings, such as water purification plants and sewage facilities, now visible to residential neighborhoods, exhibited new design strategies. The German architect and academician Kurt Ackermann, who would later be involved in a number of important works of industrial architecture, designed the Sewage Treatment Plant in Munich (1975–1988) as a prominent monument. He imbued this ignored building typology with a meaningful presence through a series of abstract, pure shapes that give form to parts of this large sewage waste "machine." In a similar strategy, the Water Purification Plant in Enkhuizen, the Netherlands (1977–1981), by Spruit de Jong Heringa, uses clear, geometric volumes and patterns to organize the purification processes and the architectural and structural elements into a common language that gives symbolic importance to the plant's primary function.

In the 1970s the influence of regional architecture first started to play an important role in the localization of industrial architecture; experiments in form and representation specific to the material cultures and traditions of regional geographies became commonplace. For example, Mario Botta and Remo Leuzinger's Crafts Center in Balerna, Switzerland (1977–1979), used a triangular steel space frame in a basic pitched-roof configuration to bridge the four principal concrete volumes of this crafts workshop, creating a relation between archetypal building forms and structure specific to Botta's regional postmodernism. Peter von Seidlein, another noteworthy German architect with a rich pedigree in industrial architecture, fused tectonic timber construction with a glass curtain wall in his Printing Plant in Paderborn, Germany (1974), creating a clear example of critic Kenneth Frampton's concept of Critical Regionalism. Additionally, Eladio Dieste generated an arched, undulating shell from bricks, mortar, and concrete for the Grain Silo in Young, Uruguay (1978), using simple building techniques to create an economic horizontal silo.

Marco Zanuso, Olivetti Factory, Scarmango, Italy, 1971

1980s

In the 1980s, at the dawn of the digital revolution, the technological transformations that would later change the nature of work and industry were starting to be felt in the development of programs for hybrid research-and-production facilities for technological companies. Guided by the spirit of engineering, technical experiments continued to influence the creation of different prefabricated and manufactured structural solutions: this later became known as "high-tech" architecture by practitioners primarily from the United Kingdom, such as Richard Rogers, Norman Foster, Michael Hopkins, Arup Associates, and Nicholas Grimshaw. It was important for sectors such as electronics, computers, and publishing, which required high technical standards for their production environments.

Projects by Rogers, such as the Inmos Microprocessor Factory in Newport, Wales (1982), and the PA Technology Centre in Princeton, New Jersey (1982), are exemplary for their continued development of the structural innovations of the previous decades, utilizing elaborate systems of steel supports in prefabricated components that can be quickly assembled on site and aesthetically integrated with the service systems to create original versions of the shed typology made popular earlier in the century. Rogers's high-tech approach can also be seen in the work of other noteworthy buildings of the period, such as Foster + Partners' Renault Distribution Centre in Swindon, England (1983), where the structural aesthetic supports the image of a technologically advanced company. Additionally, in Hopkins's Schlumberger Research Laboratory in Cambridge, England (1984), a pioneering tensile membrane roof canopy is suspended by masts over steel-truss frames and panels, while Grimshaw's Financial Times Building in London (1988) showcases its printing facilities through a large glass wall supported by a steel exoskeleton. Grimshaw also designed a factory for furniture producer Vitra in Weil am Rhein, Germany (1981), which had an extension added in 1986 and was later joined by other buildings from leading international architects such as Frank Gehry, Tadao Andao, Álvaro Siza, Zaha Hadid, Herzog & de Meuron, and SANAA.

The large sheds made from prefabricated components, originally initiated in Europe in the middle of the 20th century, were still in use during the 1980s as they were required by growing industries of the time, such as aviation, textile, and construction.

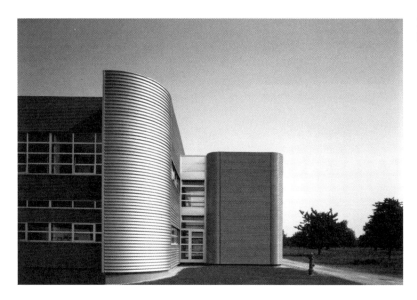

Nicholas Grimshaw, Vitra Furniture
Factory, Weil am Rhein, Germany, 1981

Hopkins Partners, Patera Building
System prototype, 1980

Hopkins Partners, Mellor Cutlery
Factory, Hathersage, Derbyshire,
England, 1988

They continued to be built using systems of trusses, frames, masts, tubes, metal sheeting, concrete panels, curtain walls, and roof glazing, and can be seen in noteworthy industrial buildings such as Afra and Tobia Scarpa's Benetton Jeans & Tops Factory in Castrette, Italy (1980), Erkki Kairamo and Reijo Lahtinen's Marimekko Factory in Helsinki, Finland (1981), Alessandro Savioli's olive oil factory Oleificio Borelli S.P.A. in Imperia, Italy (1988), and Cardete et Huet and Calvo & Tran Van's Airbus A330/340 Factory in Toulouse, France (1989).

At this point, the creative energy for industrial architecture, which had long been at the service of the organizational and operational requirements of the industry, started to flounder as the nature of industry began to change. There was a limit to how many sheds could be built, and the architectural culture of the late 20th century was largely unable to adapt to the changes that later transformed the nature of work, with the advent of automation, technology, and telecommunication, radically reducing the human element. It was only in the continuing focus on regional aspects of industry that strides were made: one groundbreaking example was the Cummins Diesel Factory in Shotts, Scotland (1983), by Ahrends, Burton and Koralek Architects, which used an existing textile mill that was integrated into the landscape to invoke the language of Scottish mines. This factory, designed in extensive consultation with the workers, would later be described as a humanist approach to industrial architecture. Another project that took on a regional approach while focusing on traditional building materials was the David Mellor Cutlery Factory in Hathersage, England (1988), by Hopkins Partners, which employed radial trusses to support the lead roof over a circular stone wall, reflecting the area's vernacular architecture. A more complex combination of a traditional and natural setting is the Recycling Plant for Domestic Waste in Oslo, Norway (1989), by Astrup og Hellern, which managed to integrate the recycling machinery into the hilly forest landscape outside of Oslo by placing the machines inside carefully arranged concrete boxes with crafted timber screens. Another low-tech approach is the Igualada Commercial Factory Warehouse in Barcelona, Spain (mid-1980s), which utilized inexpensive, locally produced elements to generate an expressive architectonic language of exposed concrete blocks, sheet metal, and thin steel structures.

Hopkins Partners, Schlumberger Cambridge Research Centre, Cambridge, England, 1984

1990s

The period from end of the 1990s into the 2000s seemed to represent a downturn in industrial architecture in general. This can be ascribed in part to the prevalence of inexpensive prefabricated concrete, steel, and aluminum elements preferred by clients for economic reasons, reducing the design capabilities of industrial architecture and consequentially degrading their attractiveness to architects. We can also associate industrial architecture's stagnation with a construction boom in residential, corporate, cultural, service sector, and public buildings that left the pursuit of industrial architecture largely hidden from the public eye. Another significant paradigm shift in the nature of industry at this time was the continuing infiltration of technology and communication systems into industry and industrial production, a shift that has yet to be fully appreciated by architects.

The 1990s was an era characterized by the widespread introduction of computation into design, directly affecting the architectural process. The result for industrial architecture was twofold: first, the structures of buildings became more complex, enabled by the formal and organizational capabilities of computational design and construction; and second, the performative aspects of buildings in issues such as energy consumption, insulation, and natural and artificial lighting became parametric data that could be factored into the design process.

The results of computational design appear in the distinctly angular forms of a number of buildings with highly complex structural systems. For example, Warehouse C in Nagasaki, Japan (1997), by Roto Architects, combines an orthogonal concrete base with a planar geometric superstructure of structural steel and steel plates, which were manufactured by local shipbuilders; a semi-transparent fabric covering tops off this complex weave of materials and forms. Likewise, the Odörfer Building in Klagenfurt, Austria (1992), by Volker Giencke, features a dramatic sloping glass roof, glass curtain wall, and a prominent, complex system of steel structural elements.

In terms of building performance, projects such as the Thomson Opto Electronics Factory in Saint Quentin-En-Yvelines, France (1990), by Renzo Piano Building Workshop, utilized data models on significant environmental control issues for this electronics manufacturer.

RoTo Architects, Warehouse C, Nagasaki, Japan, 1997

Key functional requirements in ventilation and natural and artificial lighting led to the development of the primary structural module, which extends linearly across the factory to accommodate a variety of functions. These modules, composed of curved girders with a thin structure that allows for extensive glazing and custom lighting solutions, were designed by Piano specifically for this project. A similar approach, which takes into account the workplace environment of an electronics manufacturer, was taken by Carmel Gradoli, Luis Herrero & Arturo Sanz for their Fabrica de Equipos Electronicos Inelcom in Valencia, Spain (1996). Here, after detailed lighting studies, custom vertical skylights complied with the needs of the manufacturer: the prominent steel-framed skylights on the roof play an important part in the building's internal climate as well as an expressive role in its overall thin structural system of steel.

Energy usage and sustainability also played an important part in the concept for Thomas Herzog's Wilkhahn Assembly Hall in Eimbeckhausen, Germany (1993), which utilized a system of non-ventilated green roofs of glue-laminated timber panels and plywood veneering supported by a laminated timber structure allowing for large spans. The green roof of the hall regulates heat accumulation during the summer, reduces noise levels, and delays rainwater drainage; the building embraces a commitment to ecological design.

In this period of increasing concern for ecological issues in all aspects of architecture, industrial/infrastructural building types, such as power stations, waste incinerator stations, waste transfer stations, thermal heat transfer stations, and the like grew in importance. This includes the Thermoselect Waste Incineration Plant in Verbania, Italy (1991), by Botta, which utilizes a lightweight modular truss structure to create the purposefully symbolic architecture of industry as an envelope to hide the internal functions, and the Wos 8 Heat Transfer Station in Utrecht, Netherlands (1997), by NL Architects, with its black polyurethane membrane-clad exterior envelope that provides opportunities for sporting activities. Additionally, the Geothermal Power Station Enel in Bagnone, Italy (1998), by Boeri Studio, uses an external frame, this time a series of CorTen steel ribs that arch over the technical functions, unifying and integrating the building with the wild, hilly landscape.

Gradolí & Sanz Arquitectes, Fábrica
de Equipos Electrónicos Inelcom,
Valencia, Spain, 1996

Herzog + Partner, Wilkhahn Assembly
Hall, Eimbeckhausen, Germany, 1993

Herzog & de Meuron, Dominus Winery,
Yountville, California, United States, 1997

The 1990s was a period of economic growth that sustained the globalism that had characterized the latter part of the 20th century for industry. Corporations were closely woven together in worldwide networks of production and distribution that continued to extend further into new and varying geographies. For the architecture of industry this meant a continuation of regionalism, which provided innovation in the development of new structural, architectural, and operational concepts. Noteworthy examples include the Braun Production Center in Melsungen, Germany (1993), by Walter Nageli, James Sterling and Michael Wilford, which uses a mix of functionalism and historicist archetypes based on the ancient Roman period in order to enhance the visual character of the German landscape, and the Fagar Soft Drink Factory in San Juan, Uruguay (1997) by Miguel Ángel Odriozola with engineer Elaido Dieste, which uses the latter's masonry shell construction to create barrel vaults in an inexpensive combination of concrete and brick that thrust out over the base to shade production and circulation facilities. The Dominus Winery in Yountville, California (1997), by Herzog & de Meuron, includes an iconic envelope of gabions filled with small blocks of local basalt stone that act as a mesh and heat regulator.

Technological innovation in the 19th and early 20th centuries fundamentally altered architecture by producing materials that made construction more effective, robust, and flexible. Today a similar transformation may occur through 21st century technology, producing equally dramatic results.

2000s

At the start of the 21st century, as industrial architecture transformed and industrial capitalism lurched forward, the strains of industrial architecture continued with themes that had occupied practice for many years. Modernist aesthetics, high-tech approaches, prefabrication, ecology, regionalism, and organizational and operational functionalism guided projects throughout the decade.

In Germany, the practices of leading figures in industrial architecture, such as Henn and Ackermann, produced works based on structural and modernist aesthetics. A hybrid of automation, warehousing, and structure can be seen in Erco Leuchten High Bay Storage in Lüdenscheid, Germany (2001), by Schneider + Schumacher, where the structure of the pallet warehouse is formed by the storage racks. These racks are served automatically and exposed behind a double-glazed facade that integrates the building and its architecture into the manufacturing process.

Ackermann and Partners' Marker Cement Factory in Harburg, Germany (2000), clearly organizes the main functions in volumes with pure geometries, the most distinct of which is the space underneath the circular dome that stretches over 16 arched three-chord steel-tube girders. That Ackermann is a master of visual clarity and the use of architecture to organize industrial functions can clearly be seen, even at the vast scale of this cement factory. Likewise, Henn Architekten's Autostadt in Wolfsburg, Germany (2000), is a unique building type, a warehouse parking facility that merges automation and computer control with structure. Automobiles emerging from production are temporarily brought to the glass towers via conveyor belts and elevators on their way to distributors, exposing and integrating manufacturing at the building scale.

The automated systems integrated with structural elements, such as in the Autostadt and Erco Leuchter High Bay Storage, are exemplary of the current nature of industry where the human element is almost nonexistent, and thus a minor aspect of the architectural concept. In the future, architects will increasingly have to integrate their designs with the organizational and operational aspects of computer-based automation at the cost of the "human environment," going beyond the levels only hinted at in these buildings.

The same issues confront architects when they take on buildings in which energy savings is a design priority, where an ecological consciousness must inform fundamental design decisions. The Solvis Zero Emissions Factory in Brunswick, Germany (2002), by Bain & Riecks, and the Microtech Plant in Gals, Switzerland (2002), by Crochon Brullman + Associates, are recent examples that merge the processes of nature with industry and technology to reduce energy use and environmental impact. The high-tech approach is also a part of this ecological thinking, such as in the McLaren Technology Centre in Woking, England (2004), by Foster + Partners, which factors the company's own environmental technologies into the building's architecture.

Finally, regionalism in architecture continues to be a noteworthy theme in new expanding geographies, as can be seen in a series of warehouses in India by Khanna Schultz. In particular, Schultz's Writer Warehouse in Delhi (2004) uses a combination of in-situ and precast-concrete elements to make a strong architectonic statement in a warehouse where energy savings, natural lighting, and ventilation are important factors.

BIBLIOGRAPHY

Ackermann, Kurt. *Building for Industry.* Translated by Michelle Spong. Godalming: Watermark, 1991.

Adam, Jürgen A., Katharina Hausmann, and Frank Jüttne. *Industrial Buildings: A Design Manual.* Translated by Fiona Greenwood and Jörn Frenzel. Boston: Birkhäuser, 2004.

Aitchison, Mathew, ed. *The Architecture of Industry: Changing Paradigms in Industrial Building and Planning.* New York: Routledge, 2014.

CIB-UIA. *Aspects on Industrial Architecture and Engineering.* Helsinki Building Book Ltd., 1989.

Bonifazio, Patrizia, and Paolo Scrivano. *Olivetti Builds: Modern Architecture in Ivrea.* Milan: Skira, 2001.

Broto, Carles. *Architecture for Industry.* Barcelona: LINKS International, 1997.

Cavallotti, Carlo. *Architettura industriale.* Milan: Görlich, 1969.

Grube, Oswald W. *Industrial Buildings and Factories.* New York: Praeger, 1971.

Hayes, Brian. *Infrastructure: A Guide to the Industrial Landscape.* New York: W.W. Norton & Company, 2014.

Mostaedi, Arian. *Factories & Office Buildings.* Architecture Design series. Barcelona: LINKS, 2003.

Phillips, Alan. *The Best in Industrial Architecture.* London: B.T. Batsford, 1993.

Raja, Raffaele. *Architettura industriale: Storia, significato e progetto.* Bari: Dedalo, 1983.

Reyner, Banham. *A Concrete Atlantis: U.S. Industrial Building and European Modern Architecture 1900–1925.* Cambridge, MA: MIT Press, 1986.

Smith, Virginia, Brian Ralph, Elizabeth Pisani, and Rosie Cox George. *Dirt: The Filthy Reality of Everyday Life.* London: Profile Books, 2011.

Stock, Wolfgang Jean. *Industrial Architecture in Germany—Continuity and Change: Märker Cement Works, Harburg, Architekten Ackermann und Partner.* Munich: Prestel, 2000.

Uffelen, Chris van. *Factory Design.* Translated by Alice Bayandin. Berlin: Braun, 2009.

Wild, Friedemann. *Gewerbebetriebe, Produktion, Veredelung, Dienstleistung.* Vol. 25 of *Entwurf und Planung.* Munich: Callwey, 1974.

Wild, Friedemann. *Industriebau, Fertigungsbetriebe.* Vol. 1 of *Entwurf und Planung.* Munich: Callwey, 1969.

Ackermann and Partners, Märker
Cement Factory, Harburg, Germany, 2000

Henn Architekten, Autostadt,
Wolfsburg, Germany, 2000

Schneider + Schumacher, Jörg
Hempel, Erco Leuchten High Bay
Storage, Ludenscheild, Germany, 2001

43

Interest in obsolescence arose from a major shift in thinking during the later part of the 20th century toward the reuse of existing stock and away from the excessive dominance of new building. Essentially it stems from the general understanding that buildings, like machinery and durable consumer goods, were to be eliminated and replaced when they became obsolete. In the automobile industry, for instance, the rising popularity of Japanese brands during the late 1960s and 1970s pushed US carmakers toward producing more durable models with lower rates of obsolescence. Other products including buildings followed suit, in the latter case also spurred on by a noticeable rise in historic conservation and other landmarking activities in the late 1970s. Further, the more recent clamoring in the direction of sustainability for built environments has given further rise to minimizing obsolescence and extending the longevity of buildings as physical, economic, and societal investments. Nowadays, older and blatant policies of "planned obsolescence" are often frowned upon or scrutinized in efforts to extend, or eliminate the artificial notion of, the limited useful lives of products, including buildings. Indeed, in addition to leanings toward the conservation of material content and other resources put into the construction, maintenance, and operation of buildings, a moral stance has also emerged around issues associated with building and environmental sustainability, usually embracing long-term considerations and reuse of existing stock. Certainly the advantages of planned obsolescence in the technical progress of ever-improving goods and services have been called out by claims of wastefulness and consumer exploitation, voiced by pundits like Vance Packard as long ago as 1957 in his *Hidden Persuasion.*

At root, obsolescence refers to something no longer in use, old-fashioned, and vestigial. As such, it is not a natural phenomenon but one that is a matter of human action. As the title to this short essay implies, it is also a cause rather than an *end* that, combined with sheer physical deterioration, results in depreciation of a product as an outcome, in this case a building, leading to potential demolition. On these scores demolition and replacement rates vary quite considerably. Some place the rates of building construction to demolition rates in Europe at around 11.7:1, ranging as widely as 4:1 in Germany to

Causes of Obsolescence and Building Futures

PETER ROWE

Raymond Garbe Professor of Architecture and Urban Design
Harvard University Distinguished Service Professor

William Thornton et al., Capitol Building,
Washington, DC, United States, 1793

15.7:1 in France.[1] Full depreciation—that is, the useful lives of buildings—in the United Kingdom have, on average, been placed at slightly less than 100 years, whereas in the United States it is more like 70 years. In China, with less mature markets and more uncertainty for building in play, this figure drops as low as 30 years.[2] Given a reasonable universality of building materials, the variation only further underlines the human values and actions involved with obsolescence. Basically, all other things being equal including upkeep, replacement, and so forth, the fully depreciated or useful life of a building is around 63 percent of its intrinsic physical life. In fact, not inappropriately, degradation over time has been referred to as the "fourth dimension" of building.[3]

Causes of obsolescence can be manifold—physical, economic, functional, technical, social, legal, and political.[4] Physically, for instance, some materials deteriorate more quickly or thoroughly than others in the overall composition of buildings. From a sustainable perspective this would argue for long-lived and durable materials. Economically, the type of building and its location, quite apart from quality, can often be meaningful. Again, sustainability in this context would argue for flexible building types vis-a-vis uses and locations. Also, the cost of continuing use compared to the expense of substitution, for instance, is often a pervasive economic factor. Functionally, flexibility in a building's response to use has merit, although the relative ubiquity of certain buildings to well-matched uses also seems to play a role. Technically, the components of buildings are at stake, often with different renewal cycles and among building types. Studies of buildings in the United States, for instance, have placed the renewal cycles for windows at 15 years for condominiums and 10 for retail and office uses, whereas air conditioning equipment enjoys a uniform 10-year span across all three uses.[5] Socially, market and other forces come into play in shortening or prolonging obsolescence with regard to style, area reputation, aesthetic qualities, historic significance, and related characteristics. Legally and politically, failure to comply with standards or to meet new legislation reflecting cultural trends, such as disabled compliance, can quickly and decisively result in high rates of obsolescence for nonconforming buildings.

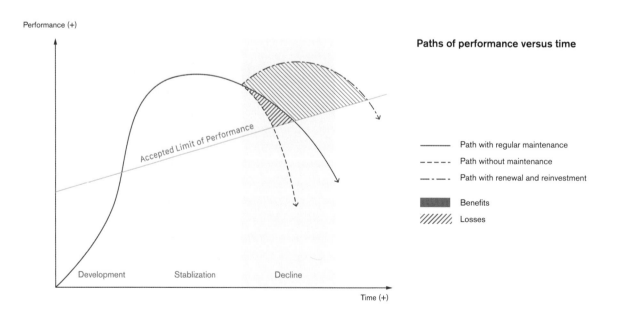

Interaction among the different attributes of obsolescence also produces varying causal outcomes and, ultimately, impacts on depreciation of buildings. As noted, different technical components have different effective lives and replacement cycles, although a particular building may be very long standing. The US Capitol Building, for example, is over 200 years old and likely to stand for a very long time to come. This will hold even as obsolescence over the years has led to changes in electrical and mechanical systems on the technical side of things, and the construction of several new buildings to provide needed accommodations when the original building proved inadequate on the functional side.[6] This case also counters the "weakest link" argument in building obsolescence that holds that it reflects the least durable or otherwise long-lasting aspect of a building's composition or function. For the US Capitol, the cultural value of the building trumps all other attributes in its continued use, appreciation, and conservation. Also the sheer convergence of numerous attributes toward significantly delayed obsolescence, even in spite of potentially substantial physical deterioration, can come into contention. Loft living, working, and retailing in New York's SoHo district is a case in point. There, use flexibility, location, social cache, and legal landmarking preserve the late 19th-century mid-rise structures, despite the rather constant maintenance and replacement that must be lavished on the cast-iron and other building facades.

Ultimately, obsolescence as a cause of depreciation and eventual demolition is primarily responsible for the conformance of a building to acceptable levels of performance in all respects over time. According to several authoritative accounts, this can be represented in a 2-space of "performance" against "time," where the profile of a building's performance rises to some higher or optimal level, usually above some overall acceptance threshold, before declining more rapidly with no maintenance than with regular attention (see figure on page 46). Further longevity can be brought about for the building through renewal and reinvestment, thus arresting depreciation at least for some period of time.[7] Clearly in cases like the US Capitol Building, this cycle can be prolonged presumably indefinitely. However, even in the field of outright historic preservation, arguments arise over how and what to preserve in perpetuity. Theoretically, if the renewal and regeneration cycle is extreme enough, the benefits deriving from the revived building will outweigh the losses, as shown by the separately shaded areas, and obsolescence and eventual depreciation will also be prolonged.

Returning to attributes of obsolescence, this may entail looking for functional flexibility, effecting mergers between two or more well-known types in order to thoroughly cover a situation, accommodating technical interchangeability in an open and accommodating manner, or even playing off of an otherwise historic and culturally significant structure by reusing it …

In yet another framework, obsolescence can be seen to be brought on along a vertical axis in gradations between the intrinsic physical character of a building through to its response to behavioral circumstances.[8] On another horizontal and orthogonal axis the variation is from endogenous circumstances concerned with the fabric and make-up of the building itself through to exogenous factors affecting the life of the building in its broader social and cultural context (see figure on page 49). Clearly, the aspect of "control" increases toward the upper left-hand corner of the 2-space, whereas "complexity" increases to the bottom right-hand corner. Moreover, it can be suggested that as a market becomes more competitive and mixed, product life spans tend to increase. For instance, presumably very few competing models will result in convergence to one or the others, eliminating significant amounts of product, in this case building types. Further, the likelihood of one continuing to dominate without change is probably remote.

In the realm of architecture and building production there are several general approaches that can be adopted toward projects, particularly from the vantage point of delayed obsolescence. In many cases some sort of adaption of familiar or otherwise-known building types is adopted. In other cases a focus is trained on making specific, necessary, and often narrowly defined requirements leading to special-built structures and programmatic accommodations. Then there is a mode somewhat akin to hedging one's bets and producing hybrids by amalgamating aspects of either well-known solutions or special-built options. Returning to attributes of obsolescence, this may entail looking for functional flexibility, effecting mergers between two or more well-known types in order to thoroughly cover a situation, accommodating technical interchangeability in an open and accommodating manner, or even playing off of an otherwise historic and culturally significant structure by reusing it, for instance. In many cases hybridization will occur in conjunction with an existing structure, although certainly not always. Returning also to the broad framework of performance with regard to time, sustained certainty in a market place for a particular generic kind of building may argue for well-trodden approaches. Extreme special-built options would seem risky unless, of course, they achieve a broadly acclaimed iconic status, in which case they may persist as parts of a cultural heritage for long periods of time. In today's world, however, such attention appears to be turning toward redevelopment opportunities rather than outright tabula rasa development. Amid the rising moral tone of sustainability, hybridization of some sort appears as the most longstanding approach by way of its inherent and incremental modification, as well as the "both-and" that results in more potential for building outcomes.

NOTES

1. Andre Thomsen and Kees van der Flier, "Obsolescence and the End of Life Phase in Buildings," paper presented at Management and Innovation for a Sustainable Built Environment, Amsterdam, The Netherlands, June 20-23, 2011.

2. Conversation with Qiu Baoxing, vice minister of Urban and Rural Development, People's Republic of China, June 30, 2016.

3. Donald G. Iselin and Andrew C. Lerner, eds., The Fourth Dimension in Building: Strategies for Avoiding Obsolescence

(Washington, DC: National Academies Press, 1993).

4. Craig Langston, Estimating the Useful Life of Buildings (Gold Coast, Australia: Bond University, 2011).

5. Iselin and Lerner, The Fourth Dimension in Building, ch. 2.

6. Ibid.

7. Thomsen and van der Flier, "Obsolescence and the End of Life Phase in Buildings."

8. Ibid.

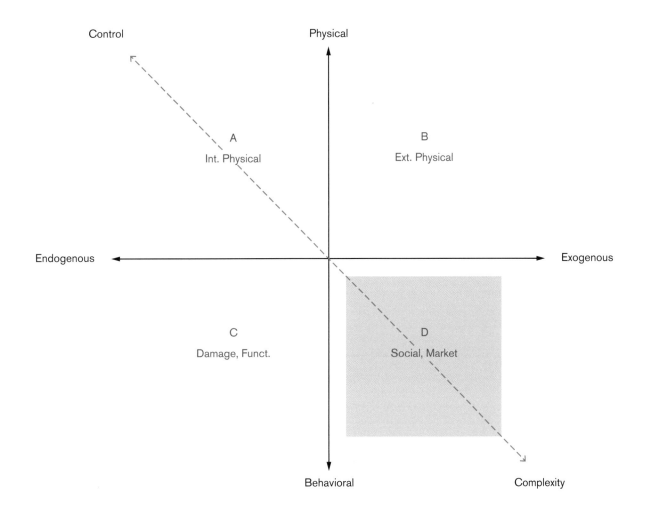

Dimensions of obsolescence

Our everyday lives are dependent on industrial and infrastructural facilities, such as large production plants, water and sewage facilities, and energy and waste treatment centers. For a society that thrives to be sustainable, we face many challenges to organize these necessities in ways that make as little impact on the environment as possible. In addition, increasing numbers and densities of people will be living in urban areas. We have to consider how to handle all demands in a new way if we are to develop into a society that takes on our current environmental challenges.

We are making efforts to reduce waste, to move toward a circular economy, but ultimately we will still generate waste that will need to be processed. As the use of landfills rightfully comes to an end, we must seek new waste management solutions. Ideally these solutions should be situated close to where waste is produced to avoid long transportation sequences.

As Sweden and other countries have shown, waste can be turned into energy, and more countries now recognize the possibilities Waste-to-Energy facilities hold. But is it possible for WtE plants to become a part of the urban landscape? Is it feasible to have these incineration plants close to where we live? Could we accept them? Is there a role for the architects who have been absent in this field?

In the early days of industrialization, design architects played an important role in designing these urban necessities. But over time, industrial plants have grown to lack expressive design and be viewed as purely functional. The plants' appearances have been governed by the processes they contain.

We are now beginning to rethink and challenge the strictly utilitarian view of WtE facilities. Can the processes be adapted to the architecture and work within the city fabric? Is it possible to treat waste where we create it? Can we can reduce transportation distances and produce energy in proximity to its users? Can design be a game changer when it comes to the general public's acceptance of WtE plants?

Aligning the necessary stages in an incineration plant with the design required for community acceptance in the urban environment is a great challenge. Sweden as a country and Tyréns as a company have been given the opportunity, along with the Harvard University Graduate School of Design, to push this important work forward and hopefully inspire cities to take on the challenge of turning waste into energy.

Another Perspective

ULRIKA FRANCKE

Chief Executive Officer, The Sven Tyréns Trust

Bjarke Ingels Architects, Amager Bakke Resource Center (under construction), Copenhagen, Denmark, 2016

A well-designed built environment contributes to a host of environmental, economic, and social benefits. Using the Waste-to-Energy plant, this work aims to show that eliciting the greatest value from infrastructure and industrial projects requires the reconsideration and repositioning of the role of design and architecture in such projects. The material presented here captures, identifies, and suggests themes that emerged during our investigations, and includes suggestions of priorities for academia, design, and industry. This will promote significant improvements in the role that design plays in industrial and infrastructural projects on many scales.

Our research was based on a number of key objectives, all designed to work toward our main goal. We aim to strengthen the understanding of what is known and not known about the role of design in WtE facilities, looking to find out why there are outstanding gaps in this area, what they are, and how they can be addressed with design. We identify procedures of good and bad design with the aim of improving future approaches. The research develops working methods and processes that enable collaboration between designers, architects, clients, policymakers and other stakeholders, and makes recommendations for future research, education, and industry.

Other objectives include identifying new integrative framework or methods are needed to better promote design, educational material that can be developed to promote work in this area, and examining the role of "planned obsolescence."

This all came from our research hypothesis—that while architecture and design are absent (if not completely neglected) in WtE projects, these disciplines can contribute significant value through programmatic hybridization, performance enhancements, contextual assimilation, and increased societal acceptance. In addition, the demand for WtE facilities is likely to increase worldwide due to waste production and the demand for alternative sources of energy locally, which helps justify our research.

We took a hybrid approach to research, consisting of three methods: quantitative, qualitative, and design. Quantitative methods enabled us to forecast demand, understand input/output mechanics of WtE facilities, and performance parameters in the facility both

Methods of Research

HANIF KARA AND ANDREAS GEORGOULIAS

as-is and in potential programmatic hybrids. Qualitative methods allowed us to identify key socio-economic enablers for WtE facilities and to understand key stakeholder drivers through semi-structured interviews. Finally, design methods helped us develop and test the proof of concept for prototypical design solutions and programmatic hybrids.

We primarily focused our research on US and Swedish cases, providing focus and a data sample through the study of two polarizing extremes. This comparative approach permits a good understanding of the issues that connect design, policy, and economics, allowing us to identify the landscape of current practice and future directions of applicable research. This maintains statistical validity due to the substantial amount of data available.

Our research was validated through the focus group approach, comprising industry and academic experts and key stakeholders (design, technology, policy, and economics). These groups met biannually to review the research output and provide recommendations for improvement.

Following the development and maturity of our findings, the research was then disseminated through graduate seminars and design studios, which have released primary findings to small groups of students and faculty. The publication of the widely completed body of knowledge then occurred three years later.

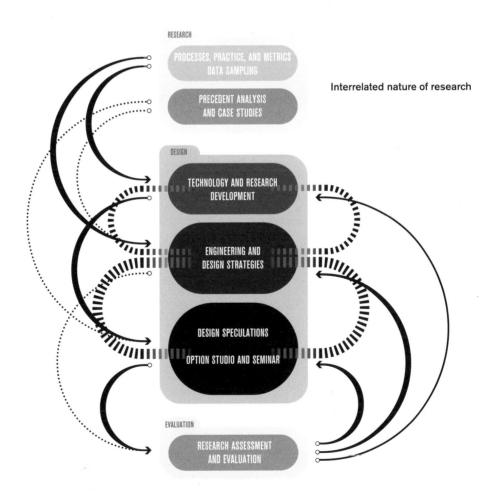

RESEARCH
PROCESSES, PRACTICE, AND METRICS
DATA SAMPLING

PRECEDENT ANALYSIS
AND CASE STUDIES

Interrelated nature of research

DESIGN
TECHNOLOGY AND RESEARCH
DEVELOPMENT

ENGINEERING AND
DESIGN STRATEGIES

DESIGN SPECULATIONS
OPTION STUDIO AND SEMINAR

EVALUATION
RESEARCH ASSESSMENT
AND EVALUATION

Alan Levine, *King of the Trash Hill*, 2013

Waste-to-Energy Primer

In ancient times, populations relied for existence on purely natural elements, such as wood, bones, and plants. These hunter-gatherers disposed of their waste by leaving it where it fell. Gradually, however, more sophisticated methods arose to deal with waste. The first recorded landfill was in the Cretan capital of Knossos in 1500 BCE. The Minoan people created dump sites where waste was placed in large pits and covered with earth. Historical records indicate that the Athenians were the first to have institutionalized waste management. In 500 BCE, the Athenians mandated that waste be deposited no less than one mile from the city and banned the dumping of refuse on city streets. However, with the end of the Classical era, it would be another 1000 years before the first policy changes would begin to influence societies in Europe (see figure on pages 58–59).

As populations and economies grew, people lived closer together in cities and towns and generated more waste. Despite some early waste management efforts, there was little understanding of the connection between sanitation and disease. Uncontrolled waste and sanitation issues prompted a series of epidemics, which swept across Europe between 1348 and 1665. The biggest of these was the Black Death during the 1340s, resulting in an estimated 75 million deaths—between 30 to 60 percent of the population of Europe at the time. From the Middle Ages and into the Industrial Revolution, people continued to die from infectious diseases—the plague, cholera, and typhoid—related to unsanitary conditions and crowding.

Across the Atlantic Ocean, America had its own interesting relationship with trash. New Amsterdam passed a law against dumping waste in the streets in 1657. In 1690, Ritten-house Mill, America's first paper mill, opened in Philadelphia, Pennsylvania, and made paper from recycled cotton, linen, and used paper. This is considered to be the first effort toward major recycling in the New World. Benjamin Franklin was a famous advocate for the proper disposal of waste. In 1739, he led an effort to petition the Pennsylvania Assembly to stop commercial waste dumping in Philadelphia and remove tanneries from the city's commercial district. Eighteen years later, Franklin began the first American colonial municipal street-cleaning operation, also in Philadelphia. Yet elsewhere in America and Europe, there were few municipally organized systems for the collection and disposal

History and Reality
of Waste

LAURA SMEAD

New York City Department of Sanitation, *Furniture Collection in New York City*, 19th century

A BRIEF HISTORY OF WASTE

FOR MILLENIA HUMANS HAVE PRODUCED WASTE. HOWEVER, THE ROAD TO REUSING REFUSE HAS BEEN ONE PAVED WITH INCREMENTAL STEPS OF TECHNOLOGICAL ADVANCEMENTS, THE RISE OF NEW MODELS OF OPERATION, VISIONARY ADVOCATES, AND POLICY CHANGES, OFTEN SPURRED BY SIGNIFICANT EVENTS THOUGHOUT HISTORY.

1834
Charleston, WV, enacts a law protecting vultures from hunters, as the birds help eat the city's garbage.

4 million tn/day

3 million tn/day

2 million tn/day

1 million tn/day

250
Archeological discoveries show that the Maya recycled their inorganic waste into fill for building projects.

1340–1350
The Black Death spreads to Central Europe and North Africa, resulting in an estimated 75 million deaths worldwide, (30-60 % of Europe's population).

1657
New Amsterdam (now New York) passes a law against dumping waste in the streets.

1690
Rittenhouse Mill, America's first paper mill, opens in Philadelphia and makes paper from recycled cotton, linen, and used paper.

1848
The Public Health Act of 1848 begins the process of waste regulation in Britain.

1500 BCE
Archeological evidence shows that in the Cretan capital, Knossos, the Minoan people created dump sites where waste was placed in large pits and covered with earth.

500 BCE
The Athenians institutionalized techniques similar to those used in Crete by mandating that waste be deposited no less than one mile from the city and banning the dumping of refuse in city streets.

1739
Benjamin Franklin leads an effort to petition the Pennsylvania Assembly to stop commercial waste dumping in Philadelphia and remove tanneries from Philadelphia's commercial district, which some historians consider the beginning of the environmental movement.

1776
The first metal recycling in the US occurs when patriots in New York City melt down a statue of King George III and made it into bullets.

1864
Health officials in Memphis, TN, hypothesize a possible correlation between the spread of yellow fever in the Memphis area and the garbage being dumped throughout the city. To reduce the threat of disease, residents are told to take their garbage to specific locations on the edge of town.

| 2000 BCE – 0 | 0 – 1500 | 1500 – 1850 |

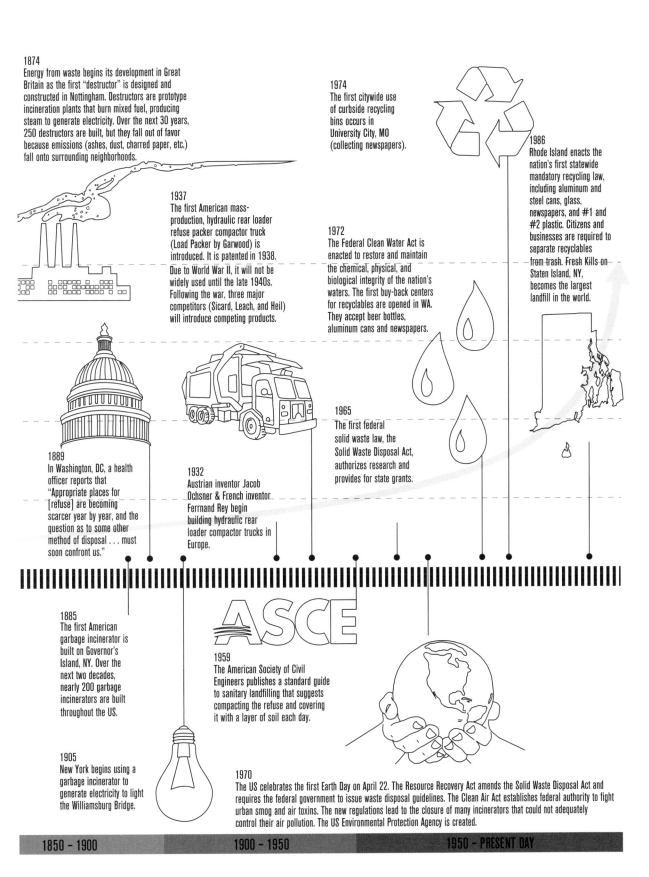

1874
Energy from waste begins its development in Great Britain as the first "destructor" is designed and constructed in Nottingham. Destructors are prototype incineration plants that burn mixed fuel, producing steam to generate electricity. Over the next 30 years, 250 destructors are built, but they fall out of favor because emissions (ashes, dust, charred paper, etc.) fall onto surrounding neighborhoods.

1937
The first American mass-production, hydraulic rear loader refuse packer compactor truck (Load Packer by Garwood) is introduced. It is patented in 1938.
Due to World War II, it will not be widely used until the late 1940s. Following the war, three major competitors (Sicard, Leach, and Heil) will introduce competing products.

1974
The first citywide use of curbside recycling bins occurs in University City, MO (collecting newspapers).

1986
Rhode Island enacts the nation's first statewide mandatory recycling law, including aluminum and steel cans, glass, newspapers, and #1 and #2 plastic. Citizens and businesses are required to separate recyclables from trash. Fresh Kills on Staten Island, NY, becomes the largest landfill in the world.

1972
The Federal Clean Water Act is enacted to restore and maintain the chemical, physical, and biological integrity of the nation's waters. The first buy-back centers for recyclables are opened in WA. They accept beer bottles, aluminum cans and newspapers.

1965
The first federal solid waste law, the Solid Waste Disposal Act, authorizes research and provides for state grants.

1889
In Washington, DC, a health officer reports that "Appropriate places for [refuse] are becoming scarcer year by year, and the question as to some other method of disposal . . . must soon confront us."

1932
Austrian inventor Jacob Ochsner & French inventor Ferrnand Rey begin building hydraulic rear loader compactor trucks in Europe.

1885
The first American garbage incinerator is built on Governor's Island, NY. Over the next two decades, nearly 200 garbage incinerators are built throughout the US.

1959
The American Society of Civil Engineers publishes a standard guide to sanitary landfilling that suggests compacting the refuse and covering it with a layer of soil each day.

1905
New York begins using a garbage incinerator to generate electricity to light the Williamsburg Bridge.

1970
The US celebrates the first Earth Day on April 22. The Resource Recovery Act amends the Solid Waste Disposal Act and requires the federal government to issue waste disposal guidelines. The Clean Air Act establishes federal authority to fight urban smog and air toxins. The new regulations lead to the closure of many incinerators that could not adequately control their air pollution. The US Environmental Protection Agency is created.

| 1850 – 1900 | 1900 – 1950 | 1950 – PRESENT DAY |

of waste, even when the economic boon of the Industrial Revolution led to a great waste increase in urban areas. By the 1800s, waste was piling up in cities, and rats and cockroaches infested most dwellings, including the White House. To deal with the waste, the city of Charleston in West Virginia enacted a law in 1834 protecting vultures, which ate city garbage, from hunters.

In 1842 a British report linked putrid environmental conditions to disease, launching the "Age of Sanitation" and resulting in the Public Health Act of 1848, which formally began the process of waste regulation in Great Britain. Similarly, in the United States in 1864, health officials in Tennessee hypothesized a correlation between the spread of yellow fever in the Memphis area and the garbage being dumped throughout the city. To reduce the threat of disease, residents were told to take their garbage to specific locations on the edge of town. A few years later, in order to prevent mass scavenging and to clean up the country, the British Public Health Act of 1875 gave authority to waste collection. From this act came the first (modern) concept of a movable garbage receptacle.

In 1874 the technology of waste disposal began in Great Britain as the first "destructor" was designed and constructed in Nottingham. These prototype incineration plants burned mixed fuel, producing steam that generated electricity. Over the next 30 years, 250 destructors were built, but they fell out of favor because of the noxious smoke produced. In the United States the destructor's American counterpart, the incinerator, was constructed in 1885 on Governor's Island, New York, and around 180 incinerators were constructed by 1900. However, as had occurred with the destructor in Great Britain, over half the incinerators were abandoned or dismantled by 1909 in response to their generation of excessive pollution.

By 1910, eight out of ten cities in the United States had a municipal garbage disposal system. With the advent of the automobile, by 1918 most US cities began switching to motorized refuse collection equipment. A few years later, in 1932, inventor Jacob Ochsner in Austria and Fernand Rey in France independently began building hydraulic rear-loader compactor trucks in Europe. In 1937, the first American mass-production, hydraulic rear-load refuse packer compactor truck was introduced.

As populations and economies grew, people lived closer together in cities and towns and generated more waste. Despite some early waste management efforts, there was little understanding of the connection between sanitation and disease.

ORGANIC

FOOD
- vegetable derived
- animal derived

- processed
- unprocessed

- animal
- garden

- unavoidable
- dead animal

GARDENING

- press/printing
- miscellaneous paper
- corrugated boxes

- animal excrement
- humid soil
- plant material

PAPER

PAPER

- folding boxes
- cartons, plates, cups
- miscellaneous board

- woody plant material
- animal straw
- books + booklets

BOARD

- PET/PETE
- HDPE
- PVC/V

- magazines + journals
- newspapers
- phone books

PACKAGING

NONPACKAGING

- LDPE/LLDPE
- PP
- PS

- advertisements
- office paper
- envelopes

PLASTIC

PLASTIC FILM

- plastic resin + ABS
- unidentified plastic
- pure plastic film
- composite plastic + metal coating

- craft paper
- other paper
- receipts
- self-adhesives
- tissue paper

PACKAGING

TABLE + KITCHENWARE

- **clear glass**
- **brown glass**

- wrapping paper
- beverage cartons

GLASS

OTHER/SPECIAL

- **green glass**

- **ferrous metal**
- **non-ferrous metal**

- cards + labels
- egg boxes + similar

PACKAGING

- human hygiene
- textiles + rubber + leather

- other board
- tubes
- diapers

METAL

NONPACKAGING

- vaccuum cleaner bags
- untreated wood

- tampons
- condoms

WRAPPING FOIL

- other combustibles

- **household ash**
- **cat litter**

- **large household appliances**
- **small household appliances**

COMBUSTIBLES

- **ceramics + gravel**
- **stone + sand**

- **photovoltaic panels**
- **lighting equipment**

OTHER

INERT

- **household construction + demolition**
- **household appliances + electronics + various equipment**

- **electrical tools**
- **toys + leisure + sports equipment**
- **medical devices + control instruments**

OTHER/SPECIAL

- **other household hazardous waste**
- **batteries**

- **automatic dispensers**

Combustible materials, suitable for WtE processing
Noncombustible materials

Waste composition

In the 1950s both the volume and forms of waste increased, and toxic waste became more commonplace. The first serious waste regulations were established during the 1960s, and the 1970s marked a turning point for waste considerations, as environmental and larger community health concerns came to the fore. A similar "environmental awakening" was likewise happening in Europe. In 1970, the United States celebrated its first Earth Day, and the United States Environmental Protection Agency (EPA) was created. Many major environmental laws and policies followed in the early 1970s, including the Resource Recovery Act, the Clean Air Act, and the Clean Water Act. These new laws led to the closure of many older incinerators and landfills that could not adequately control their pollution. The first citywide use of curbside recycling bins occurred in the United States in 1974. By 1975, all 50 states had some solid waste regulations. Three years later, the Public Utility Regulatory Policies Act guaranteed a market for energy created by small power producers and encouraged growth of the Waste-to-Energy industry. This led to incinerators being retooled as "resource-recovery" facilities, equipped with refined pollution-control devices.

Since the 1980s sustainable waste practices have become increasingly prominent. In particular, Ad Lansink of the Netherlands introduced the "waste hierarchy," which prioritizes waste prevention, then re-use, recycling, incineration (with energy production), and landfilling as the least desirable option. The hierarchy has guided waste management policy in many countries around the world.

Throughout the 1990s and early 2000s there have been increasingly widespread plans for reducing waste, incentivizing recycling, and discouraging of landfilling in Europe and the United States. Many clean WtE plants were built in the 1990s to reduce the amount of waste going to landfills. However, the amount of household waste continues to rise with increased populations, incomes, product availability, and packaging.

WASTE TODAY

Waste management is recognized as a fundamental prerequisite for sustainable development. Collection and treatment systems manage a part of the 1.3 billion tonnes of solid waste that is generated each year in cities.[1] However, a large proportion of that waste is still dumped to landfills or simply thrown away. This carries profound and multidimensional impacts for the environment and our societies at large. According to the World Bank, from 2002 to 2012, global waste generation increased by almost 100 percent, from 0.68 billion tonnes to 1.3 billion tonnes per year, while urban populations increased by just 10 percent.[2]

Ultimately waste generation becomes a part of a vicious resource-to-waste conversion cycle, perpetuated by insatiable, resource-intensive consumption and our affluent societies' constant need for more. As societies urbanize, they become wealthier, and by extension they utilize more resources and create more waste. In general, waste generation is inextricably linked with the level of economic development. However, waste generation varies greatly even within the same regions and countries. Highly developed countries and regions, such as the countries belonging to the Organization for Economic Cooperation and Development (OECD), are associated with the highest waste generation levels, often many orders of magnitude higher than waste generation levels in the least developed regions of the world (see figure on page 64). Furthermore, even though the population numbers in the OECD regions and Africa are almost equal, the OECD region produces one hundred times more waste than Africa.[3] One of the world's largest waste generators, even when compared to other highly developed regions, is the United States. During the last 50 years, per capita municipal solid waste (MSW) generation has increased by more than 70 percent in that country.[4] In 2012 the United States produced 724.6 kg per capita, while Estonia had the lowest generation rate within the OECD region, producing 279.1 kg per capita.[5] In contrast, Ghana produced 0.09 kg per capita per day (or roughly 32.8 kg per capita per year).[6]

The composition of waste also differs significantly between regions. The average MSW stream consists of hundreds of items; however, waste in affluent societies such as North America and Europe contains high volumes of paper and plastic and lower quantities of organic materials.[7] In comparison, waste composition in less-developed societies, such as in southeast Asia and Africa, is characterized by a much higher organic content and lower quantities of paper, metals, and plastic.[8] This difference in waste composition is influenced by various factors, such as cultural norms, location, and climate, but the most prominent driver is economic development. As regions urbanize and grow wealthier they witness a rapid increase in production and consumption of inorganic materials, such as paper and plastic, while the organic content of their waste streams gradually decreases.

Waste disposal also varies considerably by region and level of economic development. Landfilling is the most common disposal method throughout the world. However, most less-developed regions rely exclusively on landfilling, while affluent regions have introduced various alternative treatment methods in their waste management systems such as recycling, composting, and thermal treatment. In addition, alternative treatment methods and advanced waste management systems are also linked with a region's income level. Less developed regions are less able to source the extensive capital requirements required to operate and manage proper waste collection and management solutions, and thus rely more on landfilling practices (see figures on pages 64-65).[9]

No data available

Lowest quantile <20%

40%

60%

80%

Top quantile >80%

MSW generation per capita per day

Recycling rate

Percentage of waste to landfill

WASTE-TO-ENERGY HOTSPOTS

Converting waste into energy, or thermal treatment of waste, is the third most common method of MSW disposal globally, after landfilling and recycling.[10] Since WtE facilities require high capital investments, often significantly higher than landfills, comprehensive WtE facilities exist in middle- to high-income regions with advanced waste management systems. Other than a few exceptions, such as China, less-developed regions lack the resources and sufficient capital to introduce these facilities into their waste management systems.

WtE surpasses recycling in affluent societies worldwide, and the key hotspots are found in the United States, northwest Europe, and Asia. In Asia, key countries by size are Japan, Korea, and China; these account for nearly 90 percent of all WtE activity in the region. Similarly, the northeastern states in the United States and the northwestern regions of Europe are the major hotspots for WtE in the United States and Europe respectively (see figures on page 67).

Considering these WtE hotspots, an obvious question arises: why did WtE develop in these specific regions and not in others? A close look at the history of the regions with the most developed WtE systems reveals that all of them faced a specific set of challenges that made WtE economically feasible, especially when compared to landfilling. Among the most important contributing factors is the lack of available space for landfills. This is significant since landfill prices and gate fees tend to increase nonlinearly as the availability of space for a landfill is reduced.

Beyond the availability of space, the second key factor is environmental pollution, namely concerns with not being able to locate landfills far away from cities, potential contamination of groundwater, and environmental degradation. Importantly, all of these hotspot regions had faced substantial problems resulting from the contamination of their groundwater resources by landfills and industrial developments, which galvanized public opposition to landfills and further supported alternative waste management solutions. Finally, most of these regions are densely populated. This concentration of people leads to higher waste production and increases demand for electricity and heat. In addition, most of these regions, especially Sweden, Japan, and the European regions, lack comprehensive fossil fuel resources. As such, other than a sustainable waste management solution, WtE became a viable alternative energy source and a driving force in developing a balanced energy portfolio not exclusively reliant on fossil fuel usage and imports.[11]

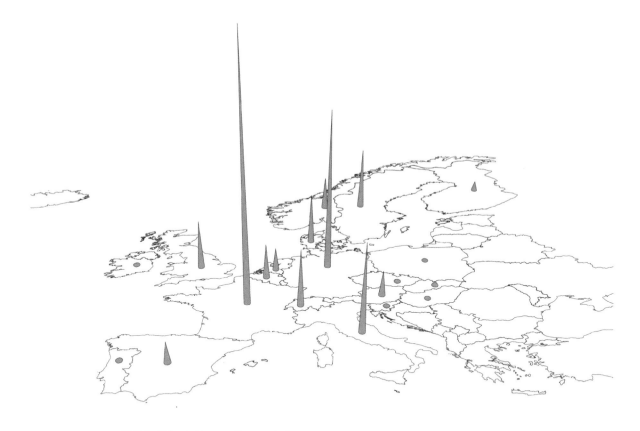

WtE facilities in Europe (by country)

WtE facilities in the United States (by state)

EUROPE AND THE UNITED STATES IN COMPARISON

Europe and the United States are the world's largest waste producers, accounting for approximately 40 percent of global waste production.[12] In 2012, both regions together generated 473 million tonnes of MSW, with the European Union producing 245 million tonnes and the United States 228 million tonnes.[13] Yet, although the composition of waste in the United States and in Europe is largely identical, the waste management systems of the two regions vary substantially. Several countries in Europe have gradually managed to minimize their reliance on landfilling through innovative systems with significant thermal treatment and recycling capabilities. Of the European Union's waste, 31 percent goes to landfills, 24 percent is thermally treated, and 45 percent is recycled and/or composted (see top figure on page 69).[14] In comparison, landfilling waste is still the most common disposal method in the United States (see bottom figure on page 69). Out of the 228 million tonnes of US waste generated, 54 percent end up in landfills, 26 percent is recycled, 8 percent composted, and 12 percent thermally treated for energy recovery.[15]

Notably, significant differences can be observed among states within the United States as well as within European regions. For example, although the northwestern European regions such as Sweden and Germany have developed highly efficient and innovative waste systems, several central and southern regions continue to rely heavily on landfilling (see figure on page 70). Similarly, in the United States, the Northeast has extensive WtE and recycling developments, while the Midwest continues to rely largely on landfilling (see figure on page 71).

Europe and the United States are among the world's largest waste incineration markets. In 2012, the European Union's 409 WtE plants treated 59 million tonnes of municipal waste.[16] Similarly, in 2012 the United States' 84 WtE facilities treated approximately 27 million tonnes of municipal waste.[17] These statistics exclude treated industrial and hazardous waste. Statistics on total waste treated in the European Union WtE plants in 2012 totaled anywhere from 79 to 137 million tonnes.[18]

Evidently, although the European Union and the United States treat comparable amounts of waste, the difference between their respective electricity and heat outputs is quite significant. This happens because the average US heating and electricity requirements are significantly higher, but also because the European WtE facilities and waste management systems are often more efficient. Incineration facilities in northern European regions such as Denmark and Sweden take advantage of widespread district heating networks to provide heat to businesses and households, which elevates the difference in efficiency levels.[19] WtE facilities can achieve about 25 percent efficiency with power generation and 85 to 90 percent efficiency with combined heat and power generation, which means enhancing the efficiency of the plant by more than 340 to 360 percent. In general, WtE facilities with combined heat and power capabilities are common in Europe, while in the United States, only 20 percent (18 out of 84) operational WtE facilities are capable of capturing heat when producing electricity. Furthermore, district heating networks in the United States are still in the early development stages.[20]

EU-27: 245 Million Tonnes of MSW in 2012

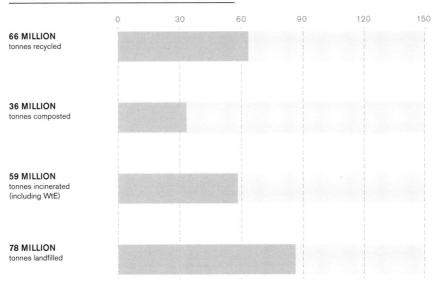

66 MILLION
tonnes recycled

36 MILLION
tonnes composted

59 MILLION
tonnes incinerated
(including WtE)

78 MILLION
tonnes landfilled

European Union waste generation

United States: 228 Million Tonnes of MSW in 2012

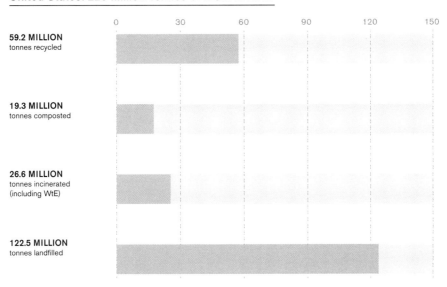

59.2 MILLION
tonnes recycled

19.3 MILLION
tonnes composted

26.6 MILLION
tonnes incinerated
(including WtE)

122.5 MILLION
tonnes landfilled

United States waste generation

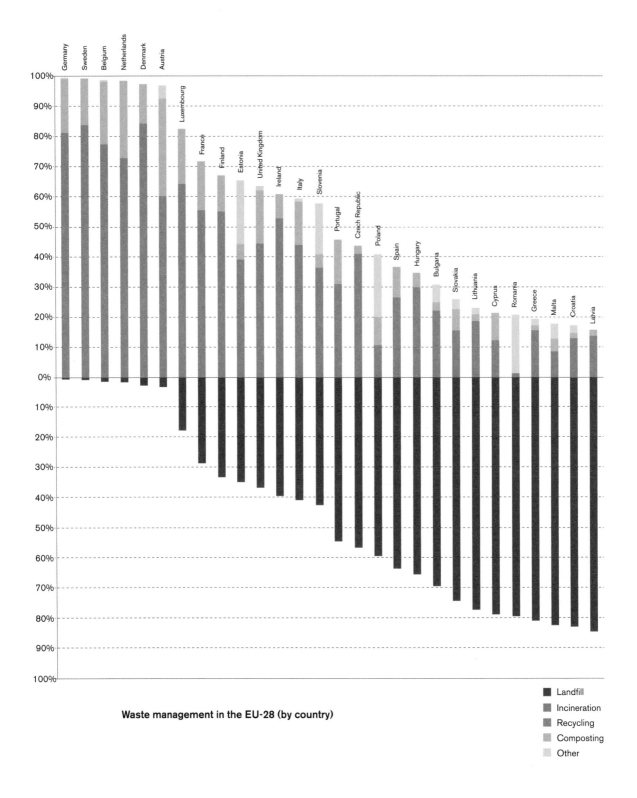

Waste management in the EU-28 (by country)

Legend:
- Landfill
- Incineration
- Recycling
- Composting
- Other

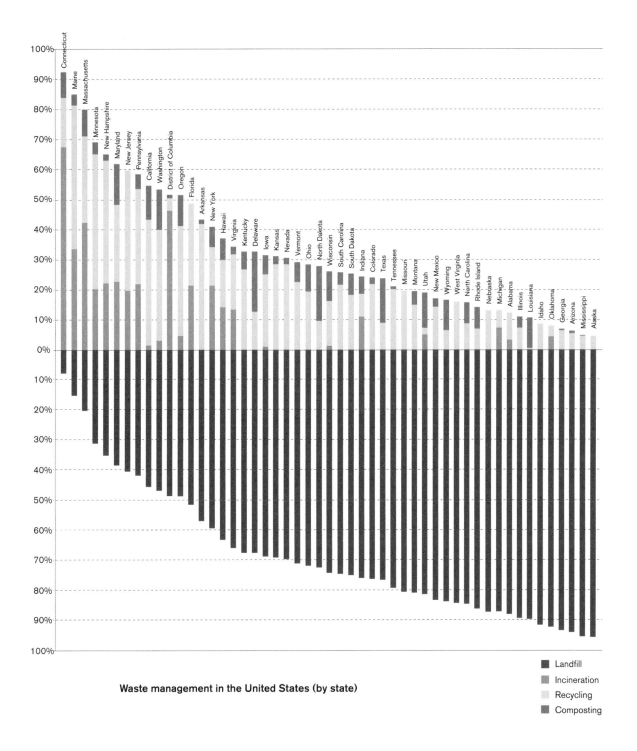

Waste management in the United States (by state)

Landfill
Incineration
Recycling
Composting

CONCLUSIONS

In response to the rapidly rising waste generation rates and volumes, Europe and the United States gradually developed sophisticated waste management systems that gather, transport, and dispose of waste very efficiently on a daily basis. In just over 100 years, the United States and most European countries have made the shift from dumping waste anywhere to safely disposing of it in landfills or even utilizing it to produce resources. This constitutes one of humanity's greatest innovations, given the variety of costs and impacts on human health that unsanitary waste disposal inflicted on global populations for many centuries.

However, it is important to reiterate that in addition to currently being the world's largest waste producers, Europe and the United States are also the regions with the most advanced waste management systems, albeit with very different efficiency levels. Notably, 54 percent of waste in the United States still ends up in landfills, compared to 31 percent in Europe. As will be discussed in the following chapters, some European countries foresaw rising waste generation rates as an opportunity to innovate; through integrated planning, these countries promoted waste as a potential resource to reduce dependency on imports and facilitate a more sustainable economy. This eventually led to the development of widespread district heating networks, and the consequent aforementioned differences in WtE outputs and waste management efficiency levels between the waste management systems in Europe and the United States.

NOTES

1. Daniel Hoornweg and Perinaz Bhada-Tata, *What a Waste: A Global Review of Solid Waste Management*, Urban Development Series, Knowledge Papers no. 15 (Washington, DC: World Bank, 2012), https://openknowledge .worldbank.org/handle/10986/17388.

2. Ibid.

3. Ibid.; and OECD, *OECD Factbook 2014: Economic, Environmental, and Social Statistics* (OECD Publishing, 2014), http://dx.doi .org/10.1787/factbook-2014-70-en.

4. US Environmental Protection Agency (US EPA), *Municipal Solid Waste Generation, Recycling, and Disposal in the United States* (US EPA, February 2014), https://www.epa.gov/sites/production /files/201509/documents/2012_msw _dat_tbls.pdf.

5. OECD, Municipal Waste (indicator), 2016, https://data.oecd.org/waste/munici- pal-waste.htm.

6. Hoornweg and Bhada-Tata, *What a Waste*, Annex J.

7. Hoornweg and Bhada-Tata, *What a Waste*; and United Nations Envi- ronment Programme (UNEP), *Global Waste Management Outlook* (UNEP and ISWA, 2015), http://www.unep .org/ietc/Portals/136/Publications /Waste%20Management/GWMO%20 report/GWMO%20full%20report.pdf.

8. Hoornweg and Bhada-Tata, *What a Waste*; and UNEP, *Global Waste Management Outlook.*

9. Lilliana Abarca Guerrero, Ger Mass, and William Hogland, "Solid Waste

Management Challenges for Cities in Developing Countries," *Waste Manage- ment* 33 (2013): 220-32, http://dx.doi .org/10.1016/j. wasman.2012.09.008; Hoornweg and Bhada-Tata, "What a Waste"; and UNEP, *Global Waste Management Outlook.*

10. Hoornweg and Bhada-Tata, *What a Waste*; and UNEP, *Global Waste Management Outlook.*

11. US Environmental Protection Agency, *25 Years of Resource Conser- vation and Recovery Act (RCRA): Building on Our Past To Protect Our Future* (US EPA, 2002), http://nepis .epa.gov/Exe/ZyPDF.cgi/10000MAO .PDF?Dockey=10000MAO.PDF; Connecticut General Assembly, *Munic- ipal Solid Waste Management Services in Connecticut* (Legislative Program Review and Investigations Committee, 2010), https://www.cga.ct.gov/2009 /pridata/Studies/PDF/MSW_Services _Final_Report.pdf; Ministry of the Environment, *History and Current State of Waste Management in Japan* (2014), http://www.env.go.jp/en/recycle/smcs /attach/hcswm.pdf; Swedish Waste Management, *Assessment of Increased Trade of Combustible Waste in the European Union* (F2012:04), http:// www.avfallsverige.se/fileadmin/uploads /Rapporter/F%C3%B6rbr%C3%A4nning /F2012-04.pdf; and Swedish Waste Management, *Swedish Waste Manage- ment System* (2013), http://www. avfallsverige.se/fileadmin/uploads /Rapporter/SWM_2013.pdf.

12. Hoornweg and Bhada-Tata, *What a Waste.*

13. This is equivalent to 251 million US tons. Eurostat, "Municipal Waste Statistics," Statistics Explained, http://ec .europa.eu/eurostat/statistics-explained/ index.php/Municipal_waste_statistics 2015; and US EPA, *Municipal Solid Waste Generation.*

14. Eurostat, "Municipal Waste Statistics."

15. US EPA, *Municipal Solid Waste Generation*, Table 30.

16. Confederation of European Waste- to-Energy Plants (CEWEP), "Waste- to-Energy in Europe in 2012," http:// www.cewep.eu/information/data /studies/m_1342; and Eurostat, "Munic- ipal Waste Statistics."

17. Ted Michaels, *The 2014 ERC Directory of Waste-to-Energy Facilities* (Energy Recovery Council, 2014), http:// energyrecoverycouncil.org/wp-content /uploads/2016/01/ERC_2014_Directory .pdf; and US EPA, *Municipal Solid Waste Generation.*

18. CEWEP, "Waste-to-Energy in Europe in 2012"; and Eurostat, "Municipal Waste Statistics."

19. Swedish Waste Management, *Swedish Waste Management System;* and Anna Chittum and Poul Alberg Østergaard, "How Danish Communal Heat Planning Empowers Municipalities and Benefits Individual Consumers," *Energy Policy*, vol. 74, (November 2014): 465-74, http://dx.doi .org/10.1016/j.enpol.2014.08.001.

20. Chittum and Østergaard, "How Danish Communal Heat Planning Empowers Municipalities."

Sweden is globally recognized as a leader and a pioneer in waste management. The country has developed an innovative MSW management system in which, as of 2013, less than 1 percent of waste ends up in landfills, 50.3 percent is treated through thermal treatment, 33 percent is recycled, and the remaining 16 percent of household waste is treated through biological treatment.[1] A quick calculation can illustrate the efficiency of the Swedish system, and the opportunity for other countries striving to improve their waste management in a similar way. In 2013, every Swede generated, on average, 461.2 kg of household waste, but only 3.5 kg of that was disposed of in landfills.[2] In recent years, the Swedish system has become so efficient that it imports waste from other European countries to keep the nation's 32 Waste-to-Energy facilities running.[3]

To reach today's level of efficiency, the Swedish waste management system went through various phases of development over several decades. According to *Swedish Waste Management*, one of the most significant factors that expedited the shift towards more sustainable waste management and energy practices was the 1973 oil crisis.[4] Although the incineration of waste without energy recovery was already common in Sweden, after the 1970s oil crisis the country became increasingly interested in developing methods to derive energy from waste in order to minimize its reliance on imported fossil fuels. Two years after the crisis, the state introduced several programs to drive investments and support the utilization of MSW for the production of energy. At the same time, municipalities started to implement strategic district-heating developments, which included households and industries, to capture heat from adjacent incinerators.[5] Despite the many benefits of energy and waste management systems, Swedish authorities hoped to avoid repeating past mistakes that led to significant industrial pollution that detrimentally impacted surrounding environments.[6] As such, after pollution concerns from air pollutants/emissions galvanized in the early 1980s, the government introduced a moratorium on new facilities in 1985.[7]

Best Practices and Missed Opportunities: Waste-to-Energy in Sweden and the United States

ANDREAS GEORGOULIAS AND LEIRE ASENSIO VILLORIA

Klaus Leidorf, *Tires*, 2006

SWEDISH POLICIES

In the early 1990s, Sweden introduced municipal waste planning mandates for municipalities, while municipalities and private companies proved that health risks resulting from the incineration of waste were significantly reduced.[8] Moreover, the pioneering "producers' responsibility" legislation introduced in 1994 further exacerbated pressure on landfills. Sweden adopted the European Union's waste legislation and started implementing a series of economic instruments designed to promote alternative means of waste management while making landfilling economically unsustainable. In 2000, an incremental landfill tax was introduced, which, along with a ban on the landfilling of combustible waste in 2002 and a similar ban on organic waste in 2005, gradually raised landfill gate fees and prices to very high levels.[9] Today landfill gate fees in Sweden are $180 per tonne of waste, in contrast to the United States' $48 per tonne. In addition, Sweden has a carbon tax, which was initially instituted in 1991.[10]

Over the last decades, Sweden has introduced more than one hundred laws that pertain to waste management. As a result, since 1994 energy recovery has increased by approximately 70 percent, recycling has doubled, and landfilling has decreased by 98 percent.[11] Evidently, these specific policies and economic instruments were fundamental in driving alternative waste management efforts and minimizing landfills (see figure on page 78) The same results can be seen throughout the European Union in countries that have enacted similar policies and economic instruments.[12]

Over the last decades, Sweden has introduced more than one hundred laws that pertain to waste management. As a result, since 1994, energy recovery has increased by approximately 70 percent, recycling has doubled, and landfilling has decreased by 98 percent.[11] Evidently, these specific policies and economic instruments were fundamental in driving alternative waste management efforts and minimizing landfills.

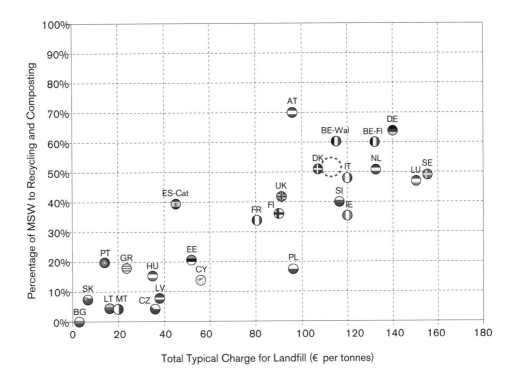

EU-28 MSW to recycling and composting (by country)

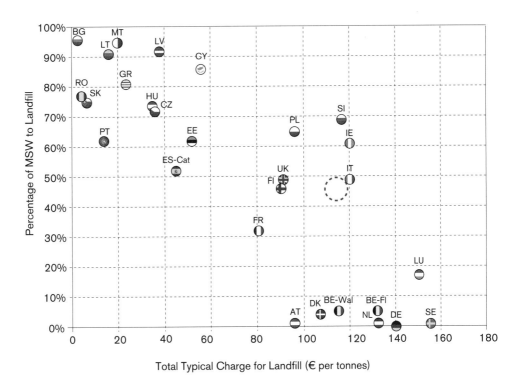

EU-28 MSW to landfill (by country)

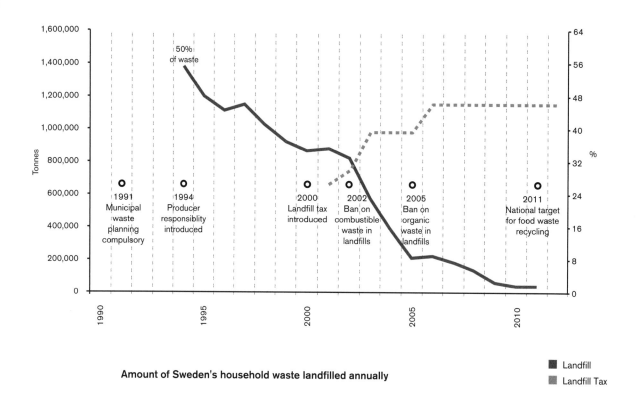

Amount of Sweden's household waste landfilled annually

Legend:
- ■ Landfill
- ■ Landfill Tax

WtE SUCCESS FACTORS IN SWEDEN	WtE SETBACKS IN THE UNITED STATES
<ul><li>Government and regulatory environment fosters WtE</li><li>Waste management is regulated as a public service</li><li>National environmental targets</li><li>Clear division of roles and responsibilities</li><li>Cooperation between and within municipalities</li><li>Communication and public engagement</li></ul>	<ul><li>Lack of communication and public engagement</li><li>Lack of state and federal support</li><li>Financing capital costs</li><li>Public opposition</li></ul>

WtE success factors in Sweden; setbacks in the United States

UNITED STATES WASTE MANAGEMENT

Unlike Sweden, the United States continues to rely extensively on landfilling. Despite a few exceptions, such as the northeastern states, the westernmost states, Florida, and Minnesota, America has developed numerous mega-landfills to accommodate the products of its vicious, and increasingly detrimental, resource-to-waste conversion cycle. In 2012, Americans generated approximately 251 million US tonnes of waste, of which 135 million tonnes headed to landfills.[13] Assuming an average landfill gate fee of $48 per tonnes, the simple act of throwing waste into landfills approaches a cost of $6.5 billion per year.

Historically, all states relied greatly on landfilling and dump disposal up until the 1970s and early 1980s. As such, they faced detrimental problems resulting from subsequent massive groundwater contamination and pollution, especially in the highly populated coastal states of the Northeast and Florida.[14] This was one of the most prominent driving forces for the Resource Recovery Act Amendment of the Solid Waste Disposal Act in 1970 and the Resource Conservation and Recovery Act of 1976.[15] This legislation facilitated a push toward waste incineration—however without requiring energy recovery, recycling, or other alternative means.

These policies were specifically designed to encourage states to develop comprehensive waste management plans, as well as to pursue more environmentally friendly waste management and disposal methods, such as incineration with energy recovery. Over the years, the policies were supported by a series of energy acts, such as the Public Utility Restructuring Policy Act and the Energy Tax Act of 1978, which subsidized privately produced power and introduced special investment tax credits. As such, WtE facilities were able to establish long-term contracts at very competitive prices.

Today, communities increasingly endeavor to introduce recycling, composting, and thermal treatment programs, among others, to facilitate resource recovery and help revitalize surrounding environments. However, although such alternative waste management methods are becoming more efficient, they are not the preferred option. In the United States, roughly 2,000 operational landfills occupy more than 6,000 acres of what would otherwise be free, open landscape.[16] Landfills are usually situated in remote locations next to forests, occupying land that could be utilized for recreation or various other purposes. They emit greenhouse gases that account for 2 to 5 percent of the country's total emissions, pose significant odor and health risks, and cause long-term disruptions to their surrounding environments.[17] If all landfilled waste were to be utilized for resource recovery, America could supply heat and electricity to millions of homes and extract millions less tonnes of coal. Why, then, are landfills still the most prominent method of waste management in the United States? Reasons go beyond the familiar "Not in My Backyard" pattern, when residents object precipitously to plans that site waste facilities in their immediate surroundings.

Money, not surprisingly, lies at the heart of the problem; the most polluting method of waste management is also the cheapest. Although the total number of landfills has decreased since the early 1970s, the vast areas of available land throughout the United States enable the development of mega-landfills that accept waste at very low charges and pose significant roadblocks to the transition toward alternative waste management methods. According to the US EPA, reliance on landfilling and landfill numbers peaked in the 1970s, but official stats are only available from the late 1980s. In 1988 there were approximately 8,000 landfills in the United States, whereas in the late 2000s—the most recent period for which data is available regarding the number of landfills—that number was reduced to approximately 2,000 landfills.[18] Similarly, although landfill gate fees have been constantly rising, the average US landfill fee is still low compared to other waste management methods, and significantly lower than several European countries and the rest of the world.

For many states, transporting waste to out-of-state landfills is the most financially feasible solution. After the landmark Supreme Court case on waste, *Flow Control,* in 1994, solid waste was designated as a commodity subject to interstate commerce laws.[19] As such, states were not able to control the final place of waste disposal or direct waste to a specific facility over long periods of time. This jeopardized the ability of WtE and other alternative disposal facilities to sign long-term contracts, while presenting the option for cities to export waste to states with much higher availability of land and disposal capacity. Taxpayers in New York, for instance, paid $2.2 billion to cover the state's waste management needs in 2012; $300 million were costs for railroad, truck, and landfill operational expenses to transport and dispose of waste in out-of-state land-fills.[20] The trucks travel 40 million miles annually, the equivalent of approximately 7,000 trips from New York City to Los Angeles.[21] The latest Congressional Research Service report estimates that in 2005 Pennsylvania received seven million US tonnes of waste from New York and New Jersey, while Ohio received 500,000 US tonnes of waste from New Jersey and 132,000 tonnes from Connecticut, both of which are located more than 500 miles away. According to the report, from 1995 to 2005 state waste imports increased by 147 percent.[22]

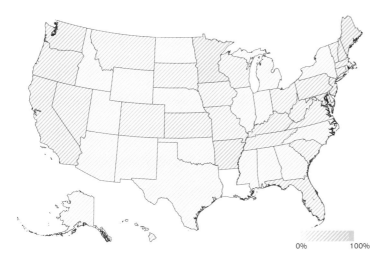

Percentage of MSW landfilled in the United States (by state)

0%   100%

Percentage of MSW recycled in the United States (by state)

0%   100%

Percentage of MSW to WtE facilities in the United States (by state)

0%   100%

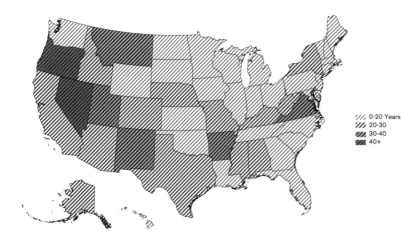

Average remaining life of US landfills

0-20 Years
20-30
30-40
40+

MSW landfill tipping fees

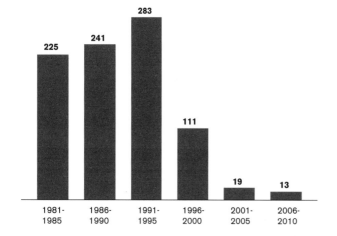

225	241	283	111	19	13

| 1981-1985 | 1986-1990 | 1991-1995 | 1996-2000 | 2001-2005 | 2006-2010 |

New landfills permitted in the United States

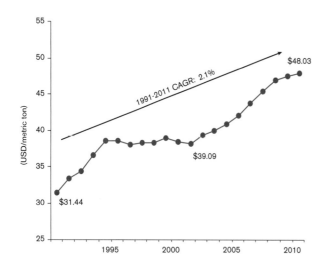

1991-2011 CAGR: 2.1%

$48.03

$39.09

$31.44

(USD/metric ton)

82

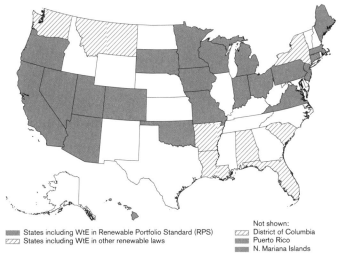

US states defining WtE as renewable

States including WtE in Renewable Portfolio Standard (RPS)
States including WtE in other renewable laws

Note: Some state RPS programs limit program eligibility to certain types of WtE technology, including CO, MO, OH, and WI. WtE is eligible in AZ if approved by the Arizona Corporation Commission.

Not shown:
District of Columbia
Puerto Rico
N. Mariana Islands

Waste exports: New York

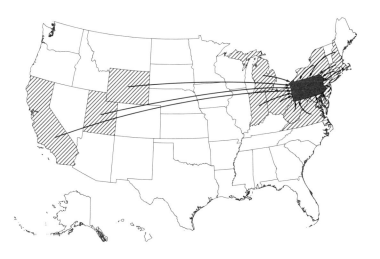

Waste imports: Pennsylvania

SWEDEN AND THE UNITED STATES IN COMPARISON

Despite a similar MSW stream composition and waste management infrastructure, Sweden has managed to develop a waste management system that relies extensively on thermal treatment and recycling, whereas the United States has been unable to move past its reliance on landfilling practices. Although the waste management systems of both countries relied extensively on landfilling 40 years ago, today Sweden sends less than 1 percent of its MSW into landfills, while the United States has consistently been landfilling more than 50 percent of its MSW (see figures on pages 85–87).

Other than the fact that Sweden is a much smaller country and produces much less MSW than the United States, several specific factors made the transition toward more efficient waste management and energy systems a success in Sweden. As we previously discussed, Sweden has developed a regulatory environment that supports WtE and alternative waste management developments through various laws, economic instruments, and governance structures. Waste management is established as a significant public service, which is supported by mandates and regulations that make municipalities responsible for all activities and services required for managing waste generated within their boundaries. Then, municipalities are further supported by a well-established governance structure that specifies a clear division of roles and the responsibilities of every actor in the waste management system, under the umbrella of long-term national environmental goals.[23] Moreover, the Swedish waste management authorities have taken extensive communication and public engagement measures to communicate and explain the importance of waste management, which not only creates a culture of environmental stewardship and widespread knowledge of waste management practices, but also minimizes the potential for public opposition.

In comparison to Sweden, the United States currently lacks comprehensive waste management policies at the federal level. As such, there are no regulations to mandate national, long-term waste management targets, and there is no clear division of roles and responsibilities at the state level. States have to come up with their own MSW management plans and policies; they are only responsible for following the EPA's waste management hierarchy. (In contrast, in Europe every country member is obligated to comply with the Landfill Directive, which specifies measurable targets and policies to avoid the use of landfilling.[24])

Furthermore, the United States lacks state subsidies and support schemes necessary to facilitate WtE developments. In Sweden, for instance, the organic portion of waste is recognized as a renewable source of energy, thus making WtE facilities eligible for specialized incentives and subsidy programs.[25] In the United States, even though the EPA has long recognized WtE as a renewable source of energy, many states do not yet include WtE in their renewable energy portfolio standards.[26]

Moreover, the 1994 Supreme Court *Flow Control* case perpetuated widespread ambiguity regarding the exact roles and responsibilities for managing waste.[27] Since this case, states have been unable to restrict or to assign the final location of waste disposal within their boundaries. As such, waste producers are not obligated to use disposal facilities within their own community or state and can choose cheaper, out-of-state alternatives. As a result, establishing long-term contracts and financing WtE projects has become increasingly difficult, since facilities are not able to secure a stable supply of waste over the long term. Without regulations and economic instruments such as a landfill or a carbon tax, the availability of land for landfill developments throughout the United States keeps the price of landfilling at very low levels and hinders the development of

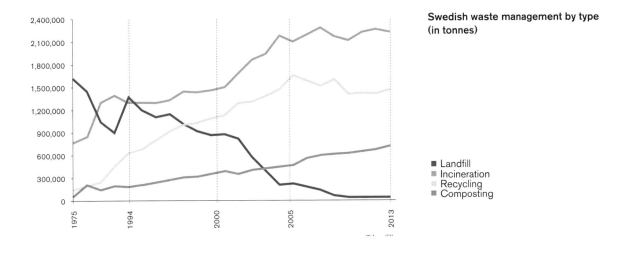

Swedish waste management by type (in tonnes)

■ Landfill
■ Incineration
▨ Recycling
■ Composting

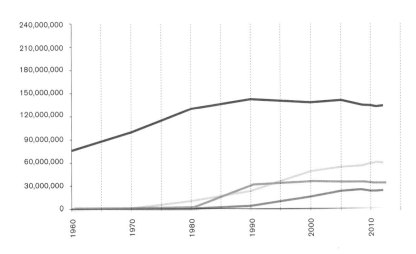

United States waste management by type (in tonnes)

alternative waste management practices. Notably, WtE is also among Sweden's cheapest energy sources, since Sweden does not have significant fossil fuel resources or other cheaper local alternative energy options. However, this is not the case in the US, where most states enjoy significantly lower energy prices.[28] Additionally, in the United States WtE facilities still face intense public opposition, since WtE is regarded as a barrier to expanding the recycling market as well as a source of environmental pollution and health risks. As such, new developments have been consistently delayed and blocked by environmental groups and communities opposed to such projects.

The Northeast of the United States shares many similarities with Sweden with regard to waste management. Although the Northeast has a much higher population rate and produces more waste, it is the only US region that has managed to develop a waste management system comparable to that of Sweden. Specifically, the northeastern states rely extensively on thermal treatment of waste and recycling, and they strive to minimize the use of landfilling practices. Furthermore, the Northeast is the region with the largest number of WtE facilities, accounting for approximately 46 percent of total US facilities.[29] Connecticut, Massachusetts, and Maine, for instance, are the US leaders in WtE and use thermal means to treat 67.1 percent, 42.2 percent, and 33.5 percent, respectively, of their municipal waste.[30]

According to the Northeast Waste Management Officials' Association, the northeastern states have developed a regional waste management system where, in contrast to other states and regions, waste is exchanged and disposed of or recycled within the region. Every northeastern state exports MSW to at least one other Northeast state, thereby taking advantage of economies of scale that minimize transportation costs, as well as circumventing any potential challenges with siting and developing disposal facilities.

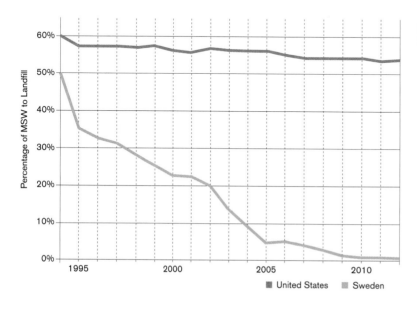

Percentage of MSW landfilled in the United States and Sweden

Similar to Sweden, the northeastern states benefit tremendously from cooperation and coordinate their efforts to reduce the generation of waste and increase alternative modes of treatment and recycling.[31]

Over the years, the northeastern states have implemented stringent policies and waste management mandates that exceeded the regional and federal requirements set by the EPA at the time. For instance, decades ago, long before the EPA made it compulsory for states and municipalities to do so, Connecticut and Maine adopted the waste hierarchy, a guideline that specifies the most preferable waste management options and policies that should be implemented in a specified order. As such, they have long been established as leaders in environmental and waste-specific policy making.

The main driving force behind these comprehensive policies and progressive initiatives, which were often initiated by the region's smallest states, was the fear of becoming a regional waste repository. Furthermore, since most of the northeastern states are relatively small, any potential issues with siting landfills and respective environmental impacts are magnified. Thus, although all states relied extensively on landfilling in the late 1960s and early 1970s, environmental degradation and landfill issues were a particularly prominent source of concern in the Northeast.[32] One of the most significant concerns regarded the contamination of groundwater bodies. For example, the state of Connecticut, which is ten times smaller than Sweden, had approximately 150 operational unsanitary landfills in the late 1960s. Connecticut was one of the first US states to prohibit open dumping of waste in 1966, and implemented the first statewide waste management strategy, the Solid Waste Management Act, in 1971.[33] Two years later, the Solid Waste Management Services Act of 1973 promoted resource recovery as a favorable waste management option and an environmental goal of the state: "Maximum resource recovery from solid

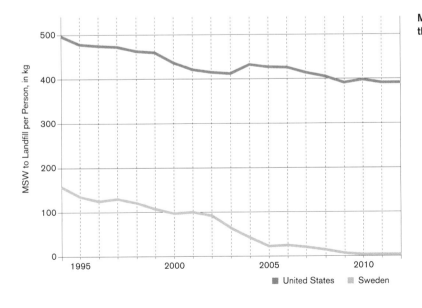

MSW landfilled per person in the United States and Sweden

waste and maximum recycling and reuse of such resources in order to protect, preserve, and enhance the environment of the state shall be considered environmental goals of the state."[34] Moreover, it established the Connecticut Resources Recovery Authority to facilitate a regional, strategic approach to WtE.[35] Finally, in addition to the federal landfill requirements that were set by the Resource Conservation and Recovery Act of 1976, Connecticut implemented more stringent regulations with regard to landfill planning standards and permits, and mandated that "beyond physical location requirements, a written determination of need from the Department of Environmental Protection commissioner is necessary for new or expansion permits for landfills."[36]

Similarly, Maine banned the construction of new landfills in 1989, and mandated the closure and restoration of unsanitary landfill sites and open dumps. This raised questions about the waste treatment capacity and whether the remaining landfill space was enough to manage the state's waste. In response to these concerns, the state facilitated widespread waste incineration and recycling efforts, aimed to avoid the use of landfills and develop a more sustainable waste management system.[37] Notably, Maine has traditionally facilitated cooperative municipal action. For instance, the Municipal Review Committee in central and eastern Maine has been established to negotiate and manage contacts for the region's 140 communities.[38]

Despite a similar municipal solid waste stream composition and waste management infrastructure, Sweden has managed to develop a waste management system that relies extensively on thermal treatment and recycling, whereas the United States has been unable to move past its reliance on landfilling practices.

PROJECTIONS

Despite the urgent need to move away from landfilling practices, the significant efforts and innovative waste management systems of a few US regions so far have not been enough to drive a systemic change toward more sustainable waste management practices in the country. However, in the United States, as well as throughout the world, rapid urbanization will continue to lead to increasingly higher waste generation. In the United States, waste generation has already increased by approximately 10 percent in the last ten years. In previous decades, that number was even higher, often exceeding the 30 and 40 percent mark. If the current trajectory holds, by 2020 the United States might be faced with unprecedented levels of MSW and no adequate capacity to manage and treat it in an environmentally responsible way. Worldwide projections are even more alarming. According to the World Bank's estimations, by 2025 urban residents throughout the world are expected to generate up to 2.2 billion tonnes of MSW per year, a 60 percent increase compared to the 2012 generation levels.[39] Currently, there is no accurate estimate on when municipal waste generation is going to peak in the United States or throughout the world.

Another aspect that further complicates the challenges ahead is that municipal waste streams will continue to change. Although the composition of waste streams will remain largely the same, the distribution of the main components across waste streams might be considerably altered as a result of technological change. For instance, the amount of electronic waste, paper, and packaging materials in US waste streams has been constantly changing during the last decades, shifts that—although not significant—add additional pressure on a recycling system that is also not supported by federal regulation.

Furthermore, the US WtE market is also set to experience considerable challenges. Although in recent years some WtE facilities have expanded their original capacity to treat more waste, the majority of the 84 operational US WtE facilities were built from the late 1980s to the mid-1990s. As such, most of the contracts are set to expire relatively soon, and the facilities would have to negotiate new long-term agreements that would not include previous beneficial terms and subsidies. Without subsidies to make them economically feasible, and in a waste management system that favors the use of landfills, most WtE facilities have been unable to continue their operations after the end of their initial contract. In addition, this issue impedes the potential for new WtE develop-ments. As a result, the number of US WtE facilities has been constantly decreasing. In 2011 there were 97 operational WtE plants in the United States, while by 2015 the number had dropped to 84.[40] In comparison, during the same period, Europe as a whole introduced 12 new WtE facilities.[41]

Yet the trend in the United States can be changed, and the stakes are high. A few quick calculations can demonstrate the opportunity the country faces, and what it stands to lose by neglecting to act now. In 2014, a study by Nicholas Themelis and Charles Mussche at Columbia University found that if all the municipal waste disposed of in landfills in the United States in 2011 were thermally treated, it could provide electricity for approx-imately 13.8 million homes and heat approximately 9.8 million homes (provided those homes had district heating).[42] Moreover, it would prevent 123 million tonnes of CO_2 from the atmosphere—the equivalent of taking 23 million cars off the road. In contrast, if the current trajectory holds, the country will continue losing precious resources as well as perpetuating environmental and health risks. States with higher population densities—mainly along the coastlines—face the biggest problems. On the whole they lack adequate space for landfills and they produce the largest amounts of waste per capita in the United States. And siting and permitting new facilities in general, not only landfills, has become very problematic due to community opposition. Thus, sooner or later states will run out of options. Several states in the Northeast, for instance, need more landfill space than is currently available. Even states that have traditionally been significant waste importers will soon lose precious landfill space. For example, Pennsylvania imported 8 million US tonnes of MSW and substantial amounts of industrial, construction and demolition, and other hazardous waste in 2005, but the state is expected to face a significant waste disposal crisis by 2020 if landfill capacities are not expanded or new facilities are not permitted.[43]

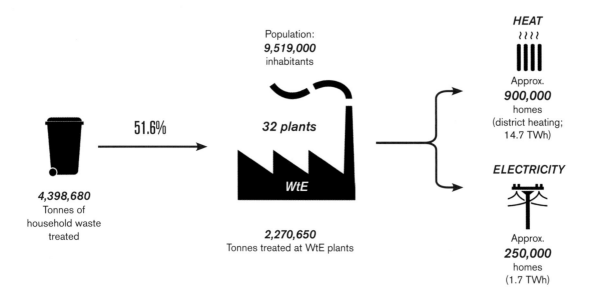

Sweden waste energy recovery as of 2012

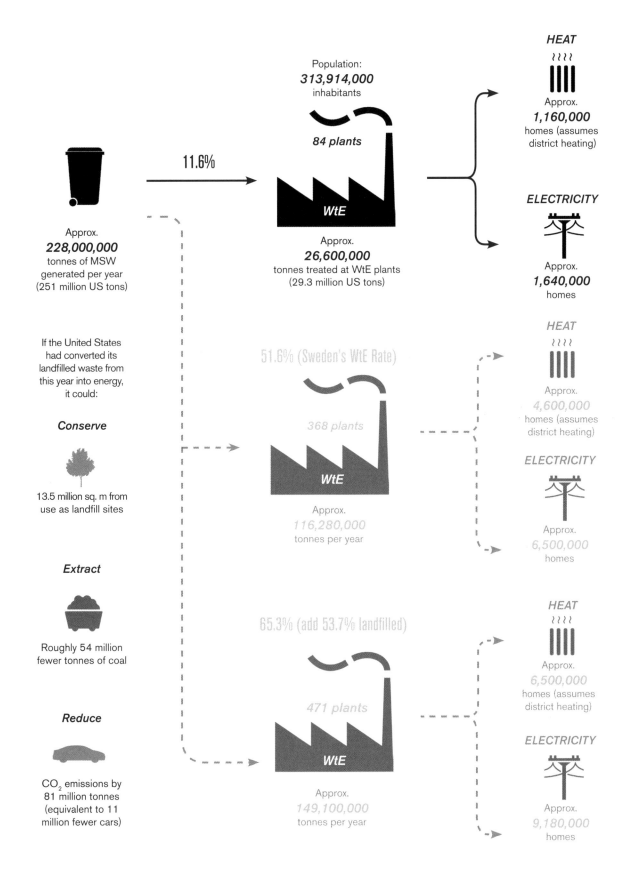

Population:
313,914,000 inhabitants

84 plants

WtE

11.6%

Approx.
228,000,000 tonnes of MSW generated per year (251 million US tons)

Approx.
26,600,000 tonnes treated at WtE plants (29.3 million US tons)

HEAT

Approx.
1,160,000 homes (assumes district heating)

ELECTRICITY

Approx.
1,640,000 homes

If the United States had converted its landfilled waste from this year into energy, it could:

Conserve

13.5 million sq. m from use as landfill sites

51.6% (Sweden's WtE Rate)

368 plants

WtE

Approx.
116,280,000 tonnes per year

HEAT

Approx.
4,600,000 homes (assumes district heating)

ELECTRICITY

Approx.
6,500,000 homes

Extract

Roughly 54 million fewer tonnes of coal

65.3% (add 53.7% landfilled)

471 plants

WtE

Approx.
149,100,000 tonnes per year

HEAT

Approx.
6,500,000 homes (assumes district heating)

ELECTRICITY

Approx.
9,180,000 homes

Reduce

CO_2 emissions by 81 million tonnes (equivalent to 11 million fewer cars)

United States waste energy recovery, actual and projected

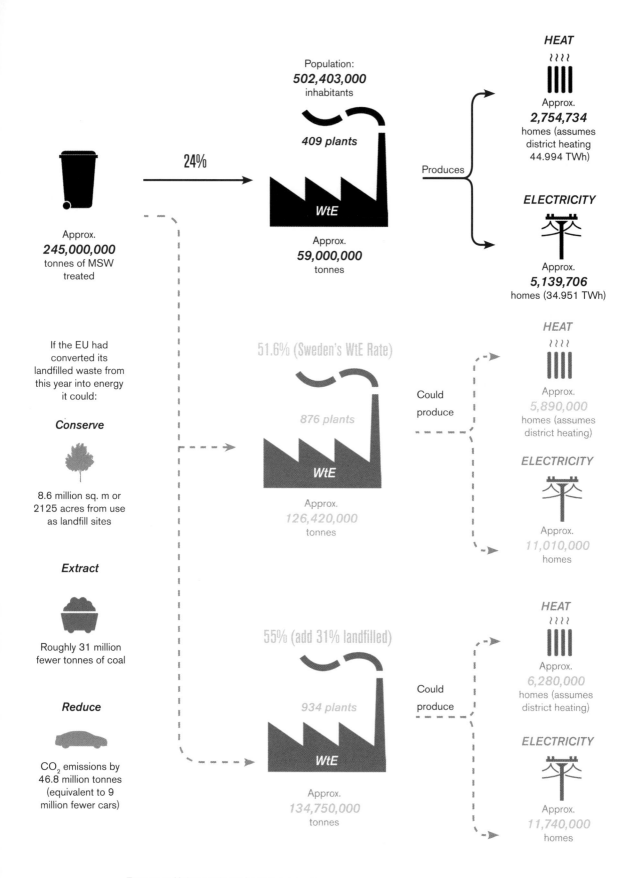

Population:
502,403,000
inhabitants

409 plants

24%

WtE

Approx.
59,000,000
tonnes

Approx.
245,000,000
tonnes of MSW
treated

Produces

HEAT

Approx.
2,754,734
homes (assumes
district heating
44.994 TWh)

ELECTRICITY

Approx.
5,139,706
homes (34.951 TWh)

If the EU had
converted its
landfilled waste from
this year into energy
it could:

Conserve

8.6 million sq. m or
2125 acres from use
as landfill sites

Extract

Roughly 31 million
fewer tonnes of coal

Reduce

CO$_2$ emissions by
46.8 million tonnes
(equivalent to 9
million fewer cars)

51.6% (Sweden's WtE Rate)

876 plants

WtE

Approx.
126,420,000
tonnes

Could
produce

HEAT

Approx.
5,890,000
homes (assumes
district heating)

ELECTRICITY

Approx.
11,010,000
homes

55% (add 31% landfilled)

934 plants

WtE

Approx.
134,750,000
tonnes

Could
produce

HEAT

Approx.
6,280,000
homes (assumes
district heating)

ELECTRICITY

Approx.
11,740,000
homes

European Union projected energy recovery

Given the significant amounts of waste that is currently treated in Pennsylvania and in states with similar histories and capacities to import other states' waste, without long-term strategies the failure to introduce additional capacity and develop synergistic solutions could lead to unprecedented consequences.

In summary, in 2015 there were 84 WtE plants in the United States. However, if the country used its waste for energy production in a proportion equal to Sweden's, it would need 368 plants in the entire country—and this is just for WtE, only a part of the waste management portfolio. In other words, it is possible to foresee the need for thousands of waste-processing facilities across the country. The potential, as well as the challenge, is similar for the European Union, where approximately 876 (467 additional) plants would be required to match Sweden's rates of WtE processing. Within this space of opportunity, new projects can offer solutions that generate clean energy and mitigate the negative impacts of waste on the wider urban atmosphere and microclimates.

As the world's population continues to rise, waste generation will also rise, along with greenhouse gas emissions and environmental impacts on the surrounding environments. In the next 10 years, the United States and Sweden will each have to add about one plant a year just to keep up with current WtE rates. The European Union will need approximately 40 additional plants by 2025 to keep up with current incineration needs. Notwithstanding the economic, social, and environmental benefits of a waste management system that is based on alternative management options, the United States has been unable to move past its detrimental reliance on landfilling, which inevitably facilitates environmental degradation and emits greenhouse gases that expedite climate change. What can be done to improve this situation?

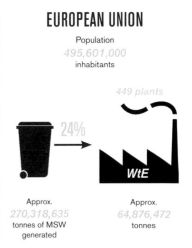

2025 projections of waste generation, population, and WtE plant needs

CONCLUSIONS

First, there is an obvious need for changes in policy and regulations. As long as landfilling waste is the cheapest option, and environmental and social externalities are excluded from the pricing of waste, fewer treatment facilities will be built and, among those that do get built, innovation will be constrained by project finances. Policies and regulations need to change and evolve in order for US cities to have more, better, and healthier waste treatment facilities. Successful examples of countries with innovative waste management systems indicate that policy, design, and planning need to go hand in hand. In Sweden, where almost 100 percent of waste is diverted from landfills, a novel regulatory environment has been fundamental in fostering the transition toward alternative waste management methods.

Next, landfill charges need to be steep enough to make the landfilling of waste economically and socially unsustainable and to make alternative methods viable financially. And cities and towns need to learn to accept waste as a resource—even if it is something that we collectively work to reduce. The utilization of economically recoverable waste streams—combustible and organic waste—can lead to new ways of powering and heating our homes. Furthermore, long-term strategic plans need to set overarching environmental and waste management goals, promoting cooperation and communication as foundations to educate and engage the public in the decision-making process. Through outreach and education, the public can be motivated and become aware that their participation is crucial. This, in turn, perpetuates a tradition of environmental consciousness and waste reuse, as well as public responsibility.

NOTES

1. Avfall Sverige, *Swedish Waste Management 2014* (Malmö, Sweden, 2014), http://www.avfallsverige.se/file-admin //sah_2014_Eng_141001.pdf.

2. Avfall Sverige, *Swedish Waste Management 2014*.

3. Avfall Sverige, *Assessment of Increased Trade of Combustible Waste in the European Union*, report F2012:04 (Malmö, Sweden, 2012), http://www .avfallsverige.se/fileadmin/uploads /Rapporter/F%C3%B6rbr%C3%A4n-ning/F2012-04.pdf; and Avfall Sverige, *Swedish Waste Management 2014*.

4. Avfall Sverige, *The Swedish Waste Management System* (Malmö, Sweden, 2013), http://www.avfallssverige.se/file-admin/uploads/swedish_waste_manage-ment_130910.pptx; and Avfall Sverige, *Swedish Waste Management 2014*.

5. Herve Corvellec, Torleif Bramryd, and Johan Hultman, "The Business Model of Swedish Municipal Waste Manage-ment Companies," *Waste Manage-ment & Research* 30 (2012): 512–18,

doi:10.1177/0734242X11427944; Avfall Sverige, *The Swedish Waste Management System*; and Avfall Sverige, *Swedish Waste Management 2014*.

6. Swedish Environmental Protec-tion Agency, S*weden's Environ-ment—Problems and Protection 1960–2010* (Swedish Environmental Protection Agency, 2011), https: //wnaturvardsverket.se/Documents /blikationer6400/978-91-620-8501-8 .pdf?pid=4183.

7. Corvellec, Bramryd, and Hultman, "The Business Model of Swedish Municipal Waste Management Companies."

8. Jurate Miliūtė and Andrius Plepys, "Driving Forces for High Household Waste Recycling: Lessons from Sweden," *Environmental Research, Engineering, and Management* 47 (2009), 50–62, http://www.researchgate. net/publication/262336629_Driving _Forces_for_High_Household_Waste _Recycling._Lessons_from_Sweden; and Avfall Sverige, *The Swedish Waste Management System*.

9. Avfall Sverige, *The Swedish Waste Management System*.

10. Swedish Environmental Protection Agency, *Sweden's Environment*.

11. Avfall Sverige, *The Swedish Waste Management System*; and Avfall Sverige, *Swedish Waste Management 2014*.

12. Emma Watkins et al., *Use of Economic Instruments and Waste Management* (Paris: Bio Intelligence Service, 2012), http://ec.europa .eu/environment/waste/pdf /final _report_10042012.pdf.

13. US Environmental Protection Agency (US EPA), *Municipal Solid Waste Generation, Recycling, and Disposal in the United States*, Tables and Figures for 2012 (Washington, DC, 2014), http: //www3.epa.gov/epawaste/nonhaz /municipal/pubs/2012_msw_dat_tbls.pdf.

14. US Environmental Protection Agency (US EPA), *25 Years of Resource Conservation and Recovery Act (RCRA): Building on Our Past To Protect Our Future* (Washington, DC, 2002), http://nepis.epa.gov/Exe

/ZyPDF.cgi/10000MAO.PDF?Dock-ey=10000MAO.PDF; Gershman, Brickner & Bratton, Inc (GBC), *Meeting the Future: Evaluating the Potential of Waste Processing Technologies to Contribute to the Solid Waste Authority's System* (Fairfax, VA, 2009), http://swa.org/DocumentCenter/View/138; and Connecticut General Assembly (CGA), *Municipal Solid Waste Management Services in Connecticut* (Legislative Program Review and Investigations Committee, 2010), https://www.cga.ct.gov/2009/pridata/Studies/PDF/MSW_Services_Final_Report.pdf.

15. US EPA, *25 Years of Resource Conservation.*

16. US EPA, *Municipal Solid Waste Generation*; and Nicholas Themelis and Charles Mussche, *Energy and Economic Value of Municipal Solid Waste (MSW), including Non-Recycled Plastics (NRP), Currently Landfilled in the Fifty States* (New York: Columbia University, 2012), http://www.americanchemistry.com/Policy/Energy/Energy-Recovery/2014-Update-of-Potential-for-Energy-Recovery-from-Municipal-Solid-Waste-and-Non-Recycled-Plastics.pdf.

17. US Environmental Protection Agency, "Chapter 7: Waste," in *Inventory of US Greenhouse Gas Emissions and Sinks: 1990–2013* (Washington, DC, 2015), http://www3.epa.gov /climatechange/Downloads/ghgemissions/US-GHG-Inventory-2015-Chapter-7-Waste.pdf.

18. US EPA, *Municipal Solid Waste Generation*; and Rob Van Haaren, Nicholas Themelis, and Nora Goldstein, "The State of Garbage in America," *BioCycle* 51(2010): 16, http://www.biocycle.net/2010/10/26/the-state-of-garbage-in-america-4/.

19. US Supreme Court Reporter, C & A Carbone Inc v. Clarkstown, 511 US 383 (1994), justia.com/cases/federal/us/511/383/case.html; and Molly Macauley, *Waste Not, Want Not: Economic and Legal Challenges of Regulation-induced Changes in Waste Technology and Management* (Washington, DC: Resources for the Future, 2009), http://www.rff.org/files/sharepoint /WorkImages/Download/RFF-DP-09-11.pdf.

20. New York City Office of Management and Budget (NYCOMB), *Fiscal Year 2013 Executive Budget*, mayor's message (2012), http://www.nyc.gov

/html/omb/downloads/pdf/mm5_12.pdf; *Fiscal Year 2013 Budget Function Analysis*, mayor's message (2012), http://www.nyc.gov/html/omb/downloads/pdf/bfa5_12.pdf; and New York Citizens Budget Commission, *Taxes In, Garbage Out: The Need for Better Solid Waste Disposal Policies in New York City* (2012), http://www.cbcny.org/sites/default/files/REPORT_Solid-Waste_053312012.pdf.

21. New York Citizens Budget Commission, *Taxes In, Garbage Out.*

22. James McCarthy, *Interstate Shipment of Municipal Solid Waste*, update (Congressional Research Service, 2007), research.policyarchive.org/18953.pdf.

23. Avfall Sverige, *The Swedish Waste Management System.*

24. European Commission, Council Directive 2008/98/EC; and Council Directive 1999/31/EC.

25. Avfall Sverige, *The Swedish Waste Management System.*

26. Ted Michaels, *2014 ERC Directory of Waste-to-Energy Facilities* (Energy Recovery Council, 2014), http://energyrecovery-council.org/wp-content/uploads/2016/01/ERC_2014_Directory.pdf).

27. US Supreme Court Reporter, C & A Carbone Inc v. Clarkstown.

28. International Energy Agency, *Electricity Information* (2012), http://www.iea.org/media/training/presentations/statisticsmarch/electricityinformation.pdf.

29. Michaels, *2014 ERC Directory of Waste-to-Energy Facilities.*

30. Dolly Shin, "Generation and Disposition of Municipal Solid Waste (MSW) in the United States—A National Survey" (master's thesis, Earth and Environmental Engineering Department, Columbia University, 2014), http://www.seas.columbia.edu/earth/wtert/sofos/Dolly_Shin_Thesis.pdf.

31. Northeast Waste Management Officials Association (NEWMOA), *2014 Annual Report*, http://www.newmoa.org/publications/annual2014.pdf.

32. Maine Department of Environmental Protection (ME DEP), *Municipal Landfill Closure & Remediation Program: History and Future Program Requirements* (2012), http://digitalmaine.com/cgi

/viewcontent.cgi?article=1055&context=dep_docs; US EPA, *Municipal Solid WasteGeneration*; and CGA, *Municipal Solid Waste Management Services.*

33. CGA, *Municipal Solid Waste Management Services.*

34. Connecticut General Assembly (CGA), *Solid Waste Management Services Act* (1973), https://www.cga.ct.gov/current/pub/chap_446e.htm.

35. CGA, *Municipal Solid Waste Management Services.*

36. CGA, *Solid Waste Management Services Act*; CGA, *Municipal Solid Waste Management Services.*

37. Ralph Townsend and Francis Ackerman, *An Analysis of Competition in Collection and Disposal of Solid Waste in Maine* (Portland, ME: Maine Attorney General, 2002), http://www.maine.gov /ag/dynld/documents/Solid_Waste_Report.pdf; ME DEP, *Municipal Landfill Closure & Remediation Program.*

38. Maine Municipal Review Committee (MRC), "About MRC", http://mrcmaine.org/about/#overview.

39. Daniel Hoornweg and Perinaz Bhada-Tata, *What a Waste: A Global Review of Solid Waste Management*, Urban Development Series, Knowledge Papers no 15 (Washington, DC: World Bank, 2012), https://openknowledge.worldbank.org/handle/10986/17388.

40. Michaels, *2014 ERC Directory of Waste-to-Energy Facilities.*

41. Confederation of European Waste-to-Energy Plants (CEWEP), "Waste-to-Energy in Europe in 2012" (2013), http://www.cewep.eu/information/data/studies/m_1342; and Confederation of European Waste-to-Energy Plants (CEWEP), "Waste-to-Energy in Europe in 2013" (2014), http://www.cewep.eu/information/data/studies/m_1459).

42. Themelis and Mussche, *Energy and Economic Value.*

43. McCarthy, *Interstate Shipment of Municipal Solid Waste.*

DISPOSING,
TRANSPORTING,
TIPPING,
SEPARATING,
SCREENING,
FLUFFING,
FEEDING,
INCINERATING,
BOILING, SUPERHEATING,
ECONOMIZING, CONDENSING,
GENERATING,
FILTERING,
MONITORING,
DISCHARGING & STORING,
DISTRIBUTING,
OPERATING & MAINTAINING

HOW WASTE BECOMES ENERGY

In order to best understand Waste-to-Energy processes, it is important to understand the facilities' physical components, what they do, and their end results. We can easily deduce that waste goes in, something happens to it, and energy comes out. However, there are additional inputs, highly interrelated internal mechanisms, and numerous outputs that inform the organization and other design opportunities within a given facility. Technological development in the Waste-to-Energy sector has advanced to the point that a radical shift in the technology seems highly unlikely in the coming years. Instead, refinements to individual components that allow for more cost-effective or efficient solutions are likely the future technology for these facilities.

AN OVERVIEW: WHAT GOES IN, WHAT COMES OUT, AND WHY COMPONENTS MATTER

The initial inputs of a typical WtE facility are waste, air, and water. The waste is brought into the plant, tipped (or unloaded), mixed, and fed to the incinerator. To aid in combustion, air from the tipping and storage areas is introduced into the furnace. The water is isolated in an independent cycle of preheating, boiling, evaporating, superheating, and expanding that drives the generation of electricity. After electrical generation, the steam condenses back to water. During this process, heat can be transferred to a separate water source and sold to utilities as district heating. In addition, cleaned gases from the incineration process are emitted to the atmosphere, while ashes can be processed for a variety of uses or landfilled as a significantly reduced volume.

This transformation of waste into energy involves a series of distinct yet related components. Like a living organism, a WtE plant has multiple possible component configurations, required connections between the components themselves and with external sources, and technical requirements for each element. This translates into complex design decisions pertaining to spatial organization, clearance zones, and component orientations. For example, some elements within the plant require significant space for maintenance, while others need constant multilevel access. Some spaces must be enclosed or open to the exterior or on a particular level, while others require specific proximities to certain elements. An awareness of the role of each component of a WtE plant is

Anatomy of the Waste-to-Energy Facility

LEIRE ASENSIO VILLORIA

WtE Design Lab, Waste-handling claw, 2016

key, not only in understanding how a plant works but also in identifying its main organizational requirements and potential design opportunities.

These parameters are powerful tools for the architect undertaking the design of a WtE plant. By understanding both the flexibility and constraints embedded in each component, we can foresee organizational modifications that may have a major impact in developing novel configurations and spatial arrangements. In other words, we can rethink the part-to-whole relationship of a plant's components in order to substantially reorganize it by expanding or compacting its footprint, weaving additional programs into the facility, and/or exposing certain processes to the public to address the issue of public perceptions.

In this chapter we offer an overview of the operations that take place throughout the WtE process as well as outline the spatial and functional requirements of each component. For quick reference, we have also included an inventory of WtE components accompanied by a brief description and a list of their typical dimensions, required connections, and maintenance needs. (Note that on first mention, each plant component appears with a number to allow for easy identification within the diagrams. These numbers reappear periodically to clarify component sequences or process flows.) Overall, this knowledge forms a base on which architects can build their design for WtE plants by arranging necessary connections, choosing between linear or layered configurations, and making decisions concerning spatial organization, materials, and so forth. Furthermore, a thorough understanding of the plant's function and its components can allow architects to address not only the aesthetic value of the facility but also the facility configurations and tectonic and structural systems that contribute to its efficiency.

Using the architectural toolset developed in this research, a number of associative models have been developed within the Waste-to-Energy Design Lab, and are provided in the Design Opportunities chapter as a sample base for architects to gain real time evaluations of design decisions against the constraints of the plant components.

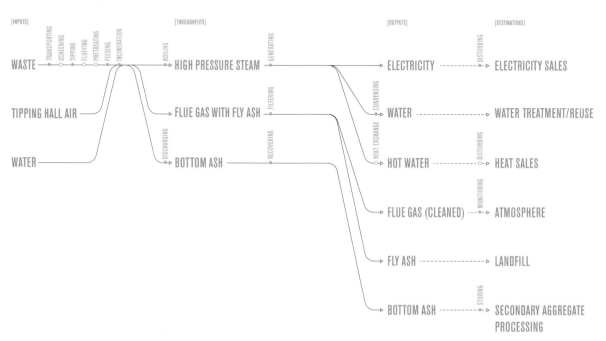

How waste becomes energy

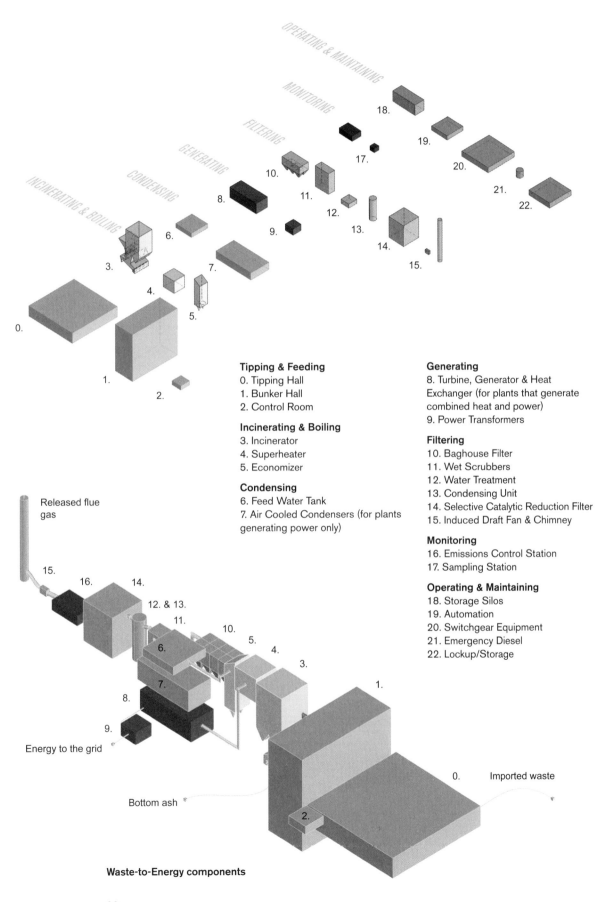

OPERATING & MAINTAINING
MONITORING
FILTERING
GENERATING
CONDENSING
INCINERATING & BOILING

Tipping & Feeding
0. Tipping Hall
1. Bunker Hall
2. Control Room

Incinerating & Boiling
3. Incinerator
4. Superheater
5. Economizer

Condensing
6. Feed Water Tank
7. Air Cooled Condensers (for plants generating power only)

Generating
8. Turbine, Generator & Heat Exchanger (for plants that generate combined heat and power)
9. Power Transformers

Filtering
10. Baghouse Filter
11. Wet Scrubbers
12. Water Treatment
13. Condensing Unit
14. Selective Catalytic Reduction Filter
15. Induced Draft Fan & Chimney

Monitoring
16. Emissions Control Station
17. Sampling Station

Operating & Maintaining
18. Storage Silos
19. Automation
20. Switchgear Equipment
21. Emergency Diesel
22. Lockup/Storage

Released flue gas

Energy to the grid

Bottom ash

Imported waste

Waste-to-Energy components

TIPPING & FEEDING

COMPONENT	SECTION SKETCH	DESCRIPTION/REQUIREMENTS

(0) TIPPING HALL

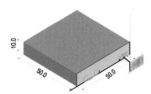

The **tipping hall** is a closed area where the trucks circulate and deliver the waste to the waste bunker. The room facilitates traffic to avoid congestion and control odor release. It also uses a negative pressure draft to reduce odor escape.

Dimensions: 50 m x 50 m x 10 m

Required Connections: Direct connection with bunker hall, road connection that ensures ease of access.

Spatial Requirements: N/A

Maintenance Needs: N/A

(1) BUNKER HALL

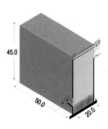

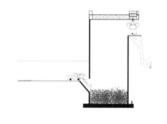

The **bunker hall** is the waste storage area and is usually a deep and narrow pit. In the bunker hall the waste is handled by a crane that stacks, mixes, and fluffs the stored waste before transporting it to the hoppers.

Dimensions: 20 m x 50 m x 45 m

Required Connections: Direct connection with tipping hall and the incinerator's hopper.

Spatial Requirements: N/A

Maintenance Needs: N/A

(2) CONTROL ROOM

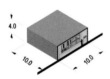

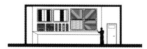

The **control room** houses the operating personnel and the necessary operating equipment. The room includes monitoring data screens and keyboards that control basic functions of the facility.

Dimensions: 10 m x 10 m x 4 m

Required Connections: Generally located near the waste bunker, the tipping hall, and the boiler to allow visual contact for supervision.

Spatial Requirements: N/A

Maintenance Needs: N/A

COMPONENT	SECTION SKETCH	DESCRIPTION/REQUIREMENTS

(3) INCINERATOR

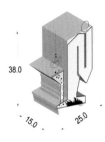

38.0   15.0   25.0

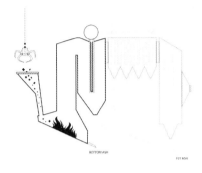

BOTTOM ASH   FLY ASH

The **incinerator** is the combustion area where waste is fed by the crane and burned. From the incinerator, the produced flue gas passes to the boilers, while the residue (bottom ash) is discharged from the bottom part of the component.

Dimensions: 15 m x 25 m x 35 m

Required Connections: Direct connection to the bunker hall and the superheater.

Spatial Requirements: Needs about 6 or 7 levels of access, 2 m distance from walls on each side and 100 sq. m at the entrance of the boiler for storage of grate parts during maintenance.

Maintenance Needs: Once per year.

(4) SUPERHEATER

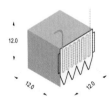

12.0   12.0   12.0

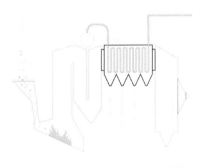

The **superheater** is a horizontal or vertical component through which tubes of steam are exposed to the high temperatures of the flue gases and heat is transferred to the steam through convection.

Dimensions: 12 m x 12 m x 12 m

Required Connections: Direct connection to evaporizer and economizer. The steam tubes from the superheater need to be connected to the turbine of the generator.

Spatial Requirements: Needs a way for the tubes to be replaced (i.e. from above, if the roof can open, or from underneath) and lifting equipment.

Maintenance Needs: Tubes need to be changed every 5 years.

(5) ECONOMIZER

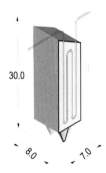

30.0   8.0   7.0

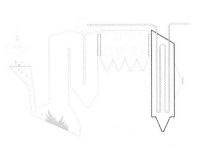

The last part of the boiler is the **economizer**. Here the water is heated before passing to the boiler drum and the evaporizer, reaching just below boiling point for those pressure properties.

Dimensions: 8 m x 8 m x 30 m

Required Connections: Direct connection to the superheater. Connection to the first part of the flue gas treatment (baghouse filter).

Spatial Requirements: N/A

Maintenance Needs: Every 10–15 years.

COMPONENT	SECTION SKETCH	DESCRIPTION/REQUIREMENTS

(6) FEED WATER TANK

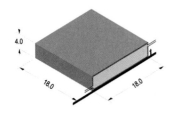

The **feed water tank** is where the steam goes after it has been condensed back to water. From there, water flows to the evaporizer to begin the steam generation cycle again.

Dimensions: 18 m x 18 m x 4 m

Required Connections: Connections to evaporizer and condensers.

Spatial Requirements: Should be inside the building. The bottom of the tank should be 10 m above the end of the feed water pumps.

Maintenance Needs: N/A

(7) AIR-COOLED CONDENSERS

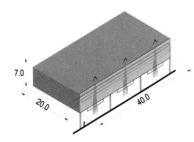

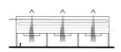

The **air-cooled condensers** are large dry-cooling components that bring the tubes of heated steam through fan-induced cooling air drafts in order to condense it back to water.

Dimensions: 40 m x 20 m x 7 m

Required Connections: Receives steam from turbine and sends condensed water to water tank.

Spatial Requirements: Needs to be outside to allow air flow for cooling.

Maintenance Needs: Low maintenance needs, mainly for fans.

HEAT & POWER GENERATION

(8) TURBINE GENERATOR

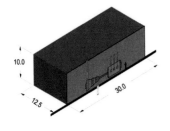

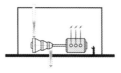

The generator room is a large space where the **turbine**, the **generator**, and (if the plant produces hot water for district heating) the heat exchangers are located.

Dimensions: 30 m x 12.5 m x 10 m

Required Connections: Receives steam from superheaters and sends it to condensers. Needs connection to the grid through power transformers.

Spatial Requirements: Needs at least 5 m around the turbine and a lifting crane for maintenance.

Maintenance Needs: Low maintenance needs.

(9) POWER TRANSFORMERS

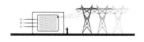

The **power transformers** are located one step before the power generated in the facility goes to feed the grid. It is used to transform electricity in both directions.

Dimensions: 9 m x 9 m x 6 m

Required Connections: Close to switch gear, direct connection to the grid.

Spatial Requirements: N/A

Maintenance Needs: N/A

FILTERING

COMPONENT	SECTION SKETCH	DESCRIPTION/REQUIREMENTS

(10) BAGHOUSE FILTER

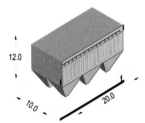

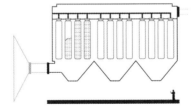

The **baghouse filter** is comprised of metal cages covered by fabric filters that capture fly ash particles. The flue gas passes from the outside of the fabric bags to the inside, leaving behind all ash particles, which are periodically cleaned by compressed air flowing in the opposite direction.

Dimensions: 10 m x 20 m x 12 m

Required Connections: Usually follows economizer.

Spatial Requirements: Needs 2 m around and some space below. Requires lifting equipment for replacing the filter bags and doors 2.5 m wide.

Maintenance Needs: Every 5 years.

(11) WET SCRUBBERS

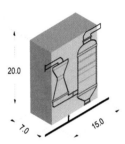

Scrubbers are filters that reduce the acidic components of the flue gas. They are towers where water is sprayed down into the upward-traveling flue gases. In the typical configuration, there is an acidic scrubber to remove HCl & HF and a neutral one for the removal of SO2.

Dimensions: 7 m x 15 m x 20 m

Required Connections: Usually follows SCR or baghouse filter when the plant doesn't use a catalytic filter.

Spatial Requirements: 2 m all around.

Maintenance Needs: N/A

(12) WATER TREATMENT

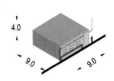

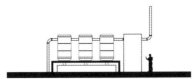

The **water treatment** area is where the water-filled dischargers lead to have residues and toxic fly ash treated.

Dimensions: 9 m x 9 m x 4 m

Required Connections: Connection to wet scrubbers to receive produced residue.

Spatial Requirements: N/A

Maintenance Needs: N/A

103

COMPONENT	SECTION SKETCH	DESCRIPTION/REQUIREMENTS

(13) CONDENSING UNIT

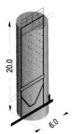

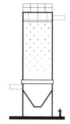

The **condensing unit** is another scrubber unit that is used to further cool the flue gases when the plant connects to district heating. Condensing steam to water improves the efficiency of the heat production.

Dimensions: Diameter: 6 m
Height: 15–20 m

Required Connections: Follows scrubbers in case of district heating.

Spatial Requirements: 2 m all around.

Maintenance Needs: N/A

(14) SELECTIVE CATALYTIC REDUCTION FILTER

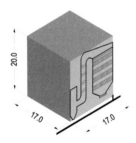

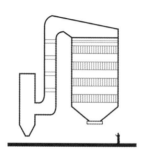

The **SCR (selective catalytic reduction)** filter is used to eliminate NOx by the use of a catalyst (ammonia).

Dimensions: 17 m x 17 m x 20 m

Required Connections: Usually follows baghouse filter.

Spatial Requirements: 2 m all around.

Maintenance Needs: Catalysts changed every 5 to 10 years.

(15) ID FAN & CHIMNEY

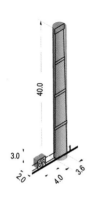

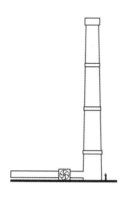

The final step before releasing the clean flue gases to the atmosphere is the **induced draft (ID) fan**, that creates a boosting draft, and the **chimney**.

Dimensions: Fan diameter: 3 m, width 1 m
Chimney diameter: 3.6 m; height: 40 m

Required Connections: Connection to emissions control room.

Spatial Requirements: Needs ample clearance space for maintenance and lifting devices for heavy equipment replacement.

Maintenance Needs: Low maintenance needs.

COMPONENT	SECTION SKETCH	DESCRIPTION/REQUIREMENTS

(16) EMISSIONS CONTROL STATION

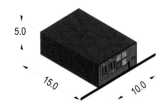

The **emissions control station** is a room where the emissions monitoring equipment is installed. It is located at the end of the flue gas cleaning line, sometimes embedded in the stack.

Dimensions: 10 m x 16 m x 5 m

Required Connections: Connection to last part of flue gas cleaning and then to ID fan and chimney.

Spatial Requirements: Long straight path needed on both sides of the station.

Maintenance Needs: N/A

(17) SAMPLING STATION

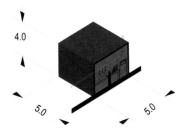

The **sampling station** is a room where manual measurements are performed once or twice a year, in order to compare them with the emissions control automated data.

Dimensions: 5 m x 5 m x 4 m

Required Connections: Usually located close to emissions control station.

Spatial Requirements: Needs good access.

Maintenance Needs: N/A

COMPONENT	SECTION SKETCH	DESCRIPTION/REQUIREMENTS

(18) STORAGE SILOS

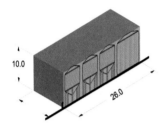

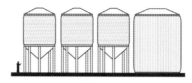

The **silos** store residues (mostly boiler fly ash and flue gas cleaning residues) until they are taken out in a dry form and transported for further treatment.

Dimensions: 26 m x 10 m x 10 m

Required Connections: N/A

Spatial Requirements: Needs road access, usually located outside on a higher level.

Maintenance Needs: N/A

(19) AUTOMATION

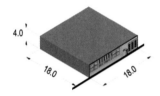

The **automation room** is where maintenance, programming, and repair works of the control system are performed.

Dimensions: 18 m x 18 m x 4 m

Required Connections: Usually positioned close to control room, but also could be close to other equipment with high maintenance needs like boiler, flue gas cleaning, or turbine.

Spatial Requirements: N/A

Maintenance Needs: N/A

(20) SWITCHGEAR EQUIPMENT

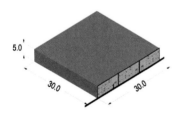

The **switch gear equipment** consists of the rooms that feed electrical power to the equipment of the facility. It could be divided in two or three different rooms locate close to the boilers, filters, and generator.

Dimensions: 30 m x 30 m x 5 m

Required Connections: In close proximity to the rooms they feed.

Spatial Requirements: N/A

Maintenance Needs: N/A

COMPONENT	SECTION SKETCH	DESCRIPTION/REQUIREMENTS

(21) EMERGENCY DIESEL

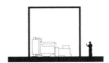

The **diesel generator** feeds the switch gear equipment that is connected to critical parts of the plant, that need to be in operation even in the event of a blackout (i.e., the parts that feed water to the boiler).

Dimensions: Diameter: 6 m, Height: 6 m

Required Connections: Connection to switch gear.

Spatial Requirements: N/A

Maintenance Needs: N/A

(22) LOCKUP/STORAGE

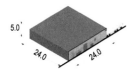

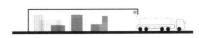

The **lockup/storage area** is a storage space for spare parts of the plant.

Dimensions: 24 m x 24 m x 5 m

Required Connections: N/A

Spatial Requirements: Needs ground level access.

Maintenance Needs: N/A

DISPOSING AND TRANSPORTING

The process of recovering energy from waste should not be thought of as occurring within a single building (the WtE plant), but rather as a complex system of waste collection that begins with household disposal, continues to various technologies for gathering and transportation, and eventually makes its way to recycling, composting, or energy recovery facilities. While municipal solid waste from households is a prominent part of the waste stream, additional sources include medical, construction, and demolition wastes.

In the United States, most municipalities have garbage collection and recycling systems that operate on independent schedules. Garbage trucks have a single compartment into which all waste is emptied. In contrast, Sweden has fostered a nuanced understanding of waste as more than just a singular entity; as a result, the country has a vastly more sophisticated management process. In certain Swedish municipalities, homeowners have two waste bins, each with four compartments for various types of wastes. Garbage and recycling collection are not two completely different systems, but instead a single process that alternates which waste type is collected each week. Lorries that have four unique compartments make the collection, ensuring that the homeowner's sorted waste remains separated.

One problem with conventional truck pickup is the traffic issues created at some plants. This is the main public concern when locating a plant in places like Sweden and the United States. Despite circulation organization, trucks may nonetheless arrive at the facility at the same time. In addition to causing congestion, these stationary vehicles surrounding the plant release greater odors from the transported waste. Since odors are one of the main nuisances for neighboring individuals or facilities, WtE plants are considered more suitable for rural environments, where they are afforded a larger surrounding buffer zone to minimize negative effects. For WtE plants to gain acceptance in a denser urban environment, odor release from garbage trucks must be effectively controlled.

An alternative to conventional truck transport is automated vacuum collection (AVC). With AVC systems, separate disposal inlets for various waste types are located throughout a neighborhood or district, and waste is collected via suction to a central transfer station. While no precedent exists of waste traveling directly to a WtE facility, this is technically possible. AVC systems are capable of a 2 km suction distance between the collection

Components of Waste-to-Energy

Garbage truck dumping waste on the tipping room floor

center and the furthest inlet, and a two-fraction system (a configuration that can store two types of waste, such as incinerable and organic) can handle the waste of 8,500 dwellings. A number of successful vacuum systems have been implemented in Sweden, Barcelona, and on Roosevelt Island in New York City, among many others, and the technology for these systems allows them to be placed below water tables, directly in water, in frost areas, earthquake zones, and high rise buildings.

Collection tubes vary in diameter from 300 mm to 500 mm, are generally buried between 1 m to 2.5 m below ground, and move the waste at about 20 to 25 m/sec. Most blockages in the collection pipes are solved within 15 minutes by adding additional suction to the system. In rare cases, the system needs to be shut down and blockages are removed manually. In case of pipe damage, a 500 mm tube can be repaired from inside by welding a cover over the damaged spot; smaller diameters, however, require excavating to the damaged section of pipe. One current setback for these systems is that their capacity is only 20 tonnes per day, equivalent to about seven crane grabs, making their contribution limited for WtE collection.

TIPPING

The first WtE process that occurs inside the facility is called tipping, where trucks deliver and unload their collected waste for further processing. In a standard configuration, tipping occurs in an enclosed room called the tipping hall (0), a space of roughly 2,500 sq. m, in which the trucks circulate and deposit the waste. In order to facilitate truck traffic, the tipping hall usually has a separate entrance and exit, both equipped with a weighing bridge to measure deliveries to and from the facility and thus track the quantity of imported waste. Contemporary facilities are typically equipped with radioactive waste detectors alongside the weighing bridges, as well as a different entrance for not-weighed vehicles.

On entering the tipping hall, the trucks must maneuver into place, unload their waste, and then exit without causing congestion, which could create unnecessary delays and cause odors from waiting trucks to be released into the environment. The unloading time for a typical garbage truck should be less than 5 minutes, but for larger multicontainer side-dump vehicles, tipping can take as long as 30 or 40 minutes. These larger trucks should be accounted for in the spatial arrangement and dimensioning of tipping areas.

Schematic diagram of ENVAC system

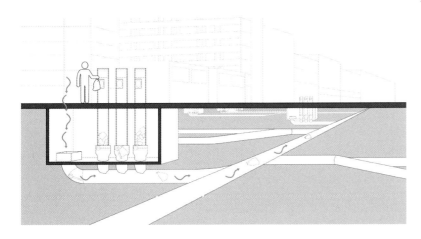

Odor control is an important issue for WtE plants and it is strongly connected to public perception. Prevailing winds should be taken into consideration when organizing the plant and orienting the tipping hall. Accounting for wind direction can reduce the spread of odors from the tipping hall. Another technique deployed in the tipping hall, in cases of malfunction or accumulated waste, is the use of perfume sprayers as a backup mechanism to mask smells from the plant.

Moving on to the bunker hall (1), we first must note that there are multiple incineration technologies—mass burn, modular, and fluidized bed systems that use refuse-derived fuel (RDF)—and they have distinct precombustion processes. Mass burn facilities input refuse that has undergone minimal preprocessing other than the removal of white goods, such as refrigerators and dishwashers, and other large items. Modular systems are prefabricated, smaller, faster to install, have smaller capital costs compared to other types, and also require minimal preprocessing. In comparison, fluidized bed systems require fuel preparation, which takes place in an RDF plant where waste is mechanically processed into a more homogeneous combustion fuel. This normally necessitates a multistage sorting and separation process prior to combustion.

In mass burn facilities, all the waste is deposited in a bunker hall, or pit, which is the waste storage area. To ensure the continuous feeding of the incinerator, the bunker hall is designed to hold approximately four days of waste. A basic visual screening can be performed here to remove hazardous trash and adjust the combustion parameters according to the type of the imported waste, for example winter versus summer, or industrial versus municipal. While most facilities employ a deep and narrow pit, a tipping floor can be used when a pit is not possible due to specific geotechnical conditions or other reasons. In a tipping floor scheme, trucks deposit waste directly onto the floor of the tipping hall, necessitating a larger footprint and more laborious waste handling by front-end loaders.

SHREDDING

For fluidized bed incineration, the ideal particle size is approximately 50 to 150 mm. Shredding the waste reduces the overall volume of the input material to about a third or quarter of its initial size and improves the quality of combustion. In "shred and burn" RDF operations, a bag breaker coarsely shreds the waste material and ferrous metals are then recovered. After this, small particles are removed while larger elements continue on to secondary shredding procedures.

Bunker hall

Although shredding increases the efficiency of the combustion process, shredding is not a very common feature in WtE plants. Shredding waste significantly increases the odors released, making it less fitting for an urban environment. However, rural landscapes offer the opportunity to install these plants at longer distances from residential or other heavily populated areas, so the smell is not as problematic. Plants that include shredding waste often shred at night to decrease the possible disturbance to neighbors with odors. Shredding also produces a large amount of noise, which can be mitigated with an appropriate insulation system similar to that used around the generator room.

SEPARATING

In RDF facilities, the feed material for combustion undergoes a fully automated screening and separating process to recover all potential recyclables from the waste before it is shredded and incinerated. Screening can be done within the plant, but is often done in a separate location called a material recovery facility, or MRF. A first step in this multistage process is trommel screening. Here unsorted waste is rotated in a cylindrical sieve, where centrifugal and gravitational forces break open household garbage bags. The loose material is separated by size, falling through holes in the cylinder, while the largest waste is expelled at the end of the trommel. A next step is air classification, in which an upward-moving air current separates lighter and heavier materials. While these processes allow for separation, material recovery is tackled by magnetic separation for ferrous metals, eddy current separation to extract aluminum, and optical sorting where appropriate or necessary.

FLUFFING

In mass burn incineration, a crane (or grapple) in the bunker hall (1) stacks, mixes, and fluffs the waste before feeding it to the incinerator. Fluffing is a process in which waste is lifted by the crane and then dropped back down, reducing the density of waste at the pit's bottom. Fluffing also creates a more homogeneous fuel by breaking up household garbage bags and mixing waste from various sources, which allows for better combustion. Other than visual screening, fluffing constitutes the full extent of waste processing for mass burn facilities.

Exterior view of shredding process

Shredded MSW

In all facility types, waste handling is done in enclosed areas, and older waste is handled first in order to avoid decomposition and odor accumulation. In addition to successful vehicle circulation and waste handling, a negative air draft is created to further control odor. This is achieved by drawing air from the tipping and bunker halls to use in the combustion process, where the high temperatures eliminate the offensive odors.

The control room (2) houses the operating personnel and the necessary operating equipment for the basic functions of the facility. It is typically a space for three to five operators who supervise the processes of waste transport, management, and incineration. The space usually has visual contact with the bunker hall for the operators to supervise the screening and feeding processes.

FEEDING

From the control room, operators feed the waste from the bunker hall or storage area into charging hoppers that lead to the furnace. Feeding is a gravity-based process comprised of the hopper, an intermediary chute, and a hydraulic ram mechanism that feeds the waste into the furnace. As waste is displaced at the bottom of the chute by the feeder, gravity slowly empties the chute and hopper until the introduction of more waste from the bunker continues the process. The hopper is composed of steel and constructed with a 45-degree slope to allow the waste to slide into the chute. As the waste enters the chute it forms an air seal that separates the bunker hall from the furnace, although there is usually a safety gate between the hopper and the chute to prevent backfires and ensure the seal. Additionally, the chute is often water-cooled to protect it from the high temperatures of incineration.

While the feeding process can be performed automatically, with cranes fluffing the waste and feeding the incinerator at an automated pace, operator supervision is critical for the adaptation of the feeding speed or of other parameters to fit the waste's characteristics. Season, furnace temperature, waste source, and waste type can significantly affect the quality of the combustion, which is why the operating personnel constantly monitor and adapt the feeding process.

Within the control room, an operator fluffs and moves the waste

INCINERATING

Incinerating burns waste to generate heat (thermal energy) that is then processed as steam or further converted into electricity. While a number of mass burn technologies exist, they all follow the same process: continuously feed waste on a grate that tumbles it from the hydraulic ram feeder, through a combustion chamber, into a discharge point for the residue, called bottom ash.

In order to do this, mass burn plants most commonly use a reciprocating grate system. Reciprocating grates have alternating stationary and moving parts and employ a back-and-forth movement to propel the waste forward across three to five primary zones, including drying, combustion, and material burnout. Modular systems typically have two combustion zones: a primary combustion chamber and an afterburner that acts as the primary pollution control mechanism. Odorous air is drawn from the tipping hall (0) and bunker hall (1) and is injected into the grate system as underfire air (below the grate) or overfire air (above the grate, into the flame). Underfire air is typically preheated and serves to dry the waste and aid in combustion. The air is injected into plenums under the grate that correspond to the different zones, allowing operators to fine-tune the amount of air for each stage. Overfire combustion air is typically not heated and is injected at a higher pressure through nozzles located above the grate. The overfire air aids in the complete burnout of the gases produced by heating the waste and creates a turbulence that sufficiently mixes the flue gas.

Alternatives to the reciprocating grate design are reverse reciprocating grates, roller grates, and rotary drums. Reverse reciprocating grates and roller grates work similarly to reciprocating grates, with minor differences. Reverse reciprocating grates push the waste upward and backward to tumble it forward, ensuring good exposure to the combustion air. Roller grates employ rotating cylindrical rollers in place of moving grates to tumble the waste. Rotary combustors are large, downward-angled drums that slowly tumble waste fed inside them. In this configuration, air is injected through the drum's membrane to aid in combustion, and the furnace is integral with the boiler.

In fluidized bed incineration, a spreader-stoker traveling grate is most typically used. In this system, the pretreated material enters the feed chute either directly from an apron conveyor or from a storage bin. As with in mass burn, the material is gravity fed, but in this case it is blown toward the back of the furnace onto a continuous moving grate that

View into a reciprocating grate furnace   Superheater

transports the material back toward the inlet. In this system, lighter materials incinerate before they land, while heavier materials fall to the grate and then burn out fully before the ash discharges into a water quench trough below the inlet. Overfire and underfire air operate similarly to mass burn technologies in this system.

In fluidized bed incineration, a bed of limestone or sand capable of withstanding high temperatures replaces the linear grate mechanism of mass burn. Aerating the material from below with high-velocity air allows it to take on the properties of a fluid. This fluidized material is then evenly heated and waste is introduced. This method of incineration melts and burns the waste, and ash discharges from the bottom of the furnace. This technology provides a more uniform temperature than mass burn and can produce a higher temperature steam without severe corrosion problems. While it can have slightly higher electrical power production and less bottom ash, fluidized bed technology creates more fly ash or flue gas cleaning residues, and the fuel preparation requires more electrical power than mass burn fuel preparation.

The incinerator is a large component with rough dimensions of 15 m x 25 m x 35 m. For maintenance and operation reasons, the equipment needs about six or seven levels of access: to the valves for ammonia level monitoring, to viewing glasses, to add grease to the grate system, and to accommodate other necessary functions. In addition, the incinerator must be at distance of at least 2 m from the walls on each side, and it requires 100 sq. m at the boiler's entrance for storage of grate parts for maintenance, which happens about once per year for this component. Incinerating produces two throughputs: residual bottom ash, which is released into a water-filled discharger at the bottom, and flue gas, which continues on to the boilers.

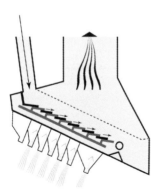

Reciprocating grate

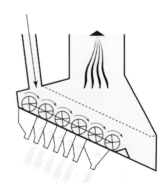

Roller grate

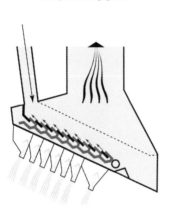

Reverse reciprocating grate

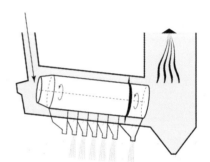

Rotary drum

BOILING, SUPERHEATING, ECONOMIZING, CONDENSING

Boiling is best understood as a heat transfer process between an isolated water cycle and the flue gases from the furnace. This process allows the water to be heated on its way to the turbine, while concurrently cooling the gases on their way to filtering and cleaning. The water cycle begins with flue gases converting the water to steam, the steam powering the turbine for electricity generation, and then the steam condensing into water to begin the cycle anew. While the flue gases travel in a sequence from the evaporator, to the super-heater (4), to the economizer (5), the water in the cycle begins at the economizer, then moves to the boiler drum, then to the evaporator, and finally to the superheater.

The flue gases produced by combustion begin at a temperature of roughly 1000 °C. While still in the furnace, the gases pass through a three-part vertical heat-exchange chamber where ammonia is added, chemical reactions occur, and the gases are cooled to approximately 600–700 °C. During this process the gases provide heat to the evaporator, an element comprised of multiple tubes embedded within the incinerator walls (3), where water is converted into steam. The water tubes in the walls of the incinerator, as well as the overfire or underfire combustion air, serves the additional role of keeping the equipment's temperature relatively low and helping diminish corrosion. After the initial passes inside the incinerator, the flue gases move to the superheater (4), a component through which tubes of steam are re-exposed to the high temperatures of the flue gases. Here heat is transferred to the steam through convection, conveying more energy to the steam and making it drier before it reaches the turbine at a final temperature of approximately 400 °C. The super-heater includes two to four parts and can be either horizontal or vertical. Horizontal components are cleaned by mechanical means, while steam cleans vertical components. Because it is easier and causes less corrosion, mechanical cleaning is usually preferred. Since the tubes are exposed to very high temperatures they typically need to be changed every five years. The facility's organization must provide a way for the tubes to be replaced—for example, from above if the roof can open, or from underneath using lifting equipment. The final part of the boiler for the flue gases is the economizer (5). Here the flue gas tempera-ture drops to around 180 °C for further cleaning.

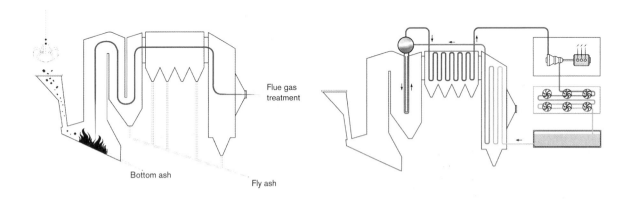

Flue gas treatment

Bottom ash

Fly ash

Waste and flue gas movement

Water and steam movement

Meanwhile, the water begins in a feed water tank (15) and heads to the economizer where it is preheated in exposed tubes to just below its boiling point. Next it passes through a boiler drum located above the incinerator, is converted to steam in the evaporator, and then moves to the superheaters for drying, as explained above. After the steam is used to produce electrical energy, in plants that do generate heat, the steam is condensed back to water with heat exchangers. Plants that do not generate heat use air-cooled condensers (14)—a large dry-cooling component that brings the tubes of heated steam through fan-induced cooling air drafts—to condense steam to water. An alternative to air-cooled condensers is using local bodies of water, if available, to cool the steam. If district heating is implemented, steam first has to pass from the heat exchangers, which warm the water that is then sent to the grid for heating. After recondensing, the water is brought to the feed water tank, where it can begin the cycle all over again.

GENERATING

Generating is where the thermal energy produced by waste incineration, in the form of steam, is transformed into electrical energy. The generator room (12) is a large space where the turbine, the generator, and (if the plant produces hot water for district heating) the heat exchangers are located. The room is spacious, with dimensions of approximately 30 m x 12.5 m x 10 m, and is equipped with a crane for maintenance needs.

Pressurized steam coming straight from the superheater (4) puts the turbine in motion, which powers the generator. Steam is then sent to the heat exchanger or, if there is no district heating, straight to the air-cooled condensers (14). Finally, the power transformer (13)—a component located one step before the facility-generated power leaves to feed the grid— transforms electricity in both directions. For example, if the generator is not in operation, the facility can take electrical power from the grid, but if it is producing electricity, it will transfer its energy to the grid. This component requires a switchgear room (18) in close proximity.

View of turbine and generator

FILTERING

In contemporary WtE facilities, filtering flue gas before it is released into the atmosphere involves the greatest number of components. Regulations for air and water emissions vary according to the location of the plant; regardless, they typically focus on the reduction of dust, acids, nitrogen oxides, furans, and dioxins, as well as the handling of the captured discharges. Throughout filtering, different residues are collected separately and either disposed of at special hazardous landfills or sold for use in other industries.

A primary consideration for flue gas cleaning is the control of particulates—comprised of unburned materials (soot) and unburnable materials (fly ash)—that remain in the flue gases from incineration. The baghouse filter (6), a metal-cage-supported fabric filter that captures fly ash—is a typical component used to address these particulates. The flue gas passes through the fabric bags, leaving behind all ash particles. The fabric bags are periodically cleaned by compressed air flowing in the opposite direction, which causes the accumulated dust particles to drop to the discharge hopper on the bottom of the component. For maintenance and operation reasons, baghouse filters require a clearance space of 2 m around and below them. Every fifth year, the filter bags have to be replaced and, for this reason, lifting equipment and access through doors measuring from 2 to 2.5 m in width are necessary. An alternative to the baghouse filter is a component called an electrostatic precipitator (ESP), which uses an electrostatic charge to remove particles from the flowing flue gases. The ESP is not as effective as the baghouse filter in terms of absorbing acids and chlorides, which makes it an inefficient solution in many cases where regulations require a low acidic discharge, especially in water emissions. A baghouse filter or an ESP is the simplest filtering configuration that can cover the full emissions requirements, although they usually operate on the limit of acceptable pollutants and are therefore only sufficient in small-scale plants or in locations where emission regulations are not very strict. Therefore, most plants include additional equipment to further improve their emissions quality.

The scrubbing of acid gases, such as hydrogen chloride and sulfur dioxide, is another critical element of flue gas filtering. Acid gases can either be dissolved into water or transformed into salts with the help of an adsorbent that is injected into the flue gas. Mercury, dioxins, and furans can be adsorbed by activated carbon injected in the flue gas.

In order to improve this process, a calcium or sodium sorbent is added to the flue gas after it leaves the economizer (5). Acid gas scrubbing involves either wet scrubbers, dry sorbent injection, or spray dryer absorbers (SDAs). Also known as dry scrubbers, SDAs are the most common scrubbing technology in use. The two types of SDAs are distinguished by their means of injection: rotary atomizers or dual fluid nozzles. Both of these technologies, however, mix water and sorbent chemicals into the flue gas. As an alternative, dry sorbent injection carries a lower capital cost, but it is less efficient and most often deployed in small plants. Semi-dry absorbent systems have become popular in both big and small plants today. In the semi-dry system the dry sorbent is moistened by adding water before injection into the flue gas. In this way the absorber can be much smaller than the typical SDA, which is a big cylinder 5 m in diameter and 20 m high. Another alternative is wet scrubbers (8). These are large towers, 15 to 20 m tall, in which water is sprayed down into the flue gases that are traveling upward. In the typical config-uration, the scrubbers are placed after the baghouse filter or ESP, and the first step—called quench—is where the flue gas is cooled to the saturation temperature (normally around 60 °C). Then it passes to the first scrubber unit (acidic), where the water comes into contact with the flue gases to absorb hydrochloric acid, hydrofluoric acid, and any possible residue of ammonia or mercury. However, sulfur dioxide is not easily soluble in water in the high acidity environment of the first scrubber. This is why a second unit is needed (neutral), this time for the removal of sulfur dioxide. Water from the wet scrubbers is sent for treatment before being discharged or reused. This takes place in the water cleaning area (11), a room around 80 sq. m that holds equipment to treat water-filled dischargers carrying residues or toxic fly ash.

Another important filtering step is controlling nitrogen oxide emissions, which chemically react in the atmosphere to create ozone and contribute to smog. A selective catalytic reduction system (SCR; 7) can be used for this process by using a catalyst and ammonia as a reduction agent. An SCR unit injects ammonia, aqueous ammonia, or urea into the flue gases, mixes them sufficiently, and then passes the mixture through catalytic modules that induce a chemical reaction to produce water vapor and nitrogen.

This reduces nitrogen oxide emissions by approximately 90 percent. The SCR is posi-tioned either after the baghouse or more commonly after the last flue gas cleaning equipment. In both cases, in order to function well, the SCR requires heat exchangers to raise the temperature of the flue gas to 180 to 250 °C. The temperature of the flue gas is typically around 140 °C coming from the baghouse filter and around 40 °C coming from the wet scrubbers, which makes placing it the SCR right after the baghouse filter less energy consuming. This system is a very big component with dimensions around 17 m x 17 m x 20 m and requires maintenance every five to ten years. A clearance space of 2 m around it is necessary.

A more common alternative to the SCR is the selective non-catalytic reduction system (SNCR). This technology injects the ammonia or urea into the flue gases while still in the furnace, using the heat to induce chemical reactions instead of the catalysts in SCR technologies. This has significantly lower capital costs that offset its higher operating costs, although it only removes about 50 percent of nitrogen oxide emissions. Additional methods of reducing nitrogen oxide emissions include the use of overfire air, overall minimization of combustion air, and the reinjection of flue gases into combustion to use up more of the oxygen. More recently, activated carbon injection into the flue gases has been shown to significantly reduce the quantity of mercury emitted, and has also reduced emissions of dioxins and furans.

In cases where district heating is incorporated into the plant's program, a condensing unit (9) is added to improve heat production efficiency. The condensing unit is another scrubber that further cools the flue gases. By condensing steam to water, the efficiency of the heat production is improved by roughly 10 to 20 percent. However, the produced water must be treated and cleaned through the water-cleaning component (11) prior to release. The final step before releasing the clean flue gases to the atmosphere is the induced draft fan (ID fan or IDF), which sucks the air through the entire filtering process and draws it to the stack (10). The fan requires a wide clearance space for maintenance as well as lifting devices for heavy equipment replacement.

One aspect of the filtering process

MONITORING

Due to strict regulations concerning water and air emissions, continuous supervision of the discharges and their chemical content is necessary for the operation of the plant. Operating personnel in the control room (2) continuously monitor data and adjust the incineration and filtering parameters to the specific characteristics of the waste, ensuring low emissions levels.

There are two additional rooms dedicated to monitoring the plant's performance. The first is the emissions control station (16), which contains all of the automatic emission-monitoring equipment. It is located at the end of the flue gas cleaning line. A long straight path is needed before and after the emissions control in order to achieve accurate measurements. The amounts of particles vary in one flow versus another; a bend in the path before or after the emissions control could affect the particle flow and hence samples taken by the emissions control. The emissions control can be performed one of two ways: by extracting a flue gas sample through a pipe, drying it, bringing it to a certain temperature, and analyzing its contents for certain substances; or by taking the measurements inside the main flue gas flow via light transmission from one side to the other. This method measures the light wavelengths that have been absorbed by the flue gases and thus calculates the contents of certain substances. The second monitoring area is the sampling station (17), a room of approximately 25 sq. m where manual measurements are performed. Once or twice a year, a consultant compares the manual measurements to those taken by the fixed equipment. The sampling station is usually located close to the emissions control station.

Operators monitor the various systems
and emissions of the plant

DISCHARGING AND STORAGE

Much of the material produced during the incineration and filtering process must be stored in the plant until it is transported to other locations. The storage silos (19), located outside the building, are used for storing chemical absorbents like lime and activated carbon, and residues such as boiler fly ash and flue gas cleaning residues, until they are removed in a dry form and transported for further treatment. The storage silos are generally on a level higher than the access road in order to have enough space underneath for a truck. In order to eliminate the spread of odors and material, the loading process to the truck is usually done in a closed space measuring at least 7 m wide and 25 to 30 m long. Each material is handled in a different way according to its hazardous or non-hazardous nature and its recycling potential.

Typically, WtE plants generate residues that are classified into three groups: bottom ash, fly ash, and flue gas cleaning residues. Bottom ash is discharged from the incinerator (3) into water and is then conveyed to a large hall, measuring roughly 25 m x 25 m x 10 m, often located off-site, for drying. Alternatively, bottom ash could be collected and stored in a bunker, 10 m x 25 m x 20 m, located next to the incinerator. In both cases, spacious storage is used instead of a silo so that the material can be regularly mixed until it dries and matures, which takes roughly four to six weeks. Additionally, during this process the bottom ash is sorted for the recovery of metals that can be sold, if such sorting did not occur prior to combustion. After drying and metals recovery, the bottom ash is the least harmful residue and can easily be reused in road construction, or it can be landfilled at 10 to 20 percent of its original waste volume. Fly ash, from the boiler and ESP, contains more heavy metals and is normally landfilled. Flue gas cleaning residues are more soluble because of their salt content, and some heavy metals can be dissolved in water because of the high pH. This material requires either specially classified landfills, or it can be deposited underground in salt mines. Today it has become common to use flue gas cleaning residue to neutralize waste acids from the metal manufacturing industry.

Enclosed ash conveyor system

View into ash hall, where bottom ash is deposited

Ash collection

DISTRIBUTING

In WtE facilities, approximately 25 percent of the energy generated by incineration can be converted to electrical energy that can be sold to the utility company. While about 20 percent of energy is lost throughout the process, 55 percent of energy created (in the form of heat) is lost to the air-cooled condensers (14) when electricity is the only sale-able output. The potential gains of district heating implementation allow for the recovery of 55 to 65 percent of that initial energy generation, and an additional 10 to 15 percent is possible with the condensation of flue gases. This also allows plants to sell district heating at competitive rates compared to other types of energy generation and, as a result, reduce tipping fees. Because of the nature of electrical distribution and hot water district heating, facilities do not need to be centrally located within their coverage area; losses exist but are not substantial.

OPERATING AND MAINTAINING

Aside from the many components for specific actions in the WtE process, the operation and maintenance of the plant necessitates a number of auxiliary components. These relate to the handling of power within the facility, maintenance needs including storage and administrative workspaces, and any potential extra programs included in the plant operation. To perform maintenance on the plant's operating system without impeding the operators' work in the control room (2), the control system's maintenance, programming, and repairs take place in the automation room (20). This space is roughly 18 m x 18 m x 4 m and can be located anywhere in the facility. While the automation room is usually positioned close to the control room, it can also be placed near equipment with high maintenance needs such as the boiler, flue gas cleaning, or turbine.

Supporting WtE plant facilities

The power system requires switchgear rooms (18) that feed electrical power to each piece of equipment. Switchgear equipment requires roughly 900 sq. m of space and is usually divided between three or more different rooms. Most of the electrical equipment connects to the boiler, although other parts connect to the flue gas cleaning, turbine, and generator. In larger plants, a switchgear room is also needed for the induced draft fan. For the plant's critical equipment that must stay in operation even in the event of a blackout, such as the parts that feed water to the boiler, an emergency diesel generator (22) feeds the connected switchgear equipment to ensure they are always supplied with power.

Except for the power supply, the plant's unhindered operation requires regular maintenance since the equipment endures very high temperatures and is therefore susceptible to corrosion. The frequency of maintenance for each part varies according to the type of equipment and thus ranges from one year to more than five. For many of the plant's critical components, spare parts are kept in storage areas roughly 24 m x 24 m x 5 m in size. These lockup/storage rooms (21) could be positioned anywhere in the plant but require ground level access for the transportation and storage of spare parts. Plants are often built to last 25 to 30 years, which relates to their economic model. However, if regular plant upgrades keep apace with emissions regulations and parts are repaired as necessary, the facility can significantly outlive this lifespan.

Heat distribution pipes connect a WtE
facility to its municipality

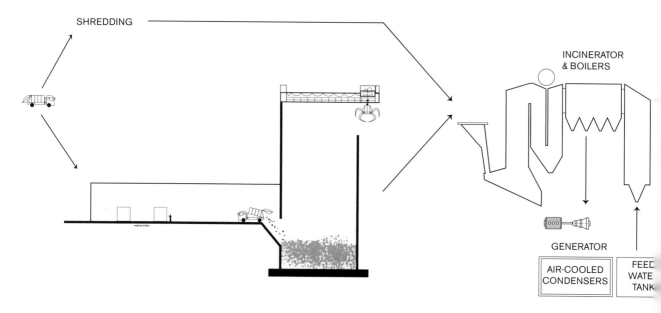

SHREDDING

INCINERATOR
& BOILERS

GENERATOR

AIR-COOLED
CONDENSERS

FEED
WATE
TANK

Potential technology configurations

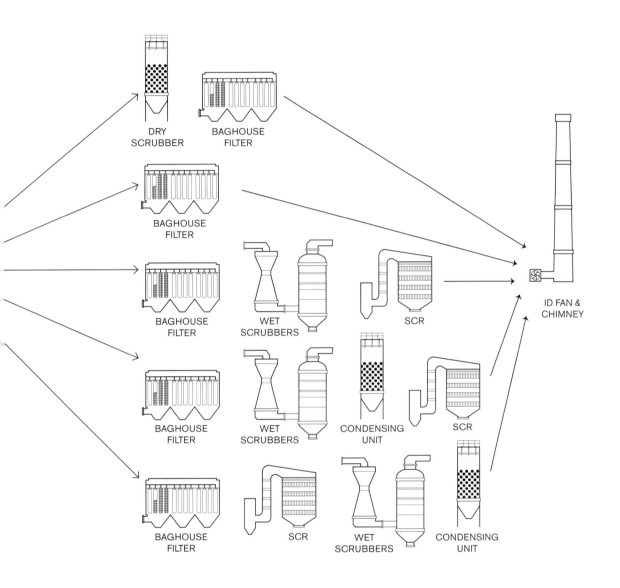

DRY
SCRUBBER

BAGHOUSE
FILTER

BAGHOUSE
FILTER

BAGHOUSE
FILTER

WET
SCRUBBERS

SCR

BAGHOUSE
FILTER

WET
SCRUBBERS

CONDENSING
UNIT

SCR

BAGHOUSE
FILTER

SCR

WET
SCRUBBERS

CONDENSING
UNIT

ID FAN &
CHIMNEY

CONCLUSIONS

Slight differences in the organization of the WtE plant's components produce a wide range of plant configurations. Each configuration has its own advantages and disadvantages, and may be more compatible with certain regions, regulations, or investments. The initial difference is in the waste handling process. Fluidized bed facilities need a lot more infrastructure than mass burn plants. Fluidized bed plants' larger footprint, greater odor release, and larger processing costs are balanced by a more energy-efficient combustion using the processed fuel and the added income from recycled materials. The incineration elements as well as the water and steam circuit generally use the same components, although the combustion grates can have a number of different mechanisms to mix the waste in the furnace and lead the ash to the dispensers.

The process that exhibits the most variety is filtering. In general, the whole circuit of the filtering process is handled differently in Europe than it is in the United States. In Europe, it is generally integrated into one building, while typically in the United States the facility is broken down into separate elements, and the filtering components can be located in smaller buildings outside the main one. Furthermore, one has to choose between different components for the same process, higher or lower levels of flue gas or residue processing, different configurations, and different connections. The residue and ash handling also differ dramatically according to region regulations or waste composition.

While we can compare possible WtE plant configurations, there is no single optimum solution, since the parameters that influence a plant's efficiency are varied. The most important factor that defines filtering processes is regional regulations on emissions control. In Europe, stricter regulations have resulted in the development of more sophisticated technologies on filtering, and the component configurations are generally lengthier. Similarly, the residue handling is more exhaustive in European countries like Sweden, where they strive for zero waste plants by recycling all hazardous or non-hazardous waste produced by the plant itself. On the contrary, in the United States recycling bottom ash as construction material is not yet allowed, and landfilling ash and residue remains the most common strategy. The relationship a facility has with neighboring industries and activities also plays an important role in determining its technology. Existing infrastructure—or the possibility of it—could give the plant the opportunity to provide district heating to adjacent grids, which would directly affect the plant's design. Ash or water treatment is related not only to existing industries, but also to the landscape of the plant's location, as water sources adjacent to the plant can replace air-cooled condensers or supply the necessary water for the plant's functions. All these factors, along with the region's economy and the initial investment, can determine which plant configuration is most applicable to a particular location.

It is generally accepted, for example, that industrial plants, including WtE plants, are better suited for rural or industrial contexts. Yet, a WtE plant could also be compatible with a more urban context—even a city center. Receiving waste directly from a plant's surroundings could help reduce transportation costs, allow for the implementation of efficient district heating, or make possible the development of hybrid facilities that integrate public life into the plant. Indeed, the role of the architect in this process can certainly go beyond a simple aesthetic flourish.

BIBLIOGRAPHY

Alstom. *Air Quality Control Systems.* http://alstomenergy.gepower.com /Global/Power/Resources/Documents /Brochures/air-quality-control-systems.pdf.

Alstom. *Air Quality Control Systems for the Waste to Energy Industry.* http://alstomenergy.gepower.com/Global /Power/Resources/Documents /Brochures/aqcs-air-quality-control-sys- tems-for-the-waste-to-energy-industry.pdf.

Alstom. *Boiler Service Solutions.* http://alstomenergy.gepower.com /Global/Power/Resources/Documents /Brochures/boiler-service-solutions.pdf.

Alstom. *GRT Steam Turbine.* http://alstomenergy.gepower.com /Global/Power/Resources/Documents /Brochures/grt-steam-turbines.pdf.

ABB. *Solutions for Waste-to-Energy Plants.* 2011. https://library.e.abb.com/.

Anderson, Christer. ÅF Industry. Personal correspondence with author.

Asgharinejad, Arash. "Mathematical Modeling of Solid Waste Incinerators." *Research Journal of Applied Sciences, Engineering and Technology* 5, no. 9 (2013): 2714–2723.

Avfall Sverige [Swedish Waste Manage- ment]. *Towards a Greener Future with Swedish Waste-to-Energy: The World's Best Example.* http://www.avfallsverige .se/fileadmin/uploads/forbranning_eng.pdf.

B&W Volund. *21st Century Advanced Concept for Waste-Fired Power Plants.* 2012. http://www.volund.dk/~ /media/Downloads/Brochures_-_WTE /Advanced_concept_for_waste-fired _power_plants.pdf.

Cabot Corporation. "Flue Gas Treatment." http://www.cabotcorp.com/solutions /applications/flue-gas-treatment.

Cardiff Energy Recovery Facility. Trident Park, Cardiff. Drawing no EfW-POR-15 .PO. SLR ARCHITECTURE. Bradford-on -Avon. 2010.

Dutch Waste Management Association. "Transformation into Energy Factories: R1 Status Drives Up Energy Efficiency." *Waste Forum,* Nov. 2011. http://www .wastematters.eu/uploads/media/waste forum_november_2011_Transformation _into_energy_factories.pdf.

Envac Group. "Vacuum Technology." Our Technology. Aug. 2009. http://www .envacgroup.com/products-and-services /our_technology.

General Electric. *GE in Waste to Energy.* 2007. https://www.gepowercontrols .com/eu/resources/literature_library /vertical_markets/downloads/WasteEnergy _leaflet_EN_final.pdf.

Hamon Deltak. *Heat Recovery Steam Generators for Combined Heat and Power.* 2014. http://www.hamonusa.com /sites/default/files/Hamon%20CHP%20 WHB%20Brochure.pdf.

Klinghoffer, Naomi B., and Marco J. Castaldi. *Waste-to-Energy Conversion Technology.* Philadelphia: Woodhead, 2013.

Konecranes. *Renewable Energy Plant Solutions Sustainable Energy Production.* http://www.konecranes.com/sites/default /files/download/konecranes_brochure _waste_to_energy_en_2013.pdf.

Lhoist Group. *Sorbacal Flue Gas Cleaning.* http://www.sorbacal.com /sites/sorbacal/files/Sorbacal_Flue%20 Gas%20Cleaning.pdf.

McGill AirClean LLC. "Acid Gas Control, Spray-Dry Scrubbers, Semi-Dry Scrub- bers, Dry Injection Systems." http://www .mcgillairclean.com/textDocs/products /acid_gas_control_systems.htm.

McGill Airclean LLC. "Air Pollution Control Equipment and Services." http://www .mcgillairclean.com/textDocs/products.htm.

Martin GmbH. *Martin Entschlacker* /http://www.martingmbh.de/media/files /technologie/update_1 /Entschlacker_08_13.pdf.

Martin GmbH. "Feeder." Waste-to-Energy Technologies. http://www.martingmbh.de /en/feeder.html.

Martin GmbH. "Reverse-acting Grate Vario." Waste-to-Energy Technologies. http://www.martingmbh.de/en/reverse -acting-grate-vario.html.

NTM-GB. *Quatro Recycling Vehicle.* http://ntm-gb.com/wp-content /uploads/2015/04/Quatro.pdf.

PWS Nordic AB. *Kärl Och System.* http://www.pwsab.se/fileadmin/images /PDF/PWSflerhj_web.pdf.

United Nations Enviroment Programme, Division of Technology, Industry and Economics. "1.5.2 System Types." In *Inter- national Source Book on Environmentally Sound Technologies (ESTs) for Municipal Solid Waste Management (MSWM).* http://www.unep.or.jp/letc/ESTdir/Pub /msw/sp/SP5/SP5_2.asp.

United States Environmental Protection Agency, Office of Air Quality Planning and Standards. *Stationary Source Control Techniques Document for Fine Partic- ulate Matter.* Report. Sept. 30, 1997. http://www3.epa.gov/ttn/caaa/t1/reports /sect5-4.pdf.

World Bank. *Municipal Solid Waste Incineration.* Report. August 1999. http: //www.worldbank.org/urban/solid_wm/erm /CWG%20folder/Waste%20Incineration.pdf.

Rudy and Peter Skitterians, *Factory by Night*, 2016

The Architect and
Waste-to-Energy Design

As cities grow and Waste-to-Energy (WtE) becomes an increasingly accepted means of dealing with municipal solid waste, a case can be made for locating WtE facilities close to or even within a city's center, as opposed to in the suburban or rural areas where such plants have traditionally been placed. Rapid urbanization in cities such as Vasteras, Sweden, also leads to an encroachment of cities as they expand toward previously peripheral WtE plant sites. Yet, the design and planning of WtE projects in urban situations becomes a more complicated proposition. Consequently, the architect's role in such circumstances becomes increasingly prominent, echoing the stronger need for a design-based solution that extends beyond technology and socio-political agendas. In fact, the timely involvement of architects can add value to WtE projects in both obvious and unexpected ways. In this chapter we explore what such contributions can be. In other words, what is the role of the architect in WtE facilities?

KEY QUESTIONS AND SYNTHESIS

To investigate the possible roles architects can play in the design and delivery of WtE plants, we approached select and diverse individuals representing major stakeholders in the WtE process—plant owners and operators, engineers, politicians, academics, and architects who have designed WtE plants. In keeping with our research's geographic scope, we focused on individuals and companies located in either Scandinavia or the United States. For each group of stakeholders, we used a semi-structured interview approach: to set the discussion's general agenda, we developed a list of questions that addressed issues specific to the interviewee but that also left space for new and unexpected subjects to emerge. With the interviewee's permission, we recorded the discussion for further analysis.

For example, of plant owners we asked, "In your country, how much of the waste produced makes it to WtE plants, landfill, or other systems? What are your general thoughts on the business case for a WtE plant in America?"

Of engineers we asked, "Which WtE technology would be easier to combine with hybrid typologies? How do you see a hybridization of technologies?"

Of politicians we asked, "How can we reduce centralized waste transportation and its impact on highways?"

Of architects we asked, "Is there a scope to make plants compact? What is the role of design in this process?"

The Role of the Architect

ANDREAS GEORGOULIAS

Ábalos & Herreros Architects, Northeast
Coastal Park Waste and Recycling Plant,
Barcelona, Spain, 2004

After each interview concluded, the research team transcribed the discussion. Then, after all interviews were completed and transcribed, we applied the axial coding method to identify findings and key themes. We decided against using the hypothesis-based method because our research topic lacks extensive published treatment, and we wanted to avoid using predefined relationships that exist in industry between owner, engineer, architect, and politicians, which might bias our approach. Instead, we followed a grounded research approach, where we dive into the primary data without preconceptions and let the findings emerge; some may confirm our assumptions and hypotheses, some may contradict them, and others may address issues we had not even considered.

Therefore, we selected the axial coding approach as the most relevant to our data sample and the state of existing research. We read the interviews multiple times and identified key themes that reoccurred in different interviews. These themes formed our research "codes," which range from intangible qualities like "aesthetics" through defined aspects such as "site context." We then carefully re-read each interview and marked each phrase, conclusion, or response that matched one of our codes. Finally, we isolated all phrases that fell under a specific code and listed them in a separate document, which serves as an "axis" of arguments related to specific themes that emerged during our inquiry. In this way, we consolidated the collective experience and knowledge of various WtE stakeholders. The findings of our research appear categorized below in a narrative that links the themes.

ROLE OF THE ARCHITECT AND THE FUNCTION OF DESIGN VALUES

THEME: HISTORICALLY, INDUSTRIAL BUILDINGS HAVE NOT NEEDED AESTHETIC CONSIDERATIONS. When we think about a WtE plant, often a negative image comes to mind. Plausibly, the first waste combustion plant in 1874, located in Nottingham, England, set an aesthetic norm for a WtE building. While the technological innovation and evolution of these facilities has progressed, unfortunately little attention has been given to the overall aesthetic quality of such industrial typologies. This in part stems from a lack of need due to WtE sites being distant from the city, a lack of designated budget for architecture, or a

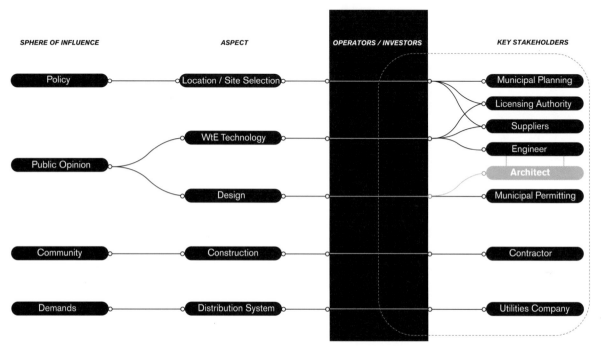

strict implementation of the mandate "form follows function," which in this case translates into forms driven by the machine aesthetics that govern the process, step by step.

As was noted by a Swedish architect, "The architectural shell is built around the process. It is not a building to enclose the equipment; rather it is built in at the same time." With a few contemporary exceptions that break this norm, this approach has changed little.

THEME: AESTHETICS ARE IMPORTANT FOR MITIGATING NEGATIVE ASSOCIATIONS WITH INDUSTRIAL BUILDINGS AS WELL AS INTEGRATING WTE PLANTS INTO THE COMMUNITY.

In dealing with the integration of a building into the neighboring community, design is unarguably an important factor. Even though WtE plants offer numerous benefits, the unpleasant industrial aesthetic prompts most people to shun such buildings in their neighborhoods. For example, since the 1900s, the image of a long chimney emitting plumes of black smoke has been viewed as evil. Of course the pollution and climate degradation concerns associated with these industrial buildings were then quite valid; but since the environmental movements of the 1970s, there has been a constant implementation of increasingly strict environmental regulations. Even though today black smoke has been replaced by extremely controlled emissions—the majority is just steam—the stigma of the chimney remains.

The "evil chimney" is just one of many historical associations linked to the form of a WtE plant. Other factors like height of the facility, location of the site with respect to the city center, and integrating the building with its context and landscape are very important points to consider when designing a plant. A WtE plant expert elucidated this concept by noting, "If you are close to one of the main roads leading into the cities, if you are in the city-center itself? Well, then [the WtE plant] simply has to look very nice." The conversation highlights the need for these buildings to have a rich visual quality—not only to change people's perceptions, but also for the building to better integrate with the surroundings. The call for innovation in the external appearance of such industrial buildings stresses the importance of the role of the architect in the design of such plants.

Architect's role in WtE plant design

Architects need to first address what is most problematic: WtE plants' purely functional appearance. "I think trying to take some of the industrial attitude away from [WtE plants] could ultimately be very beneficial," said a materials and community affairs manager for a US WtE plant. The challenge for architects lies in solving the problem of how to make a plant "aesthetically pleasing" without compromising the functionality of the processes within. As rightly pointed out by one WtE plant expert, the architectural considerations are dictated by all the processes of a WtE plant from incineration to flue-gas cleaning and from ash treatment to release of gases. Rather than opposing the flow of this process, what can architecture provide to add value or remove complexity from this process, which also incorporates better industrial aesthetics? Is it possible that a building that produces energy from waste can look pleasing?

Another Swedish architect who specializes in WtE plant design referred to a general plant and noted, "This ugly plant should be nice looking to make energy, and people care about how it looks. It must not smell nor produce smoke." In Sweden, in some cases the public is involved with voicing opinions on whether a particular design is acceptable or not. For obvious reasons a plant that visually appeals to its neighbors may be more readily accepted and integrated within a community.

A good design can alter much in a facility's functioning. Provided smell is not a factor, the well-designed plant can be located closer to the city or even within the city itself, which reduces the distance a garbage collection vehicle has to travel before it can dump a load of waste into the collection pit. It also reduces complexities in thermal energy distribution to the households; since the distance is greatly reduced, the steam-carrying pipes need not be of a larger diameter to accommodate for heat losses with distance. The optimum heat distribution distance for a WtE plant is about 5 km, a number agreed on by most of our interviewees. To facilitate this scenario, the role of design can be crucial and understood as adding value to the community through allowing for cheaper energy costs.

In fact, it is possible to make these plants symbolic, where they become the face of a neighborhood. A Swedish architect noted, "My concern is to make these huge investment plants look good, make them icons." He feels that the intervention of design goes beyond merely making the plant visually appealing. Rather, it should have an identity of its own. This identity also plays an important role in making people aware of the importance of this building, to them and the community. A Swedish WtE plant owner stressed the importance of the plant's appearance, saying, "Yes, it's important for me, because I am proud of my plant. I can say, 'See that plant that looks so nice? It's my plant. I love it.' I get proud of it. And that's actually how important it is for me."

Of course, we must also consider the larger picture, including the multiple impacts a plant has on its context. The design should reflect the nature of the surrounding space, whether it is a rural context where sensitivity might reflect a modest, subtle building, or an urban context where the overall cityscape needs to be examined and respected.

A Swedish WtE plant owner emphasized how in his approach to build the next plant, he is prioritizing the form of the building and making sure that the design integrates well within the city skyline. He added, "[in] the next Waste-to-Energy plant we are going to build, the boilers will be about 60 m high. That will also have a very high impact on the skyline of the city. It is also very important to find heights that are attractive and the design to get acceptance from the municipality." He went on to stress another important virtue of good design is that an attractive building is more likely to be accepted not only by the public but also by municipal approving bodies. He further added that a good design creates opportunities to induce favorable future developments for the site and surroundings, which are welcomed by the regulatory authorities. Regarding his upcoming plant he said, "They [municipality and stakeholders] would like [the WtE plant design proposal] to be something that can create and generate further development in our neighborhood and also create value." This illustrates that thinking about the larger picture and not just aesthetics is beneficial to all the stakeholders involved, including the people living in the area.

In investigating the design of WtE buildings, time is another important aspect to consider. Since these types of buildings are now being designed to last for 30 to 40 years, it is imperative to project the building designs into the future and consider the lifetime of the structure with respect to the city and neighborhood. In order to sustain a plant for the proposed lifespan, it is crucial to adopt flexibility rather than rigidity in design. This applies to accommodate both the changes in technology as well as the context around the buildings. As was elaborated by another architect specializing in WtE plants, "It's my mission to have things looking good, not a junk yard, [and] you have to plan before you build. It's very important to have the flexibility, right now and in the future. You can't tell how it is [going to be] in 10 years. It will need flexibility to change in the next 10 years with technology. It's a big investment, [and] it needs to be working for many years." Flexibility allows for a degree of adaptability with respect to the context's aesthetic needs. This illustrates one of the emerging design principles for industrial buildings that stresses an architect's role in attempting to consider a community's future growth and context beyond a singular building.

The larger context, such as energy infrastructure, is an important criteria for site selection

TOWARD EFFICIENCY OF SPACE AND SYSTEMS

THEME: THERE IS A HUGE EMPHASIS ON SITE LOCATION AS A PRIMARY DRIVER FOR EFFICIENCY.
Since available land is quickly becoming a scarce resource in many regions around the world, there is often a need for spatial efficiency when designing WtE plants. In the case of WtE buildings, there is always a cost trade-off between the distance from the city center a plant intends to service and the effective collection of waste and the distribution of heat energy. In usual scenarios, there has to be a compromise in prioritizing either of the two. A good design is crucial to the harmony and efficiency at the site location, the visual appearance, and the building's relationship with its surroundings. A Swedish WtE plant owner noted, "I think if you have a district plant, then it is very beneficial to try and stay in the same location. But if you are going to open a new site, then you can compare with other competitors who have tried to find a location very close to the city. There is usually a very strong opinion [about] a new location of a WtE plant close to cities."

THEME: VERY COMPACT DESIGNS ARE DIFFICULT TO ACHIEVE, DUE TO SPACE NEEDED FOR INTERNAL PROCESSES AND MAINTENANCE.
Since the late 1900s, efficiency has been one of the major discussion points for all the stakeholders involved with WtE plants. However, in order to achieve efficiency, we need to look at WtE in terms of its component systems and at various scales. Efficiency of space is a major component that often is very difficult to achieve because plants need a certain amount of space for internal processes and maintenance. According to a Swedish architect, "Whether it is possible or not (to have these plants more compact)—that's very much related to process. The most important thing, in these kinds of plants, is efficiency. Maybe it's hard from an architectural point of view to be able to make it smaller because it might not work with the processes." This throws light on a conflict between incorporating all the processes and supporting programs and making the plant "compact."

Compact and small are relative terms; while it is beneficial to aim for compactness, it is not feasible to make smaller WtE plants. As a Swedish architect noted, "If it's too small, it cannot be efficient." He also added that a WtE plant needs more space for maintenance (especially technology upgrades). This idea was restated by the materials and community affairs manager for a US WtE plant referring to specific US WtE plants, who noted, "Going too compact might turn out to be a hindrance for maintenance and upgrades." The role of an architect, then, is to know exactly how much space each process along with the space required for circulation and maintenance consumes. Then the architect must try to project future upgrades and find spatial requirements for the same. Only then can the facility be designed with proper spatial sensibilities. A WtE plant expert from Sweden described flue gas cleaning as a substantial part (almost 50 percent of the entire process) of the investment as well, and this component requires a huge building volume. Through our interviews and site visits, we found that the maintenance aspect is often overlooked, and it becomes a herculean task to perform maintenance or upgrade operations due to space limitations.

Another component of efficiency is found at the scale of energy distribution networks. Heat distribution is a concern at all stages, including selecting a new site location. Achieving maximum efficiency in heat distribution means maximum profits or a greater number of households served in the neighborhood. For this reason many WtE plant owners and stakeholders try to locate the plant as close to the city as possible. This increases the demand for an attractive building that compliments and works with its surroundings. As explained by a Swedish WtE plant expert, "District heating and cooling of homes uses water and steam, so the closer the plant is to the cities the better. This also implies better architecture of the plant would be needed to fit into cities." He further noted, "If you can run [waste] directly to the facility with your collection trucks, that would be a preferred location." On being asked about an approximate range from his experience he added, "I would say that 5 km could be a ballpark figure for a heating and cooling network, or it could be less, but once it reaches more than 10 km it becomes challenging." The architect has to work with engineers and city planners to develop a distribution master plan so that energy can be distributed in the best and most efficient way possible.

In the context of WtE plants, a very important avenue toward achieving efficiency is through hybrid typologies. The hybridization of programs is still largely an untapped opportunity. A good architectural design recognizes these opportunities and helps to create such symbiotic relationships. Another WtE architect seconded the idea of hybridization. "Certainly, to have a building where there is a creative way of producing energy that can be used on a 24-hour basis . . . some creative symbiosis between different uses—I think that would be an excellent idea," the architect asserted. He further expanded on the point of establishing this symbiotic relationship by saying, "some new function that itself produces a lot of waste located in or near the WtE facility that burns the waste, minimizing transportation but also increasing efficiency," would offer a good

Maarten Struijis, Purifying Plant Roteb, Rotterdam, Netherlands, 1993
Originally, this plant was located at the edge of the city. Over time, the city grew outward to meet it. When the plant was replaced in the early 1980s, gas purification equipment was added and much attention was paid to the exterior since it was now located in close proximity to a busy road and other buildings. The plant connects to the local district-heating network.

combination. Architects by nature of their profession have the capability to identify such programmatic pairings, which is beneficial to both the typologies. Especially in today's scenario where land is often a precious resource, to couple a WtE plant with, for example, a mall, which produces a lot of waste and uses a lot of energy, makes sense.

THEME: A MORE HOLISTIC APPROACH TOWARD EFFICIENCY ADDRESSES THE ENTIRE LIFE CYCLE OF THE BUILDING.

What happens when a plant becomes obsolete? Can its materials and various components be used for some other tasks, perhaps another WtE plant? Explaining the current scenario of obsolete plants in Sweden, a Swedish architect said, "Usually it's not the buildings that are obsolete; it's the boilers and stuff. In the old days, they were usually highly sought after for other purposes, for offices or schools. If you look at shipping, the plant parts that were erected in the 1970s and 1980s, they refurbish them, they tear down part of the building, and they reuse the building site, built with a new technology." The lifecycle of the plant is discretized into the lifecycle of its various components, which often have multiple uses even if the plant is out of commission. Likewise, a Swedish WtE plant expert emphasized the advantages of keeping the same site for a WtE plant, as all the required permissions are already in place.

THEME: COLOCATION SHOULD INCLUDE A SYMBIOSIS BETWEEN RECYCLING AND INCINERATION.

Presently colocation WtE facilities often sit in isolation on sites close to the city, and they could also include a colocating of incineration and recycling. As a Swedish WtE plant owner noted, "We don't say that recycling and incineration are competing with one another. They should both be able to work and help each other. It should not be a competition between those two—energy recovery and material recovery. We should try to take the part that's best for incineration, to us, and the parts that are best for material recovery that goes through these steps to find overlaps." Establishing even such small pairing can go a long way in reducing many overhead costs and increasing numerous benefits in operations.

Hence, the concept of efficiency aims to establish energy dependencies and symbiotic systems both within the plant and between the plant and other typologies. The materials and community affairs manager for a US WtE plant illustrated future WtE projects, noting, "One of the things we have been promoting for quite a while is what we call an eco-industrial park. We would be the energy supplier to a variety of other waste-related industries, like a recycling facility, a composting facility, and virtually anything else because we could then provide very inexpensive energy to these other insular projects, which would help them make their rate very competitive." In summary, to achieve space efficiency, good energy distribution networks, material lifecycle assessments, and to design and plan ambitious projects such as eco-industrial parks, architects can play a crucial role in finding relevant correlations and translate them into design.

GENERATING POSITIVE PUBLIC PERCEPTION AND AWARENESS

THEME: NEGATIVE PUBLIC PERCEPTION AND A CULTURE OF NIMBYISM NEED TO BE
OVERCOME BY DESIGN.

All stakeholders found the public perception of WtE plants to be a delicate topic. In most
cases, the ultimate success or failure of developing a WtE facility on any site depends
to some extent on how the public perceives the plant. Unfortunately, WtE plants inherit
(along with other industrial buildings) a mostly negative public perception. As previously
discussed, this perception is partly attributed to certain elements like the chimney and
its association with environmental degradation, but largely to the design quality of the
buildings and their settings. Even today, this forms a stigma in the minds of the people
when it comes to WtE buildings. Consequently, it is imperative for architects to respond
to these issues when designing a new plant. As a WtE plant expert noted, "When we
are discussing WtE, I think it is more a question of public perception, rather than scale."
He further added that it is difficult to positive a good public perception, especially when
people are unaware of facts and statistics, and they see the plant through a historically
biased lens. In his words, "It takes such a huge amount of effort in building a public
opinion in favor of WtE. If you have no tradition, if you are in a country or, in the case of
the United States, in a state that has no previous experience, then you are starting with a
blank piece of paper; you are starting to convince people that this is actually the best you
can do with your waste." Another reason why creating good public perception is difficult,
explained a WtE architect, is that "because there have been so many of these plants that
have been designed without the right sensitivity, there is a stigma about them." The stigma
is due to various reasons, but primarily it can be attributed to smell, the lack of public
involvement in plant matters and important decisions that affect the neighborhood, and
the sight of steam (perceived as smoke) coming out of a large chimney.

THEME: CHIMNEYS RAISE CONCERNS AMONG THE PUBLIC THAT THE WtE PLANT
CREATES AIR POLLUTION.

Unfortunately, this misconception still exists today. The materials and community affairs
manager for a US WtE plant, referring to WtE plants in the United States, explained,
"The chimney represents the old industrial United States of America that built with black
smoke. We don't have smoke. Steam is what you see in the wintertime."

**Babcock & Wilcox Vølund, chimney
at the Högdalen WtE facility, Högdalen,
Sweden, 2004**
Prominent chimneys can raise public
concerns that WtE plants create air
pollution.

She mentions that even today it is very hard to create a good or even neutral public perception: "We are still working hard to get over the perception that we are a polluter." Another architect confirmed that the chimney is a bad-reputation generator. He noted, "Certainly, if a WtE plant has a big chimney stack in the context of a medium-sized facility, it's going to stand out and this may not be what the people are going to be happy with." The architect indicated an important point where the role of the architect becomes crucial. The sizing of plant versus the stack is determined by the processes and the capacity, but the way the stack is handled in design and the way the plant responds to its surrounding landscape can affect people's perception of the plant as a whole.

THEME: POORLY DESIGNED AND BADLY LOCATED WtE PLANTS SMELL AND CREATE A NUISANCE TO NEARBY COMMUNITIES.

In addition to the stack, in poorly designed and improperly located WtE plants, there is often the huge problem of smell. This is the second reason why many neighborhoods want the plant to be somewhere outside the city and not in their backyards, noted a Swedish WtE plant expert. While there is a tremendous effort on the part of plant operators to tackle or minimize this problem, odor is still an issue. Especially with plants that are located close to the city center, the offensive odor becomes a major problem in determining public perception and hence public acceptance. A Swedish plant owner highlighted the efforts taken at his plants, noting, "We depend on on-time delivery to avoid these problems of smell because we are located very close to the center of the city."

THEME: THE PUBLIC NEEDS ENGAGEMENT AND THE RAISING OF AWARENESS.

In most cases, a major step toward creating good public perception is educating all the stakeholders, including the general population, about the plant's operations. "I think it's an important infrastructure [to show] what happens to waste; everybody could use the waste. And it is important [in terms of] education for kids as well as adults to see the plants," a Swedish architect said. It is imperative to have the public be a part of the plant and for them to feel comfortable around the plant. She continued, "It is challenging to create a good place as well as a nice building that people can understand, to educate people, so they can see the process going on. I think from an architecture standpoint, it is hard to make [the plant] more compact, but it would be easier to fit [plants] into cities more" by increasing awareness through education. Creating places for people to come, sit, and learn about the plant's processes, having open spaces in the landscape that are open to the public—these are a few design strategies that increase public participation and hence awareness of the plant. Understanding the importance of educating people and increasing awareness, a Swedish WtE plant owner noted that in a new plant design, he would like "the possibility to have larger groups within the plant and show them our activities."

In terms of the relationship with the public, a Swedish architect said, "It's very important to visualize. Making pictures and renderings, it's very important to show the public by renderings, gather people to talk about what's going on, make people participate in this project. We will gather their opinion and we have respect for the people." He mentioned that architectural drawings and renderings can play a very important role in educating people about the positive points WtE facilities offer to communities. "A well-designed plant with the right amenities around it—I think people might actually want one in their neighborhood," noted another architect while discussing the role of the architect in shaping public perception through design.

STRENGTHENING THE BUSINESS CASE FOR WtE

Like all other projects, a WtE plant usually comes into existence only when the project is financially feasible and viable. This scenario is preferred for the public sector, but it may not always be the case. This is almost always true, however, for private-sector owners who own and run a WtE plant. The financial feasibility of WtE plants is driven by several factors, the most important of which is the size and scale of the facility. Specifically, larger plants with higher waste inputs and electricity and/or heat outputs require fewer operational costs for procuring and managing waste throughout the plants' lifecycles. They also generate higher amounts of energy and byproducts, which facilitate higher revenues.

The most important way design can strengthen the WtE plant business case is through improving the efficiency of spaces, which enables owners to build large-capacity plants on smaller chunks of lands. A main finding from our interviews indicates that smaller plants are economically unfeasible, thus establishing a relationship between plant size, capacity, and feasibility. A Swedish WtE plant expert noted that today, only plants above a particular capacity are feasible economically, noting that "if you look at what the trends are in the market now, then the economy of scale has a huge say." These points were reiterated by many of the interviewees. Another expert mentioned, "it's much better if you can build a large [plant], because you have much startup cost in a project like this. So it's cheaper, so to say, to build a large one. And it is typical to build one that can take 200,000 tonnes and then build more lines if you want to have more than that. Then you build them beside each other." Similarly, the materials and community affairs manager for a US WtE plant mentioned, "for any WtE facility, you have to consider the economy and scale. So you could not build one economically for 100 tonnes a year." She also added, "You get that economy and scale and labor at 600 tonnes per year but, between 600 and 1,000 tonnes, you utilize your investment and equipment in a better way at 1,000 tonnes than at 600 tonnes." She explained, however, that in order for a WtE plant to be feasible in the United States, we would have to develop district-heating scenarios.

Yet, establishing a direct relationship between waste input, plant size, and operational cost is often challenging; overall costs decrease as facility size increases, but operational costs are influenced by additional factors, both external and design related (see figure on page 143). These factors, which can reduce or increase operational costs, include the necessary technologies for waste treatment, energy or heat generation, and emissions-treatment requirements. Technological advances have driven some specific WtE technologies and plant arrangements toward high efficiency levels, which create significant operational costs. Nevertheless, an optimized plant arrangement with state-of-the-art technologies might recover up to three times more electricity and/or heat compared to a conventional plant, which would make it more profitable, albeit more expensive to run, over the operating period. Furthermore, the continuous modifications in emissions-treatment regulations and advancements in flue gas cleaning technologies are, for many experts, the principal factors that determine operational costs. The costs for procuring machinery and implementing maintenance programs for emissions treatment alone can account for more than 60 percent of investment and operational costs over a WtE plant's lifecycle.

Sometimes a project's existent circumstances render it unfeasible. Factors such as the location of the site determine its distance from the city service area as well as requirements for waste transfer stations or other supporting facilities, which can significantly increase operations costs in trash collection and heat distribution. In certain countries, or even regions within a country, a specific technology might be more preferable than others, emissions treatment standards might be more stringent, the market price of electricity and heat might vary, and the waste gate fee might be higher or lower (usually depending on the regional waste system and its reliance on landfilling); all of these factors considerably influence operational costs. Furthermore, a plant's proximity to widespread district-heating networks can significantly drive revenues upward. Another important factor is the cost of upgrading technology in existing plants. When the design of the facility in place does not allow for these changes, a total shutdown can result. Giving design importance from the project's initiation can be a determining factor in creating a successful business case. "The economical side is the main drive," notes one architect.

To strengthen the business case, then, the architect's role is to design spaces for efficient use. Compact program arrangement, efficient internal planning, and intelligent use of site resources can greatly improve profitability and lead to the development of more WtE plants across the country.

IMPLICATIONS

In the 21st century, the architectural expression of industrial buildings is adopting a new language. As will be seen in the following precedent analyses, now a number of successful plants are emerging with unique and innovative aesthetic appearances, and these facilities are challenging norms regarding how WtE plants can be designed and perceived. It is up to the architect to delegate these rich expressions to industrial forms and show sensitivity, not only through design but also through a nonverbal dialogue with the surrounding buildings. As an architect emphasized, "one should really spend some time thinking about the local context, what the facility is going to look like, from the eye of the person on the street who lives there and knows this area better than those architects will ever know it." This statement summarizes a basis for contemporary WtE design. There are diverse opportunities to add value through simple design interventions and aesthetically pleasing WtE plants. These interventions can go a long way toward changing public perception, creating a scenario where people will embrace WtE facilities as a viable source of energy and beneficial community amenities.

Costs related to creating and maintaining a WtE facility

Cost per waste tonnes

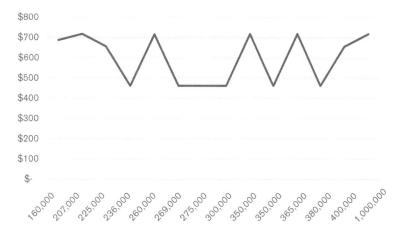

Cost per sq. m

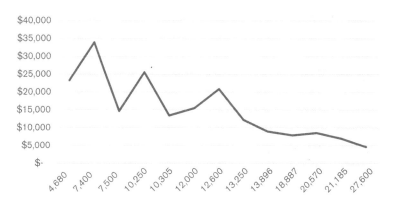

Cost per electricity output

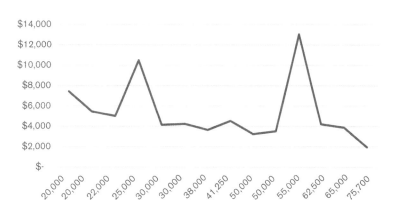

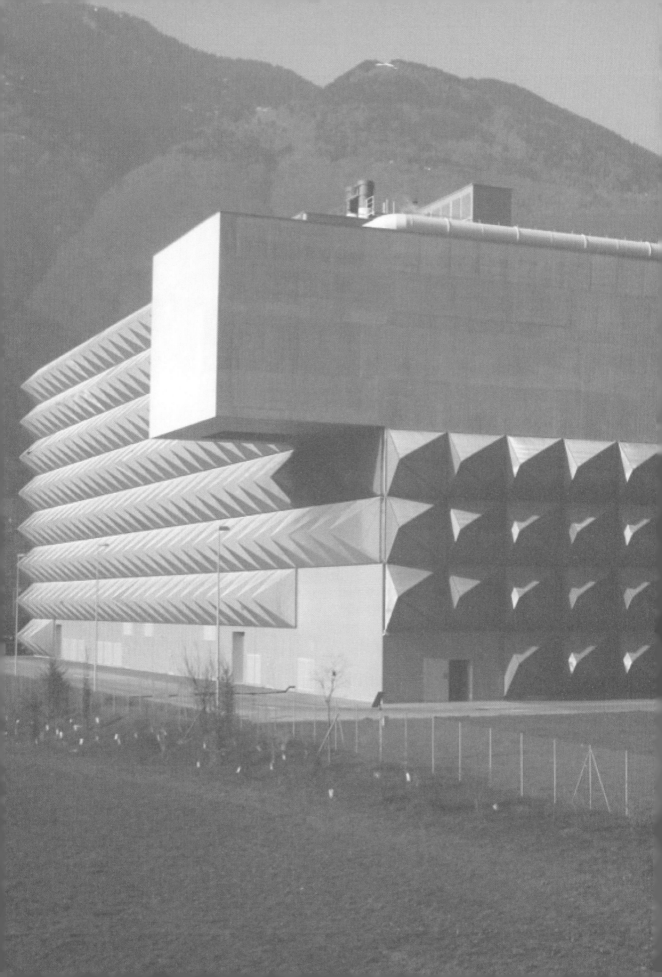

INTRODUCTION

This precedent analysis of Waste-to-Energy (WtE) facilities does not attempt to look at every WtE facility. Rather, it focuses on plants where an architect collaborated with engineers, and where a clear design element was introduced for the purpose of creating a better facility. Note that while there are many cases of architecturally interesting WtE facilities in Asia and elsewhere, this precedent analysis details only European models, as this book compares the European and American contexts. Another reason for our emphasis on European models stems from the increase in architects being used for these facilities in Europe, as the landscape is denser than in the United States and plants must be built close to cities, within view of homes and work places.

Early examples of architectural WtE facilities are largely aesthetic interventions—we find either highly stylized plants linked to a certain point in time (e.g., the Bauhaus era) or plants with architect-designed facades or stacks, such as the Spittealau Incinerator in Vienna. Yet as we look to the more recent past, namely in the past five to ten years, we see architects becoming increasingly involved in the design and arrangement of WtE plants. The facilities themselves become less recognizable as power plants and instead display larger artistic and organizational moves. Finally, we arrive at contemporary examples, such as the Amager Bakke Resource Center (ARC) ski slope facility design by the Bjarke Ingels Group (BIG). This Copenhagen plant is perhaps the most relevant example we can use to begin to reevaluate the relationship of the plant to the city, and reassess the role architects can play in such industrial projects.

Future WtE plants will legitimately requisition what these power plants are able to do, what the facilities' needs and timelines are, and how they relate to the city in terms of location and services. Today as we take stock of the more recent plants in which architects have been involved, we recognize that these facilities have yet to achieve their full potential in terms of public necessity, the future of environmental change, and basic changes to public policy.

Precedent Analysis

LAURA SMEAD AND LEIRE ASENSIO VILLORIA

Studio Vacchini, Giubiasco Incinerator,
Giubiasco, Switzerland, 2009

PRECEDENTS

Spittelau Waste Incineration Plant, Vienna, Austria, 1989
Architect: Friedensreich Hundertwasser

The Spittelau Waste Incineration Plant was modernized in 1989 with flue gas cleaning equipment. At that time artist and architect Friedensreich Hundertwasser was commissioned to redesign the facility's facade and chimney. It became a unique, internationally known work, combining technology and the arts while simultaneously reducing urban pollution. The architect's vision was to show something in direct contrast to what he saw as the depressing monotony and anonymity of industrial construction.

Chaux-de-Fonds Waste-to-Energy Plant, La Chaux-de-Fonds, Switzerland, 1995
Architect: Pierre Studer

The Chaux-de-Fonds Waste-to-Energy Plant, located on the site of an old gas works, is designed around the old gasometer. Architect Pierre Studer was tasked with finding an eco-friendly solution to the technical problem of expanding and combining this industrial site. Since waste was delivered by truck rather than by rail as with other Swiss incinerators, the entrance and exit to this facility needed careful control. The architect designed an innovative curved glass wall that marks the location where waste vehicles enter and exit. This huge wall is suspended from an external metal frame, which may be lowered or raised to compensate for winter snowfall. It automatically returns to its original height once the snow melts. The wall also functions as a window and provides sound insulation.

Rotterdam Waste-to-Energy Plant, Rotterdam, The Netherlands, 1996
Architect: Maarten Struijs

The original Rotterdam incinerator was built in 1912 just outside the city. Over time the city grew to meet it, so that in 1989 flue gas cleaning equipment was needed to protect environmental and public health. This required a new building almost as large as the original plant. The architect, Maarten Struijs, was asked to design a facade for the facility that would be visually appealing to the adjacent neighborhoods. The architect wrapped the building in a reflective uncoated metal that mirrors the changing conditions of the sun, sky, water, and weather, echoing the time and season through neutrally shifting whites, grays, and blues. The facade reads as a continuous curving wall. Windows and barred openings allow illuminated glimpses of the machinery within.

Calce Waste-to-Energy Plant, Calce, France, 2003
Architects: Luc Arsène-Henry Jr. and Alain Triaud

Architects Luc Arsène-Henry Jr. and Alain Triaud sought to increase local community acceptance of the project through architectural beauty. In their words, "The plant must be beautiful, because it represents proof that society is looking after you. It's no longer necessary that it declares its industrial purpose, since its advanced technical nature can nowadays be assumed. A sports car shows its styling, not its engine." Undulating bands of champagne-colored stainless steel comprise the Calce plant's facade. The site contains landscaped embankments and a rough, exposed concrete base to echo the local geology. The building and panels are positioned to minimize wind noise. By carefully distributing the machinery within, the facility's footprint has been reduced so it does not exceed the line of the adjacent ridge. To avoid evoking the idea of pollution, the architects shortened the chimney to 3 meters above the building elevation.

Spittelau Waste Incineration Plant
Vienna, AT - 1989
Friedensreich Hundertwasser

Chaux-de-Fonds Waste-to-Energy Plant
La Chaux-de-Fonds, CH - 1995
Pierre Struder

Rotterdam Waste-to-Energy Plant
Rotterdam, NL - 1996
Maarten Strujis

Calce Incineration Plant
Calce, FR - 2003
Luc Arsene-Henry Jr. and Alain Triaud

Rouen Waste Processing Plant
Rouen, FR - 2004
Claude Vasconi

Marchwood Energy Recovery Facility
Hampshire, UK - 2004
Jean Robert Mazaud and S'PACE architecture

Northeast Coastal Park Waste Plant
Barcelona, ES - 2004
Ábalos & Herreros

Uppsala Block 5 CHP
Uppland, SE - 2005
Arkitekt Magasinet AB

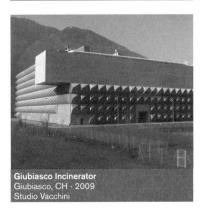

Giubiasco Incinerator
Giubiasco, CH - 2009
Studio Vacchini

Kara/Noveren Thermal Power Plant
Roskilde, DK - 2014
Erick van Egeraat

Veolia Energy Recovery Center
Leeds, UK - 2014
Jean Robert Mazaud and S'PACE architecture

Amager Bakke Resource Center
Copenhagen, DK - 2017
Bjarke Ingels Group

Rouen Waste Processing Plant, Rouen, France, 2004

Architect: Claude Vasconi

This cutting-edge plant was a pilot feature in an ongoing plan to redevelop an abandoned industrial area in Rouen, France. To accomplish this, architect Claude Vasconi enveloped the plant with an imposing metal shell that features wide glass windows, which allow a great degree of natural light to penetrate the interior. The plant's series of chimneys pays homage to the French ships once built in the nearby port.

Marchwood Energy Recovery Facility, Hampshire, England, 2004

Architect: Jean Robert Mazaud and S'PACE architecture

The Marchwood ERF has a unique design: an aluminum dome covers the entire plant. This massive dome stands 32 meters tall, and the chimney is 65 meters tall. The design was created collaboratively with local residents, councils, and a team of architects, led by Jean Robert Mazaud. The plant uses nearby estuary water to cool the steam, which powers the generator turbines.

Uppsala Block 5 Combined Heat and Power Plant, Uppland, Sweden, 2005

Architect: Arkitect Magasinet AB

A new waste incineration (combined heat and power, or CHP) plant was built in Uppsala, Sweden, in 2005. Situated on a flat landscape, the city of Uppsala can be seen from a great distance. Therefore it was important that the design for the new plant not interfere with the view of the city's historic landmarks, especially as seen from the nearby highway. An architectural competition was held to find a thoughtful design that integrated the size and shape of the plant with the surrounding landscape. The result is a humble and inconspicuous profile characterized by red-colored brick and aluminum sheets.

SUEZ Energy-from-Waste Facility, Suffolk County, England, 2014

Architects: Grimshaw Architects

The architectural firm Grimshaw designed the SUEZ (formerly SITA UK) Energy-from-Waste Facility. They sought to minimize its visual impact on the landscape by organizing the technical systems and components into more aesthetically pleasing massing than found in most WtE facilities. The torqued louvers of Grimshaw's plant reflect light, while its transparent facade lets visitors view the inner working of the energy production process. The plant also features a visitor's center where the public can be educated on the process of WtE technology.

The **Northeast Coastal Park Waste and Recycling Plant, Inceneritore Giubiasco, Kara/Noveren Thermal Power Plant, Veolia Recycling and Energy Recovery Center,** and **Amager Bakke Resource Center** are described in more detail on the following pages.

BIBLIOGRAPHY

Arch Daily. "Incineration Line in Roskilde." http://www.archdaily.com/544175 /incineration-line-in-roskilde-erick-van -egeraat.

BIG/Bjarke Ingels Group. "ARC: Amager Resource Center." http://www.big .dk/#projects-arc.

Cardani, Elena. "L'esempio pilota. Energy Exploitation Unit, Rouen." *L'Arca* 186 (December 2003): 62–67.

Dawson, Layla. "Wrapping the Machine: Emission cleansing plan in Rotterdam, Struijs, Maarten Architect." *Architectural Review* 200, no. 1195 (September 1996): 65-65.

Della Fontana, Jacopo. "Presenza garbata: Cridor Plus Incineration Plant." *L'Arca*, no. 98 (1995): 29–31.

Energitårnet. "Kara/Noven: About the Project." http://www.xn--energitrnet-38a .com/about-project-energitaarnet.

Green Build & Design Magazine. "On the Boards: Recycling and Energy Recovery Facility." http://gbdmagazine.com/2016 /on-the-boards-recycling-and-energy -recovery-facility/.

Grozdanic, Lidija. "Gorgeous Green 11MW Bioenergy Plant in Leeds will sort 214,000 tons of waste each year." Inhabitat. http://inhabitat.com /gorgeous-green-11mw-bioenergy-plant -in-leeds-will-sort-214000-tons-of-waste -each-year/.

Litt, Steven. "BIG Projects in Copenhagen, Another Northern Waterfront City, Offer Lessons for Cleveland." Cleveland.com (blog). http:// blog.cleveland.com/architecture//print . html?entry=/2013/05/big_projects_in _copenhagen_ano.html.

Mialet, Frederic. "The Calce Incineration Plant." Euro Inox. http://www.euro-inox.org (discontinued).

Reed, Peter. *Groundswell: Constructing the Contemporary Landscape.* New York: Museum of Modern Art, 2005.

Seward, Aaron. "Trash as Treasure." Architect 100, n. 9 (September 2011): 106–08.

Tekla. "Amager Bakke: One of the Largest Environmental Projects in Europe Exploits BIM." http://www.tekla.com /us/company/news/amager-bakke-one -largest-environmental-projects-europe -exploits-bim.

Tyrens. "Example of consultation: Trying to establish an incineration plant and a CHP in Uppsala." Technical document. "Uppsala." Uppsala. http://powerplants .vattenfall.com/uppsala.

Van Egeraat, Erick. "Waste to Energy Plant, Rosklide, Denmark." http:// designerickvanegeraat.com/project /waste-to-energy-plant/.

Veolia. "Energy Recovery: Marchwood." http://www.veolia.co.uk/hampshire /energy-recovery/energy-recovery /marchwood.

Veolia. "Energy Recovery: Building Marchwood." Video. http://www.veolia .co.uk/hampshire/energy-recovery /energy-recovery/marchwood /building-marchwood.

Veolia. "Introducing the Facility." http:// www.veolia.co.uk/leeds/our-proposal /our-proposal/introducing-facility.

Wien Energie. "Spittelau. The thermal waste treatment plant." Technical brochure. http://www.fernwaermewien.at.

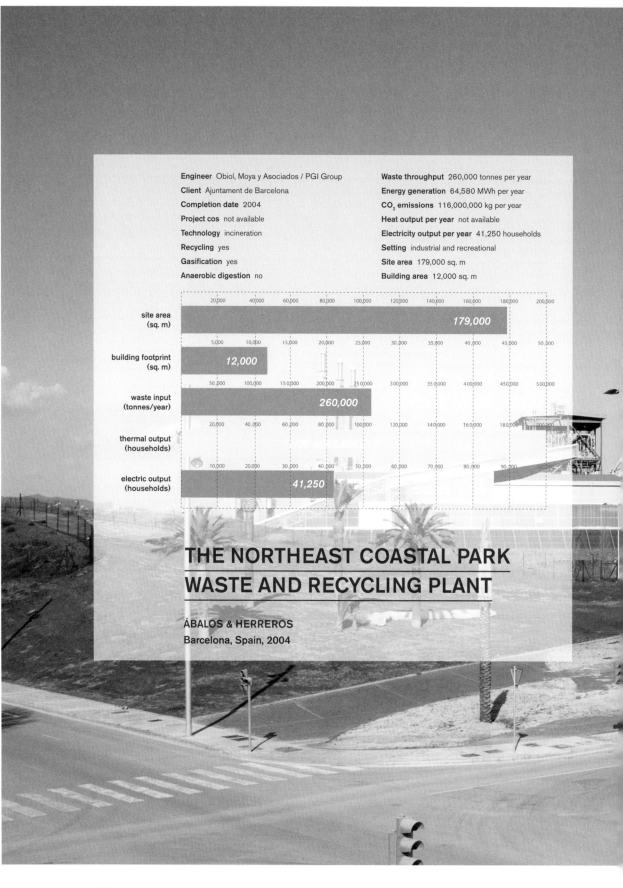

Engineer Obiol, Moya y Asociados / PGI Group
Client Ajuntament de Barcelona
Completion date 2004
Project cos not available
Technology incineration
Recycling yes
Gasification yes
Anaerobic digestion no

Waste throughput 260,000 tonnes per year
Energy generation 64,580 MWh per year
CO_2 emissions 116,000,000 kg per year
Heat output per year not available
Electricity output per year 41,250 households
Setting industrial and recreational
Site area 179,000 sq. m
Building area 12,000 sq. m

site area
(sq. m) — 179,000

building footprint
(sq. m) — 12,000

waste input
(tonnes/year) — 260,000

thermal output
(households)

electric output
(households) — 41,250

THE NORTHEAST COASTAL PARK
WASTE AND RECYCLING PLANT

ÁBALOS & HERREROS
Barcelona, Spain, 2004

Designed by Ábalos & Herreros, Barcelona's Northeast Coastal Park successfully combines two unusual uses: municipal waste management and a waterfront park and beach. Originally, this site was cut off from the city and contained a nonoperational sewage treatment plant, an artificial landfill, and an electric generator. The contaminated site was rehabilitated, regraded, and filled with recycled sand to extend a new coastline over 100 meters into the Mediterranean Sea. The WtE plant, the "Mountain," acts as a noise barrier. It also features recycling and education centers so the public can learn about these advanced technologies.

On arrival, visitors travel on a wide, paved promenade past the Mountain and education center. The palm-tree-lined path opens to a panoramic view of the sea, a large boardwalk, lawns, and beach. The paved boardwalk contains a mosaic by artist Albert Oehlen, continuing Barcelona's strong tradition in the decorative arts. The mosaic of playful fish is so large in scale that at ground level it reads as fields of color. From elevated positions, however, such as the deck on the west lawn or the train by the Mountain, visitors see the pattern come to life.

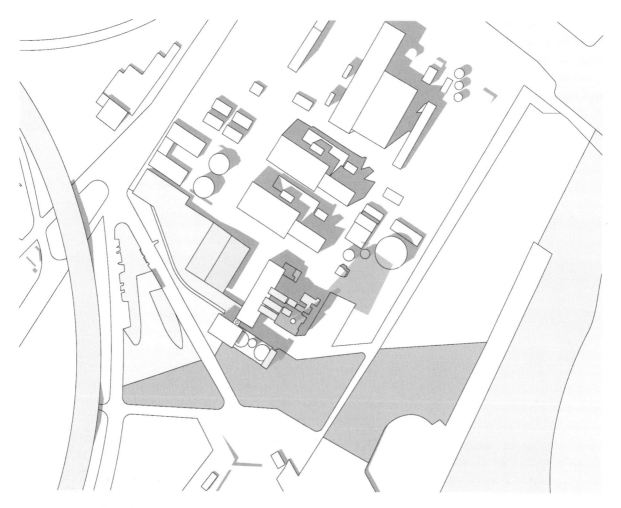

Northeast Coastal Park, site plan

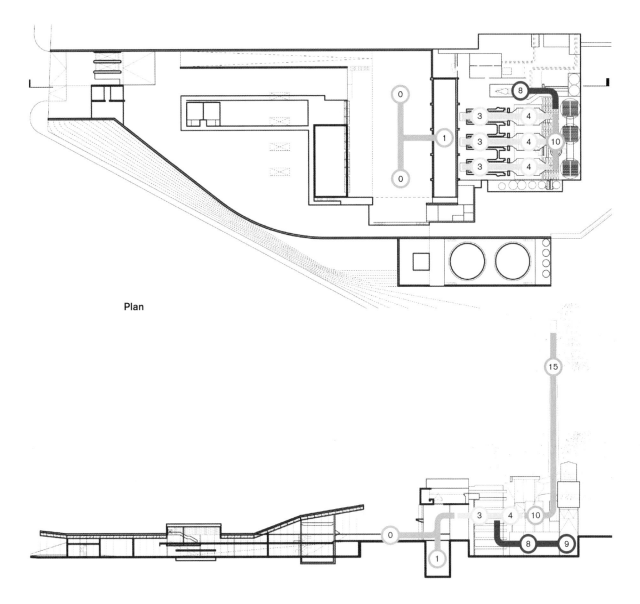

Plan

Section

Tipping & Feeding	Condensing	Filtering	Monitoring
0. Tipping Hall	6. Feed Water Tank	10. Baghouse Filter	16. Emissions Control Station
1. Bunker Hall	7. Air-Cooled Condensers	11. Wet Scrubbers	17. Sampling Station
2. Control Room		12. Water Treatment	
		13. Condensing Unit	Operating & Maintaining
	Generating	14. Selective Catalytic	18. Storage Silos
3. Incinerator	8. Turbine & Generator	Reduction Filter	19. Automation
4. Superheater	9. Power Transformers	15. Induced Draft Fan	20. Switchgear Equipment
5. Economizer		& Chimney	21. Emergency Diesel
			22. Lockup/Storage

*Component index as shown in Anatomy chapter

153

Interview with Iñaki Ábalos

Northeast Coastal Park, view of
waste digester

Iñaki Ábalos has been a professor in
residence and chair of the Department
of Architecture at the Harvard University
Graduate School of Design since 2013.
He cofounded the Madrid-based firm
Ábalos & Herreros in 1984; in 2006, he
formed Ábalos+Sentkiewicz with Renata
Sentkiewicz. In May 2016 Ábalos spoke
with Leire Asensio Villoria about the
architect's role in the creation of industrial
facilities and his experiences as a designer
of the Northeast Coastal Park Waste and
Recycling Plant, in Barcelona, Spain.

Leire Asensio Villoria (LAV): This is a preamble to our discussion. Are you interested in pursuing projects related to Waste-to-Energy facilities in the United States?

Iñaki Ábalos (IÁ): No. Rather, I am interested in knowing how the United States can address such projects. I am especially interested in the dispersion proposal of WtE treatment residues, which can be used for heating and cooling. WtE facilities are usually placed outside cities, and waste is transported to them. Yet the location of treatment facilities within cities offers possibilities for local energy use as well as a reduction in traffic. In Madrid, for example, I have seen entire avenues congested with continuous traffic through the whole day and night. This causes pollution and many problems, including a kind of traffic no one wants to experience.

LAV: Before moving onto other matters, such as of the practical differences between Europe and America, and the role that the architect has in the design of these types of facilities, I would like to discuss your design solution for the Barcelona and Madrid plants.

Based on previous discussions with the different interested parties in the WtE realm, it seems that in most cases architects have been relegated to the design of the facade, if they are involved at all. In your experience, what does the architect contribute to the design of industrial large-scale projects, and what adds value to these projects?

IÁ: It depends on the client organization. In Barcelona, the Northeast Coastal Park Waste and Recycling Plant (2004) was a special case because there was already an incinerator, and there was a European regulation that the client had

to match; the client had to transform the incinerator into a recycling plant that would fulfill new regulatory terms and adopt new technologies. Curiously all these were the agents of the Forum 2004 and Barcelona's Metropolitan Agency for Urban Development and Infrastructure, directed by architect Josep Acebillo. This big group in regional Barcelona still exists, and its leaders were aware of the opportunities this project presented. In our competition entry we emphasized that the park is not the important thing; the important thing is how the transformation of the incinerator into a recycling plant can expand and connect the city, and demonstrate a different way of handling the industrial and the urban processes. This is what won the competition. It was simply the expression of these clear ideas, more or less an image that prioritized the public character of the space and the urban community, as opposed to the industrial engineering of the processes.

In Madrid, with the Recycling and Compositing Plant (1999) everything was the opposite. We were simply given a location and told that the processes were to be rehabilitated but they had not even bought the new machines. The client showed us several examples and we had to create a project without knowing how the modernization was to be done. It was a miracle our design matched the investments; there were practically no major changes between our schematic design and what was built! Here the project was not about creating a public character for the space, but showcasing the industrial processes. The emphasis on the architecture was minimal, and the competitors who presented before us were equally focused on the industrial processes. The only difference was the architecture. We spoke of matching colors with the hillside, of organizing things to minimize the environmental

impact, of regulating the constructive systems to be recyclable. This last idea was key. And there was an educational circuit intended for schools and other visitors. So in the two cases of Barcelona and Madrid, we had different approaches, and both were right. It is very important to make this point.

LAV: Can you talk about when architects lost their place or role in this type of industrial building? Did this shift come from the industry itself, from poor education, or from sheer laziness?

IÁ: I do not want to overlook the responsibility architects surely have, but I do not believe that there is a problem with either the architect or the real estate market. Rather, there came a moment in which building solutions were semi-technical, semi-industrialized, especially in the Anglo-Saxon and American models, in which container construction was absolutely systematized, and for a client it was not necessary to engage an architect. That persisted for a few decades, and now we are moving into a different phase. This is happening with wine vaults, for example, and now Frank Gehry and Norman Foster do wine warehouses. There are containers that have demonstrated that the architect can represent an important qualitative change. Marqués de Riscal now sells in America; it is a very popular wine brand thanks to the company's Gehry-designed City of Wine complex in Rioja, a strategic investment that successfully targeted the American market.

A certain industrial territory has been recovered, a culture that was previously open only to painting and movies and music has now embraced architecture, thanks to some architects. But there was a moment in which industrial culture didn't embrace architecture. The modernization of other constructive processes swept the architect from the scene.

LAV: Yes, and now the architect is hopefully becoming more engaged in industrial work. Our investigation tries to promote a promising future for the architect, not only at the level of design but also in how the architect may be involved in defining this new type of building, what role the architect may play. Can you speculate on the future of the architect with respect to industrial typologies?

IÁ: The architect has to have a technical mentality to work in the industrial realm. It is not conducive for a postmodern historicist, for example, to design a water purification plant. In other words, to have a voice and a vote, the architect must be able to speak the appropriate technical language. In addition, the architect must show that he or can interact reasonably and rationally with the industrial projects' mechanisms and systems, and contribute positively to the problems of saving time and optimizing processes. This is where the architect can make a difference, proposing a small change that adds value. This change may help with community perception, now or perhaps in 20 years when it is necessary to recycle the building, and it will have more value. This is another very important thing to consider: architects are capable of projecting where the city will go, if it is going to be smaller or if it is going to be this orientation or another, and this can influence industrial projects to increase their value. These things, when you have already obtained minimal credibility, can have an impact. Interventions in the urban, aesthetic, and public aspects are the ways that we can introduce this extra value and create a certain authority.

LAV: What were the architectural strategies behind the design of the Barcelona plant? What were their purposes, and what is the history behind this project?

IÁ: Northeast Coastal Park Waste and Recycling Plant was the product of a very fast competition for the ugliest site in Barcelona. They called it "Chernobyl." It was an abandoned area where prostitutes and drug addicts gathered. Yet the site held interest precisely because it offered an important urban perspective of Barcelona, an open letter to the city . . . and it was interesting because it was a public space and on the sea front. It was a park and it had a recycling plant and incinerator. We had already worked with recycling plants, and we knew that there were a few new European regulations that had to be adopted in a short period of time. So our proposal was that this is not a small park; it is a whole assembly of parts that will coexist with new parts of public space. Then we assembled a recycling plant that extended the park with an unforeseen artificial beach. It fit like a glove. Renata and I worked on the competition entry over a weekend, and it was all pretty much there. We decided it was a collage, and the main idea was that we could invent a kind of ideal scenographic frame, but like a cubist collage. We could do a few fragments that were all of the same weight, without any hierarchy. So there are pavements, there are planted areas, there are a few clustered landforms. Other fragments turned in mountains, and there are four or five things that create an effect when you put them together with the chimneys. The design convinced others and it convinced me of the type of effect we can achieve today with modern city waste.

LAV: Why did you adopt an approach that promotes the generation of a public space for an incineration plant?

IÁ: Nowadays recycling and incineration plants have a political dimension. They are not simply productive processes; they affect quality of life, and they require a big public investment despite what is often a lack of interest. Because the city invests in it, from the first moment we recognized the project as both public and political. We wanted to make visible things that up until then had been invisible. This added a political dimension that gave us an advantage over our competitors in the short term while actually allowing us to create architecture, which is very important to us.

LAV: Regarding public opinion, did you encounter significant opposition from neighbors toward the Barcelona plant?

IÁ: This was not a problem. The Northeast Coastal Park Waste and Recycling Plant was a well-made media operation from the beginning. Its first interation was drawn up by Acebillo and Enric Miralles, and there was minimal opposition. It was an operation of restituting and completing the coastal region, of conquering an area that was completely degraded and relatively close to the city center. The idea was to regenerate the most marginal neighborhoods. All this sold well because it made political and urban sense. The first phase worked very well, then did little; it did just enough to open . . . But it is necessary to give time for these operations . . . Regardless, this is a brave project for an area that was very degraded and largely abandoned. It is an urbanistic project, even though everything was not done, only the most public thing was done, and then there are the

Northeast Coastal Park, view of incinerator

neighborhoods, which have been made. There are some beautiful pieces, others that are quite nice, and others that are worse, but it has had a regenerative effect on the most important sites of the city, a huge piece of the city. This was a very well-sold operation because it was good town planning.

LAV: So there was not any public resistance to the initial program?

IÁ: There was not, in Barcelona or Madrid. The locations were strategically selected because they were very remote, but close enough become urban when the processes were finished. In Barcelona the public actually welcomed the plan to recreate a beach and a public space. In the Recycling and Composting Plant on the periphery of Madrid, the area is up and coming now, and I am sure that it will be the most important public infrastructure of the southeast regional park, where it is located.

LAV: In Barcelona, the regeneration of this old incinerator plant into a WtE plant and recycling center, the introduction of the public space and other things . . . were catalysts for the area's growth. With several of their hybrid projects, our students intended to create similar catalysts. One option that you have mentioned in the past, which it is very much in line with the students' discussions, is the idea of reducing the plant's footprint. This idea can be accomplished by fragmenting the processes in a series of smaller buildings that have similar dimensions to the urban fabric so that, when the area grows, it absorbs these buildings as part of the urban fabric. So when we mention Barcelona now, we are discussing two strategies: how we bring the processes to the city, and also how the city can regenerate itself.

Shifting topics, I'm wondering: as an architect with studios in Cambridge and Madrid, what are the differences between

the United States and Spain regarding the politics of waste processing and the public perception of these types of facilities?

IÁ: The first time that I came to teach in the United States, at Columbia University, I proposed a recycling plant as a studio topic. It sounded as if I had proposed throwing stones at the dean. At that time Columbia had gone paperless and people were all chummy, and it was completely disconcerting. I did not know how to integrate into the group of colleagues, and the students acted in a very different way than I was accustomed. But one of our students, Mitchell Joachim, later a cofounder of the firm Terreform One, since then has devoted his life to the topic of recycling. What he does is marvelous.

Since then I have seen plenty of interest in recycling plants, likely due to of the interest developing in the United States as a result of things that northern Europe has exported with a certain naturalness

Northeast Coastal Park, waste delivery area

to southern Europe. In the United States they like high-speed trains and reducing energy bills. The idea that we are condemned if we don't do these things is the key problem, and it is not going to be solved rapidly.

LAV: True, I believe that this is a problem, an important and deep-seated one. Do you see a contextual difference in the architect's role in the United States and Europe when designing WtE facilities?

IÁ: There is a different attitude. In the United States these are almost utopian projects, and there are many projects. I know this is a topic of interest academically. In almost all of the schools you can find these types of studies, analyses, and proposals. Students appreciate the topic, but it remains hypothetical.

LAV: How can the architect achieve a major role in infrastructural projects in the United States? Would the country need

a change of politics from the top down, or more grassroots, bottom-up? Through an architectural movement promoted by more visible projects like yours in Barcelona?

IÁ: The ability to challenge the status quo within the United States' established systems of production is quite limited; the systems that exist are based on propagating the accepted systems, so they are not going to progress or change very much, or with any rapidity. However, the universities do make efforts, as we are doing at the Harvard GSD. The only possibility of the profession making a contribution, and it is precisely something that we are trying to achieve in schools, is by cultivating the understanding that alongside its formal and cultural dimension, architecture has a technical and performative dimension. The combination of the two dimensions is what has social and political aftereffect; focusing on only one of the two is

useless. The schools lead the country's cultural trajectories, introducing topics such as thermodynamics and energy in a way that is creative and not purely technological, thereby informing the ideology of a new generation.

LAV: Where is the topic of public perception in this cycle of transformation of the architect's position? Can public perception change, allowing a change of politics and the architecture that it bears? Is it public opinion that gives way to better architecture, or something else? Can good architecture change public opinion?

IÁ: It is the chicken or the egg. But it depends on societies. We have seen it in Europe, and we all agree that the change is from the bottom up in northern Europe. The Green Party in Germany contributed incredibly to the change of political attitudes because they reached the government. Because it was bottom-up, they came up. If you do not come up, it does not happen. More conservative policies have a relatively big social conscience. The Social Democrats have integrated these politics, and it was more top-down, as it happened in southern Europe. It is logical. There are cultures in which well-being is more measured. In northern Europe well-being is quantified; in the south it consists of a good generic life. It is very cultural.

LAV: Your project in Barcelona is different, partly, for its social ambition and the architectural strategies that frame this relationship of the public with waste. How can this social ambition be implemented in projects of a lesser scale than that of the Barcelona plant? How can we approach this in smaller plants?

IÁ: I am quite interested in this topic, namely the relatively homogeneous distribution of WtE facilities in the city and the use of the energy on a neighborhood scale. This practically turns the facility into a neighborhood utility that could provide energy for not only the lighting of the public spaces, for example, but also for residential heating. As your studio proposes, interesting hybrid public facilities could exist in neighborhoods and provide energy at no cost. This is how we should use urban WtE facilities. In a city of three million inhabitants, the dispersal of hybrid centers could introduce much value, especially to peripheral neighborhoods.

LAV: This interests me as well.

IÁ: It is interesting technically, typologically, and at a thousand levels.

LAV: Generally one tends to think that a good design is more expensive. How do you communicate the value of your design to your clients?

IÁ: I do not communicate it. There is a way of communicating, but it precedes our arrival. This is an operation for the town-planning agents—the quarter politicians, the representatives of the neighborhood associations who do the work. Or, you must enter as an immersed person in a team that comes to give input, and when you explain what you are doing, you have to be rigorous. And you also have to understand what the people are hoping to hear, and that if you do not give it, it will go badly. You must bear in mind that stakeholders are different: the elderly, minors, women . . . all have different needs. If suddenly you concentrate only on the men who are like you, and say that you are going to put in a marvelous bowling alley and a nightclub, the others are going to say, "And what happens to the old men?" It is necessary to have a social sensibility that allows the agents that have invested in you, and those who hear you for the first time, to see that you are representing them.

LAV: How do you communicate the extra cost of a design to the public? For example, in the United States with community consultation, you always know that a neighbor's complaints can stop a project. In Spain there are a series of regulations that exist beyond this . . .

IÁ: Yes, in Spain there is a filter that is urbanistic, perhaps too meticulous, that supposedly operates like a mediator of all the agents and of all the conflicts. Although then the neighbors' associations can be annoyed. We have one more way, belonging to the tradition of the French centralist state, in which the decisions come from above to below, in a much fragmented process, with many steps. Here there must be great communication, which talls to the urbanistic agents, the

social partners who represent the groups. One model is not better than another . . . the democratic city is not necessary the best, just as the construction of the city from fragmented decisions has problems. But I see good and bad, quite balanced.

Time is a key point. One of few things that modernized Spain, in the period in which the European Union was giving the country funds, is the speed of production, from a project's initiation to the users' occupation of the space. While American and northern European societies can tolerate projects dragging out for years and years, other societies cannot. The fragility of the politics does not allow it. Some democratic processes result in the tremendous waste of money, so much that, in general, there are not many benefits. Sometimes there are none. There is not yet a system of managing the city that could be said to be better than another. In this sense, in a weak economy, the economic factor should prevail.

LAV: Returning specifically to the design of WtE facilities, do you foresee other architectural opportunities, such as the burying or vertical superposition of plant components, to rethink the conventional organization of these facilities and allow them to better adapt to an urban context?

IÁ: I would like to investigate the points at which the heat watts concentrate, the maximum temperatures, and up to what point components can be isolated or reconfigured safely within their surroundings. This speaks to what typologies we can better employ, what typological organizations can make better use of the energy resources that are generated. Let's think of an outline almost like an onion. This would be what I would explore right now.

159

Northeast Coastal Park, recycling area

LAV: Today have many ways to eliminate the odors from the facility, such as negative pressure inside the bunker hall. Now the biggest problem is seen in peak hours, when the trucks back up outside waiting to unload the rubbish, almost as if they are caught in highway traffic.

IÁ: I see the possibility of diminishing the scale of and increasing the dispersal of the facilties as the most important, alongside generating typical, reusable spaces. These plants surely must attend to the components' organization, but the more typical these spaces are, the more chance there is that they will be reused in the future. In other words, once the initial program has become obsolete, you look at the building and say, "This can be 20 things." It can be a laboratory or a recreation center, a storage facility, or support another intermediary use. We must think about its next life, about how the project can be reused later.

LAV: Exactly. Do you foresee that the hybridization of WtE plants with other programs can instigate the placement of these facilities in urban centers?

IÁ: I hope. As soon as possible!

LAV: In Sweden and in many of the Scandinavian countries they speak about the circle economy, the idea that if we upcycle materials, we are going to be able to reuse them infinitely or not need to treat and dispose of them. Yet we have spoken with many engineers, experts on the topic, and even if they believe completely in the circle economy, they acknowledge that there is always going to be a lower loop, something to treat, to bury in a landfill, or burn. The premise of our design research exploration is the idea that despite the progress we will make with "reduce, reuse, recycle," there will always be something remaining.

IÁ: Yes, this is true.

LAV: When you are working on WtE or other industrial facilities, how does everyday professional practice compare, for example, to when you are engaged in working on other typologies, such as housing or museums?

IÁ: It has its high moments and its low moments. The high moment is the speed of the processes. One of the more difficult things for the architect is the slowness with which projects often

proceed. Industrial works, however, always have the swords of the time and money, and often you can use them in your favor. It is necessary to know what the materials are, the building systems that allow you to obtain a certain quality with economy and speed. A low moment is that there are often difficulties in finding the people who enjoy doing this work. In my experience, there are many who would rather be doing luxurious neighborhood housing and believe they are degraded by doing industrial work. When you find a colleague in these processes, someone who really likes what he or she does, it is a pleasure, it is an authentic delight.

LAV: One last question: in what ways can educational institutions better prepare architects to undertake industrial work? What can be done better?

IÁ: Education can do so much, and simultaneously we are greatly compressing educational time to reduce expenses and to maximize operations . . . For me it is very difficult to choose, with such limited time, what is essential to teach. Of course, the most essential thing to teach an architect nowadays concerns the capacity and the quantity of resources

Northeast Coastal Park, walkway to the beach

that we have to design, and the cultural character that design has. It sounds a little ancient, but this is the success of the Harvard GSD. Design has a real effect; the ability to design has an enormous, great social impact, more than knowing only about hospitals or about a particular typology. Of course, then you can specialize. Often, educators now have to worry, almost like medieval monks, about keeping the flame of the essential thing alive because almost the whole reality that surrounds us in practice matters very little. But this is why architecture is important.

It is absolutely essential to be able to work on a variety of scales, topics, and problems. For many years American architectural education eliminated social housing explorations, and now it is returning in many places. This is logical and natural, and it is essential to

understand the city and what 70 square meters mean in the life of a person. To think of the other extreme and look to the infrastructural scale would be ideal. But of course, the student is free to choose, and there are a thousand factors. The only thing that we can do is provide a menu that could inspire diverse careers and help students find their place. This is what we as educators can do.

Engineer unknown
Client Azienda Cantonale dei Rifiuti, Switzerland
Completion date 2009
Project cost 331 million Swiss francs
Technology combined heat and power incineration
Recycling no
Gasification no
Anaerobic digestion no

Waste throughput 160,000 tonnes per year
Energy generation 117,300 MWh per year
Emission control standard not available
Heat output per year 4,000 households
Electricity output per year 22,000 households
Setting not available
Site area 40,000 sq. m
Building area 7,500 sq. m

site area
(sq. m) **40,000**

building footprint
(sq. m) **7,500**

waste input
(tonnes/year) **160,000**

thermal output
(households)

electric output
(households) **22,000**

GIUBIASCO INCINERATOR

STUDIO VACCHINI
Giubasco, Switzerland, 2009

163

Given the increase in waste, Switzerland decided to hold a competition by invitation for the construction of a new WtE facility in Giubiasco. Studio Vacchini designed the plant to concentrate its contents into a compact cube shape. In order to do this, the normal arrangement of the machinery was turned to line the facades. A tetrahedral module breaks down the large areas of the facade into smaller surfaces, and the shapes also protect from solar radiation, provide thermal insulation, and absorb noise from the nearby highway. The square follows the lines of the landscape, surrounding fields, and existing roads.

This plant sets new standards as the most modern in Switzerland, and at the time, one of the most advanced in the world. All emissions are well below the national limit. The plant disposes of nonrecyclable municipal waste, including sewage sludge, and also takes certain types of medical waste. Giubiasco CHP incinerates approximately 160,000 tonnes of waste per year. The flue gases are treated in four stages: an electrostatic precipitator, a three-stage scrubber, a catalyst, and a tissue filter. The plant generates 100 GWh of energy per year, with residual heat supporting the district-heating network, saving some 5 million liters of heating oil per year.

Giubiasco Incinerator, site plan

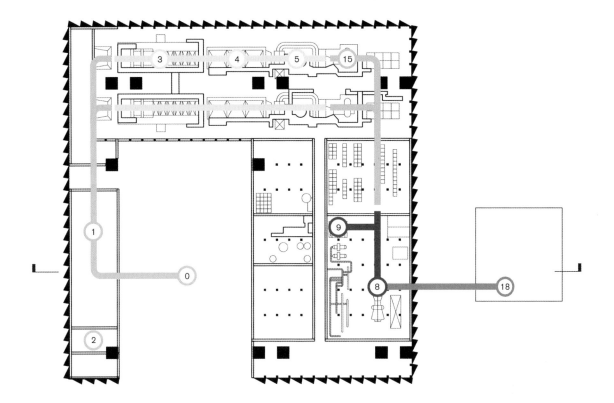

Plan

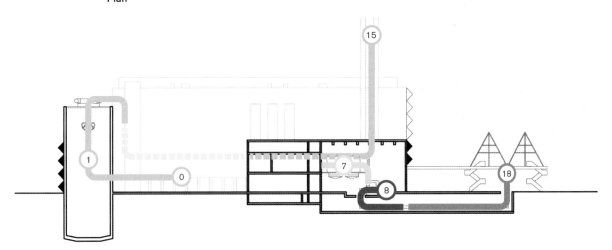

Section

Tipping & Feeding	Condensing	Filtering	Monitoring
0. Tipping Hall	6. Feed Water Tank	10. Baghouse Filter	16. Emissions Control Station
1. Bunker Hall	7. Air-Cooled Condensers	11. Wet Scrubbers	17. Sampling Station
2. Control Room		12. Water Treatment	
		13. Condensing Unit	Operating & Maintaining
	Generating	14. Selective Catalytic	18. Storage Silos
3. Incinerator	8. Turbine & Generator	Reduction Filter	19. Automation
4. Superheater	9. Power Transformers	15. Induced Draft Fan	20. Switchgear Equipment
5. Economizer		& Chimney	21. Emergency Diesel
			22. Lockup/Storage

*Component index as shown in Anatomy chapter

Giubiasco Incinerator, exterior views

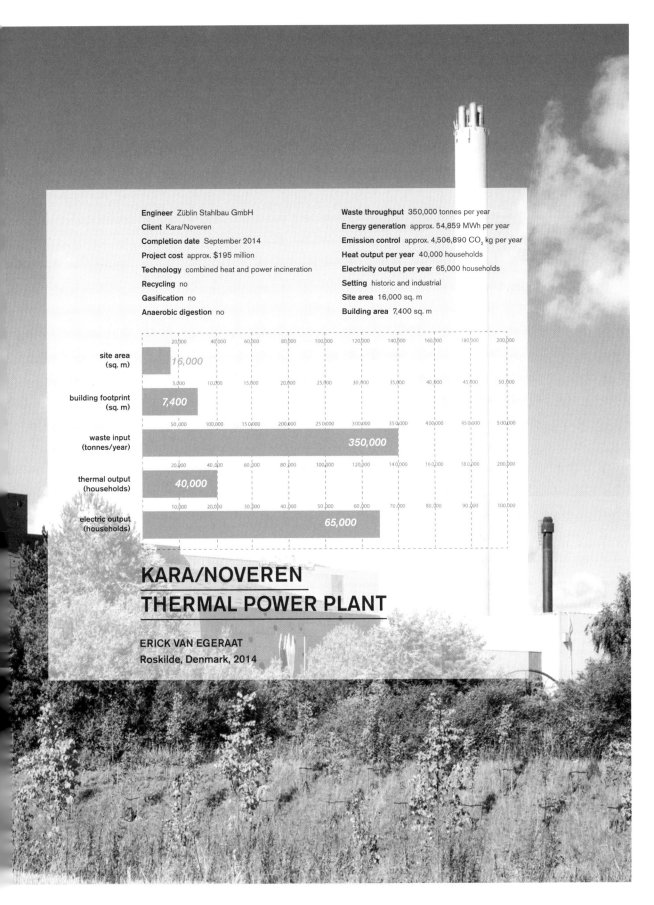

Engineer Züblin Stahlbau GmbH

Client Kara/Noveren

Completion date September 2014

Project cost approx. $195 million

Technology combined heat and power incineration

Recycling no

Gasification no

Anaerobic digestion no

Waste throughput 350,000 tonnes per year

Energy generation approx. 54,859 MWh per year

Emission control approx. 4,506,890 CO_2 kg per year

Heat output per year 40,000 households

Electricity output per year 65,000 households

Setting historic and industrial

Site area 16,000 sq. m

Building area 7,400 sq. m

site area (sq. m)	16,000	
building footprint (sq. m)	7,400	
waste input (tonnes/year)	350,000	
thermal output (households)	40,000	
electric output (households)	65,000	

KARA/NOVEREN
THERMAL POWER PLANT

ERICK VAN EGERAAT
Roskilde, Denmark, 2014

Located approximately 2 kilometers from the Roskilde city center, the Kara/Noveren Thermal Power Plant burns waste from nine surrounding municipalities and other places abroad to produce electricity and heat for the whole Roskilde region. The project was the result of a competition organized in 2008. In order to fulfill the technical requirements for ventilation and wind and water tightness, the facade is composed of two layers. The inner layer provides all necessary openings for daylight and air circulation. This liberates the outer layer from functional requirements and allows for flexibility in the patterning. The design rests on standard, readily available products and simple construction details, and it uses cutting-edge manufacturing technology to minimize the facade's production costs.

The Kara/Noveren Thermal Power Plant presents an iconic expression for the otherwise functional architecture of local waste management company Kara/Noveren's next generation incineration line. Due to its large scale, this incinerator is destined to become an outstanding structure in Roskilde's wide, open landscape. The architects recognized this, as the new incineration line is clearly engaged in a dialogue with its historic and industrial surroundings. Close to the ground the building reflects the angular factory roofs of the immediate surroundings, and toward the top it culminates in a 97-meter-tall spire, creating a contemporary counterpoint to the steeples of the city's historic cathedral.

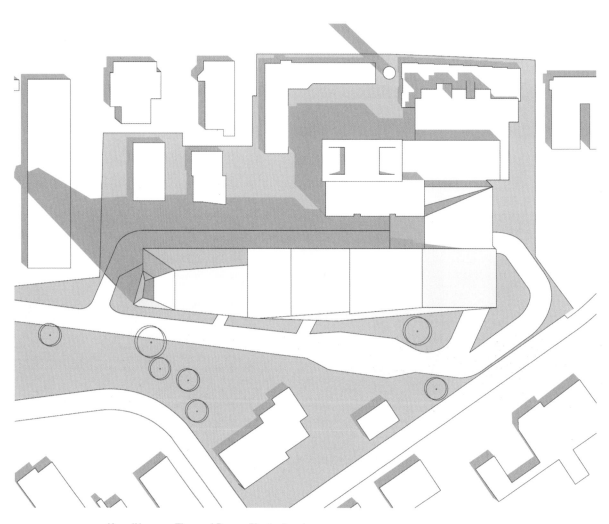

Kara/Noveren Thermal Power Plant, site plan

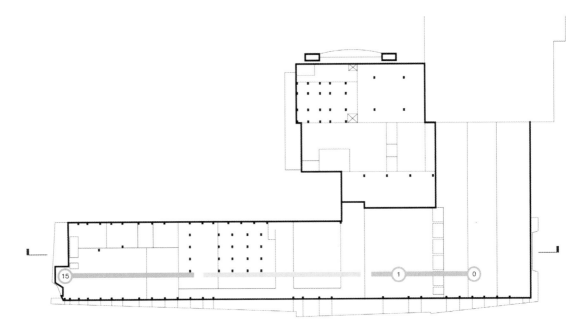

Plan

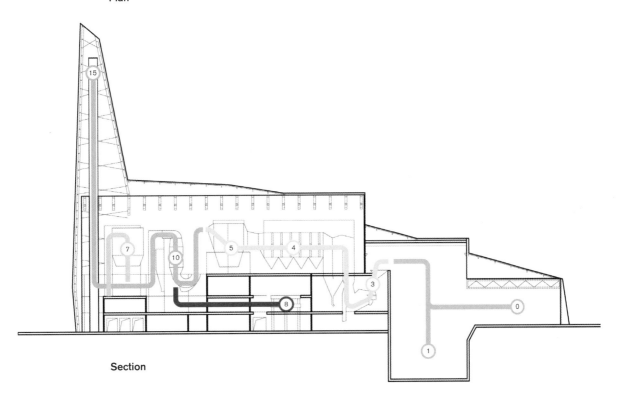

Section

171

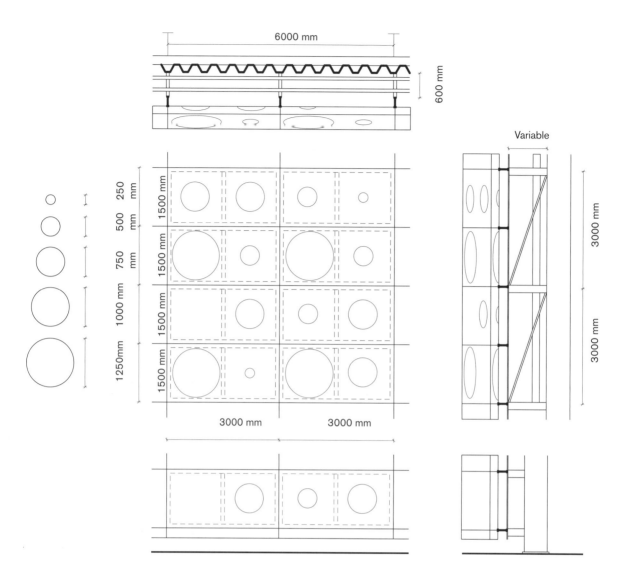

6000 mm

600 mm

Variable

250 mm
500 mm
750 mm
1000 mm
1250mm

1500 mm
1500 mm
1500 mm
1500 mm

3000 mm

3000 mm

3000 mm

3000 mm

3000 mm

Kara/Novern Thermal Power Plant, facade detail

Facade construction

Laser-cut circular openings cover the raw umber-colored aluminum facade. Programmable lighting installed between the facade's two layers acts as a visual metaphor for the energy production processes occurring within. "At night the backlit perforated facade transforms the incinerator into a gently glowing beacon—a symbol of the plant's energy production," said plant architect Van Egeraat. To hide the light sources, the light fixtures have been attached to the outer skin and the light reflects from the inner surface, creating an even glow through the perforated facade. A pattern of differently sized and spaced circular holes adorns the aluminum facade panels and increases in density as it reaches the spire. For a few minutes every hour a spark gradually grows into a blazing flame, enveloping the entire building. The metaphoric fire then ceases, and the building appears as a mound of burning embers.

Kara/Novern Thermal Power Plant, exterior views

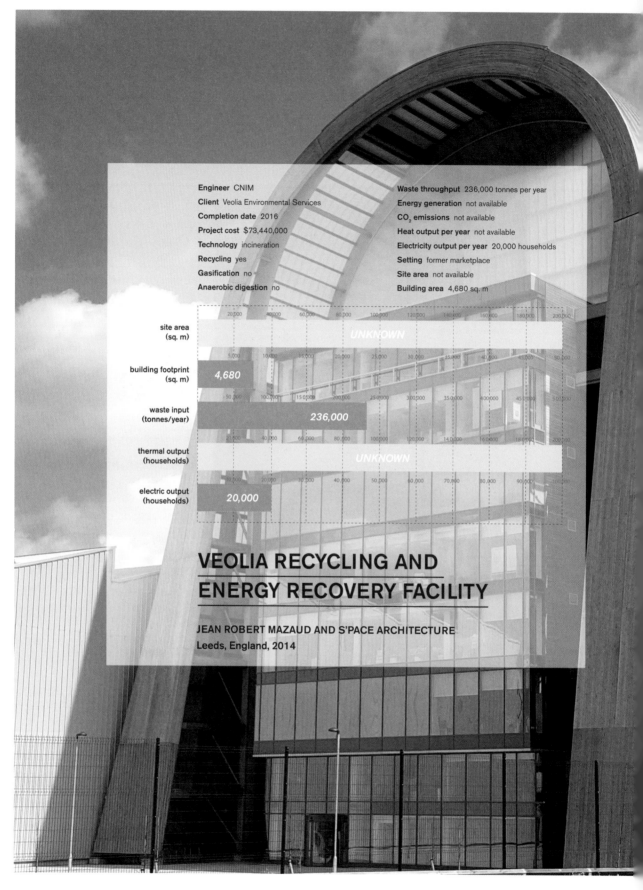

Engineer CNIM
Client Veolia Environmental Services
Completion date 2016
Project cost $73,440,000
Technology incineration
Recycling yes
Gasification no
Anaerobic digestion no

Waste throughput 236,000 tonnes per year
Energy generation not available
CO_2 emissions not available
Heat output per year not available
Electricity output per year 20,000 households
Setting former marketplace
Site area not available
Building area 4,680 sq. m

site area (sq. m)	UNKNOWN
building footprint (sq. m)	4,680
waste input (tonnes/year)	236,000
thermal output (households)	UNKNOWN
electric output (households)	20,000

VEOLIA RECYCLING AND ENERGY RECOVERY FACILITY

JEAN ROBERT MAZAUD AND S'PACE ARCHITECTURE
Leeds, England, 2014

Jean Robert Mazaud of S'PACE architecture designed this new Veolia Recycling and Energy Recovery Facility in Leeds, England. The facility is able to process approximately 214,000 tonnes of recyclable household waste annually, and will generate around 11 MW of electricity for the national grid, enough to power 20,000 homes. The plant has a unique construction of glass and timber framing, creating a living wall, or "vertical woodland," to promote biodiversity. This wall is one of the largest of its type in the United Kingdom. The facility also boasts several energy- and water-saving features, such as the ability to harvest rainwater and other sustainable drainage techniques. The building is 42 meters high with a slim chimney design. In addition, the plant offers a visitor's center so the public can learn more about sustainable waste management and the facility's operations.

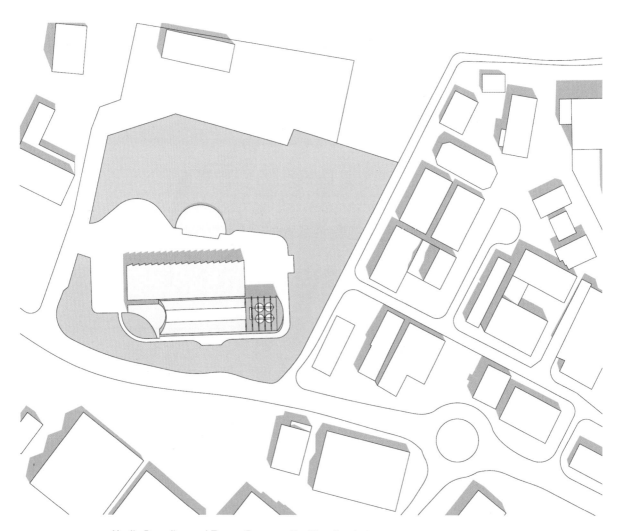

Veolia Recycling and Energy Recovery Facility, site plan

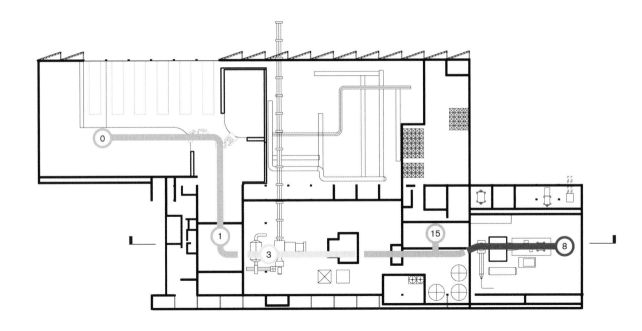

Plan

Section

Veoila Recycling and Energy
Recovery Facility, construction views

Herzog & de Meuron, Tate Modern
(turbine hall), London, 2000

For a city, having factories is not a defect. Such a statement requires some explanation.

Industrial activity, often symbolized by chimney stacks and their smoke, peaked in many developed countries and then declined before being considered hazardous and therefore undesirable, at first near human settlements and then everywhere else. From the 19th to the mid-20th century the stacks had been synonymous with progress. They then came to represent the ecological negligence of the latter half of the 20th century before finally emerging as treasures of our heritage, of work and production, when they had ceased all activity and utility.

Suffice it to say that designing a factory is a particularly ambitious challenge if the buildings continue to express vertical ducts or other visible devices that may discharge steam, heat, cooled or warmed water, or other pulverulent material (slag, dust, and various residues). Nevertheless, we find numerous activities connected with our cities and their health (diet, digestion, treatment, disposal, transpiration) requiring local infrastructures, which become an integral part of the cities' landscapes. If numerous installations, such as incinerators, are properly positioned to access energy, water, transportation (ports, highways, railways), and many others aspects related to our daily needs (wastewater treatment; waste, thermal, or power plants; data centers; transport service centers), such

Having Factories Is Not a Defect

JEAN ROBERT MAZAUD

French architect Jean Robert Mazaud started S'PACE architecture, centered around the idea of sustainable development, in 1980. The firm specializes in large-scale industrial projects, most recently the Veolia Recycling and Energy Recovery Center in Leeds, England, completed in 2015. Mazaud wrote this essay for the WtE Design Lab in 2015 to discuss the necessity and opportunity that industrial buildings offer cities.

facilities have no other choice than to move closer to urban centers, to integrate with them and reduce operating costs.

Making a factory virtuous in order for it to become acceptable, even desirable, is a challenging and rewarding task for teams composed of urban planners, architects, landscape architects, and engineers. The teams face three major obligations: to ensure that their project is contextual, conceptual, and consensual. Each of these dimensions merit explanation and development. Indeed, the designers must constantly oscillate between the search for a forward-looking vision to improve what exists and a pragmatic approach to real facts. Thus such projects provide a possibility of exploring the dialectic between the openness of creativity and the closed boundaries of reality.

If, after having violently rejected it, Rem Koolhaas has returned to context in his commission of the 2014 Venice Biennale of Architecture, it is because in a systemic and progressive approach, the context represents the most powerful part of inspiration. It creates a sociological and political anchor—the identity of place but also of situation. It explores the limits of public expectations that are sometimes buried under layers of irrelevance.

The context has so many different forms: economic, social, technical, societal, environmental, topographic, climatic, cultural . . . and it continues to impose its law even if one tries to ignore it. So many factories fight with the terrain before eventually succeeding by destroying a landscape! So many buildings opt for a uniform treatment that causes an aesthetic shock expressed by disproportion, unnecessary massification, or absentminded banality.

The concept cannot be addressed without being first persuaded that modernity (in the words of Arthur Rimbaud) is an absolute necessity. It must be modern, it must be new, or

the designer will not be considered an architect. Once one is able to consider complexity as a solution and not as a problem, vast possibilities open in the industrial field. Architecture would become a simple idea of form were it devoid of mechanical truth. Designing a factory becomes, then, an exercise in the fabrication of meaning and not just one of style. Finding the links between people, their machines, their production, and their territories then becomes a study of culture, science, and humanism.

The consensual is not a result. It is just as inspiring as the context or concept. Not trying to understand what causes adhesion in others is as great a mistake as not taking into account a functional or dimensional program. The popular posture can have very different causes: ignorance, manipulation, imagination. It may communicate itself through a lack of interest or through aggressiveness, and it requires exploring the tensions and their causes, which are sometimes far removed from initial preconceived ideas. Introducing responsiveness or flexibility often allows for the use of exchange and dialogue as a source of enrichment for a project, but also as a means of consolidating positions when faced with uncertain programmatic requirements that are dictated by machines with little or no concern for architectural requirements.

The immense catalog of a factory's detached parts, especially the incredible diversity of spatial equations that components entail and their connected juxtaposition, open up endless perspectives regarding their harmonious organization and formal translation. The arrangement of components is a process that enables designers to, in a certain way, exercise power. The load transfers in height and surface, short- and long-term storage needs, material flows of people and of vehicles all require a rational yet evolutionary response by the architect, and therefore are the carriers of invention. Although the term "innovation" often

does not have a place in an industrial program dictated by control, experience, and necessary repetitiveness, it never excludes introducing, for example, new mobile equipment such as overhead cranes, conveyor belts, or tires, which may upset conventional wisdom and established patterns.

The risk culture increasingly present in industrial activities brings new challenges to the procedures. Personal safety, fire prevention, anti-pollution treatment of air and water, and the eradication of noise, odors, sensory, and even mental factors are steps forward that require representations that valorize and consolidate them. The architect can only welcome this development and engage as an actor, thus becoming a benefactor and using these considerations to create new emblematic structures, symbolic structures accompanied by such mottos as "working for the welfare of man and the beauty of its environment."

There is not a fundamental difference between the architect of Henry Ford, Albert Kahn, who in his great works in the former Soviet Union or in the United States (like Willow Run manufacturing complex, outside Ypsilanti, Michigan), was able to bring the added value of creativity associated with the rigorous work of the designer, and Mario Botta, who on the Lake Maggiore in Switzerland, about twenty years ago, was able to reinterpret all the codes for the waste treatment center and make a black jewelry box next to a work of art. If in London the Battersea Power Station became an icon of pop culture in the 1960s, or if with the Tate Gallery Herzog & de Meuron were able to give a former electrical plant the same standing as a contemporary art museum, it is because what has remained engraved in the mind of every inhabitant are the values of work and technical progress. Lastly, the Amager Bakke project of the Bjarke Ingels Group in Copenhagen brilliantly shows that, for a city, having factories is not a defect.

B-24 bombers under construction at
Willow Run, circa 1942

Mario Botta, Church of San Giovanni
Battista, Mogno, Switzerland, 1996

Battersea Power Station, England,
1930-1950
The decommissioned power plant is
now under redevelopment.

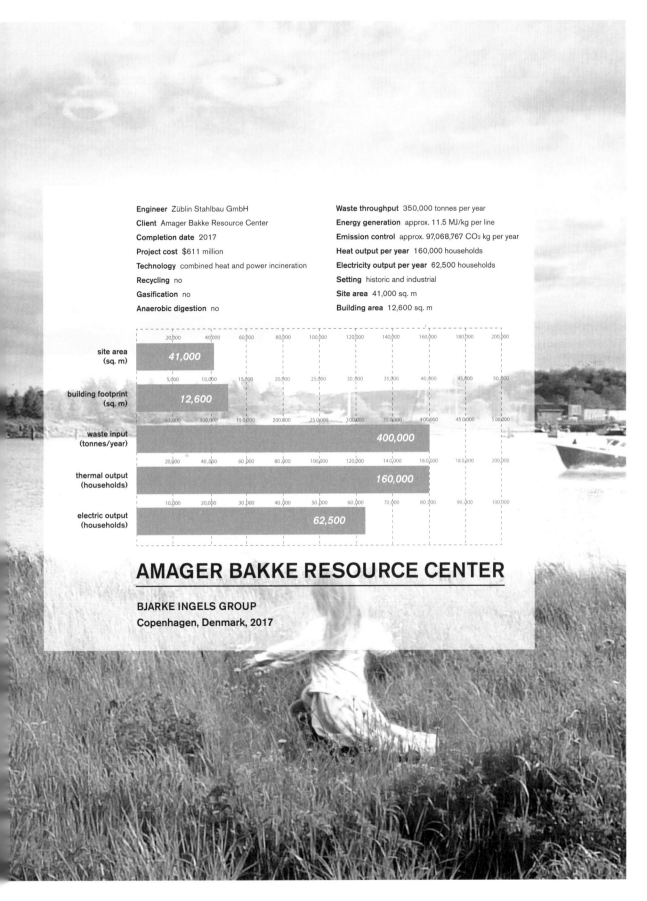

Engineer Züblin Stahlbau GmbH

Client Amager Bakke Resource Center

Completion date 2017

Project cost $611 million

Technology combined heat and power incineration

Recycling no

Gasification no

Anaerobic digestion no

Waste throughput 350,000 tonnes per year

Energy generation approx. 11.5 MJ/kg per line

Emission control approx. 97,068,767 CO_2 kg per year

Heat output per year 160,000 households

Electricity output per year 62,500 households

Setting historic and industrial

Site area 41,000 sq. m

Building area 12,600 sq. m

site area
(sq. m) — **41,000**

building footprint
(sq. m) — **12,600**

waste input
(tonnes/year) — **400,000**

thermal output
(households) — **160,000**

electric output
(households) — **62,500**

AMAGER BAKKE RESOURCE CENTER

BJARKE INGELS GROUP
Copenhagen, Denmark, 2017

Located in an industrial area near the city center, the new Amager Bakke WtE plant will be an exemplary model in the field of waste management and energy production, as well as an architectural landmark in the cityscape of Copenhagen. The project is the single largest environmental initiative in Denmark with a budget of 3.5 billion DKK, and replaces the adjacent 40-year-old Amager district incinerator plant, integrating the latest technologies in waste treatment and environmental performance. The huge facility covers an area of 41,000 square meters (around seven football fields) and rises to a height of 80 meters. Construction began in March 2014 and should be completed in 2017.

Instead of considering the new Amager facility as an isolated architectural object, the building is conceived as an opportunity to create a destination in itself, thereby reflecting the progressive vision to create a new type of waste treatment facility—an outdoor recreational park. The roof of the new plant is comprised by a 31,000-square-meter ski slope of varying skill levels and a climbing wall, all for the use of city residents and visitors. This design of this facility uses architecture to redefine the relationship between the waste plant and the city by expanding the area's existing recreational activities through a new breed of WtE plant.

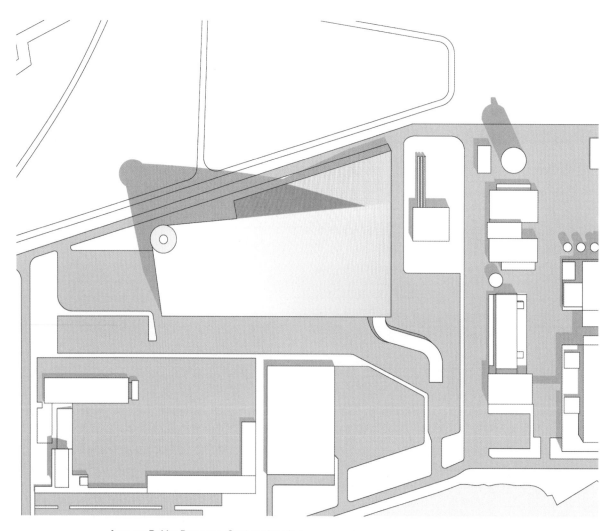

Amager Bakke Resource Center, site plan

BIG has often incorporated the roof as a dynamic, usable place in their buildings, and the Amager Bakke WtE plant is one of their most ambitious projects. The idea of incorporating the 100-meter-high smoke stack into the building form led to the design for the ski slope. According to David Zahle, a partner at BIG, the design team studied alpine slopes and designed the entire roof around criteria for what makes a good ski slope. It features different runs for skiers of different abilities, and its artificial surface allows for year-round use.

Sustainability is a major theme in the design for the Amager Bakke WtE facility. BIG describes their philosophy as "hedonistic sustainability," because they believe that living sustainably should be both positive and pleasurable. They criticize sustainability rhetoric that is penal or guilt producing. To draw awareness to the issues surrounding carbon dioxide and allow bystanders to visualize its creation, BIG has proposed a smoke-ring generator atop the facility that will release a smoke ring every time the building's internal processes produces one ton of carbon dioxide.

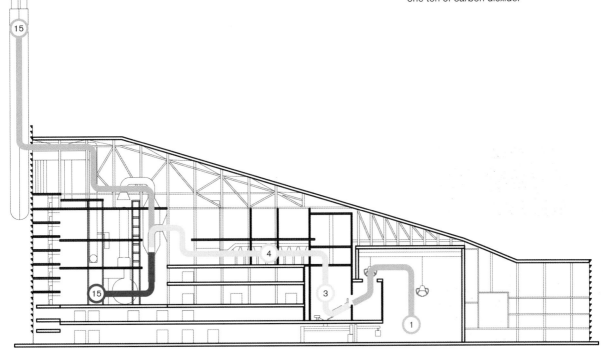

Section

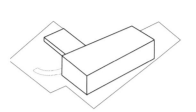
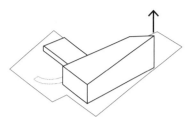
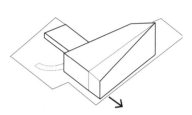
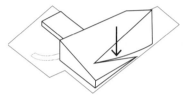
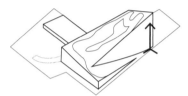

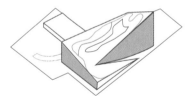
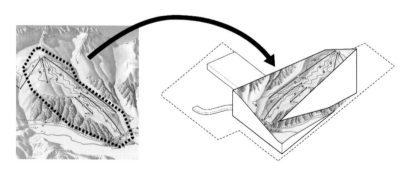

Amager Bakke Resource Center, ski slope diagrams

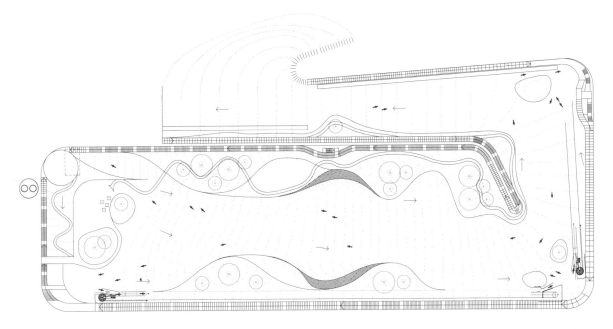

Roof plan

Ski slope rendering

Interview with Bjarke Ingels

Bjarke Ingels started Bjarke Ingels Group
(BIG) in 2005 after cofounding PLOT
Architects in 2001 and working at OMA
in Rotterdam. Through a series of award-
winning projects, Ingels has developed
a reputation for designing buildings that
are as programmatically and technically
innovative as they are cost and resource
conscious. Ingels joined Leire Asensio
Villoria in August 2015 to discuss topics
ranging from the history of industrial
architecture to his role as the architect
of Amager Bakke Resource Center
in Copenhill, Copenhagen, due for
completion in 2017.

Leire Asensio Villoria (LAV): I would like to discuss your design for Amager Bakke Resource Center, and then move on to the differences between American and European practices, and the differences in these facilities.

But first, I would like to ask: what can architects contribute to the design of large industrial projects? What specifically do architects bring to the table that adds value to these kinds of projects?

Bjarke Ingels (BI): Large infrastructural projects are often designed by engineers, who tend to break things into the different disciplines. And each discipline has experts that know about energy, or fumes, or other elements. For each issue they design machines so that, often, these things end up being an accumulation many different nonintegrated, nonholistic elements, like a machine with many components. In the end the components become quite good at what they are doing, since each is quite well designed, but they haven't been put together with a holistic point of view, and they haven't been assembled with the idea that this is a building that is going to be a part of a city.

Traditionally, these power or production plants have been placed far away in sort of an industrial park with no concern or consideration for the surroundings as being urban. They are more utilitarian. They typically appear as gray areas on city maps. If you look on Google Maps or a street map, the city will be yellow, monuments will be red, parks will be green, and all the other space where industry, warehouses, logistic centers, and power plants are located is gray. So what architects can really contribute is the fact that we think in terms of urbanism, in terms of public life. We think in terms of

the flow of people, of human enjoyment. We think in terms of adjacencies between different neighborhoods and different parts. We think about continuity of public space, urban flow, in addition to all the necessary things that our plant must address concerning logic, waste management, and power production. By adding that architectural urban approach, you end up not only designing buildings that are efficient at their core function, but also buildings that become good citizens of the cities that they are a part of, rather than big boxes that cast shadows on their neighbors and cause discontinuity. They actually can become well-integrated parts of the city that belong to their surroundings.

BI: We had already been given a layout of the rough machinery that would go into the building, so we had some insight into what different components would be combined, and in what sequence they would be combined. We understood more or less the outline of what the plant needed to contain. And in that sense our job was pretty much to design a container for it. And then it was quite clear when we went through the specs that this was going to be the cleanest WtE plant in the world. It would hardly have any toxic emissions, it would have lower CO_2 emissions, it made a little bit of steam, but it would essentially be clean and very, very safe for the surroundings.

We wanted to show this cleanliness, somehow. And in the brief there was the idea of having a visitors' center, where school classes could come and learn about WtE. We wanted to find a way

to enjoy and explore the potential of what happens when a power plant is no longer a fuming, toxic, hostile element that needs to be as far away as possible, but is actually so clean that it can be in the middle of the city where people live. We tried to imagine apart from just trying to make it look pretty, could we make it perform differently? Essentially the site occupies the waterfront in an industrial neighborhood of Copenhagen. It is very close to Amager Beach, which is the biggest beach park in the city, so the area doesn't need much more park space. But one thing Copenhagen does not have is topography. And it's right next to the Copenhagen Cable Park, where the local kids go waterskiing, so we thought that maybe this idea of extreme sports made sense. Since Copenhagen does not have hills but it has snow, we thought about snow skiing; that's one thing we could offer here because we have 100 meters of vertical drop. We could offer an actual alpine ski slope in the middle of a capital city that lacks mountains. It then became clear that downhill skiing made a lot of sense. It would create a destination. It would make people love the fact that the power plant was in their neighborhood. It would attract people to go there in order to ski or hike or climb, and then once they were there it would tempt them to learn about WtE, so it would become a perfect ambassador for the place. It could be operated autonomously with its own budget, and by renting skis or selling lift cards it could be somewhat sustainable financially. It would still remain open as a park for people who just wanted to take a hike up the hill and look out. Also, and this is why we were able to win the competition, it would be the perfect way to make blatantly visible something that was otherwise invisible. It would be instantly recognized that this is a different kind of power plant. Because if people were skiing on it, it couldn't be a toxic environment. The CEO of the company really liked the idea that this power plant made visible something that would otherwise be invisible.

LAV: Could you describe the political situation that surrounds WtE projects, and your Copenhagen project in particular? Was there public resistance to the project? Was there resistance to bundling such explicitly public programs?

BI: The project has been incredibly well received by the public. There was a significant political equation that needed to happen. Some parties believe that Denmark should be even more progressive and not have any waste at all, even though that's not going to be a reality within the next half century, and statistics show that the waste quantities are slightly growing, although they're not growing as much as they did 20 or 30 years ago. Denmark is around 40 to 42 percent recycling. According to some experts in resource recycling, this is above full exploitation. This is the point you actually start spending more resources recycling than you extract from the recycled material. So certain factions thought that it would be stupid to make any kind of WtE power plant, no matter how progressive, because they thought we shouldn't have any waste at all. Eventually they found a compromise so that the plant could be built but there's an artificial cap on how much waste it's allowed to convert to energy. So for now it will be run under capacity.

LAV: How did you leverage the public component against local resistance to the private program?

BI: Honestly, there was no resistance against the ski slope. Everybody loved it, and we actually got emails from people asking when it was going to be done. I'd taken taxis in Copenhagen, and the taxi drivers recognized me and asked when the ski slope would be operational. It was fully embraced by the public.

LAV: That's great. So how did you convince the public in Copenhagen to back this plant?

BI: We just simply presented the idea and everybody wanted it.

LAV: Even the plant operator was on board from the beginning?

BI: One lucky thing is that the woman who is the CEO of the power plant is very progressive. She was very much the person from day one who totally understood our thinking.

LAV: As an architect with offices in Copenhagen and New York, you are in a unique position to experience these practices in both regions first hand. What differences do you see in the waste management policies and the public perception of WtE facilities in general?

BI: It is quite clear that the United States has very sophisticated structural engineers. They've been building huge highway bridges and skyscrapers and all kinds of complex structures. In comparison, Denmark is a country built out of prefabricated concrete elements, so everything is very simple. So American engineering definitely has an edge. But when it comes to environmental performance—energy efficiency, noise

reduction, resource extraction, and here I mean like extracting waste products and turning them into resources—the United States is very, very inefficient. Perhaps this stems from an abundance of relatively inexpensive energy. And then there's been very little state regulation of the area, so that means that the skills are simply not there. Also, the WtE incineration plants that have existed in America have been very, very crude, basically burning trash. Therefore WtE has been deemed as polluting and very inefficient. There has not been enough focus, because oil and gas have been so cheap, on the energy value that WtE actually offers. In that sense, it is seen in the United States as a sort of third-world activity. And there's so much land in the US that landfilling has never been seen as an issue. In Denmark, people abandoned landfilling a long time ago because we don't have much available space.

LAV: Do you see a difference in the American and European contexts in the architect's role with regard to designing WtE facilities?

BI: Presently, the United States doesn't really see this as an architectural service but rather as something engineering driven. But actually, the building we're building here in New York, West 57th, is right next to a steam plant by Con Edison, which was designed by Stanford White, the architect of the Flatiron. So at some point, it was more seen as something associated with civic pride and civic significance that deserved architecture. Eventually it became a strictly utilitarian accumulation of machinery, with no holistic thought for integrating it successfully into its environment.

Construction view at night

LAV: How might architects be able to regain that position in infrastructural and industrial projects in the United States? Is it going to require a top-down policy change? Or a bottom-up architectural movement with a highly visible project, perhaps similar to Amager Bakke? How do we begin to change public perception?

BI: Built examples are almost always the best at facilitating change. I've presented Amager Bakke at a few American conferences, and it always triggers a very exciting response, so there's some openness or interest in the possibilities.

But, I don't know . . . I think about what we've experienced with our work with the Dry Line, which we actually call "social infrastructure." It's the idea of creating infrastructural projects—in this case for resilience—that have a positive social side effect in the form of park space or public space or amenities. We did the project as part of the US Department of Housing and Urban Development's (HUD's) Rebuild By Design, with the Hurricane Sandy money. But we've seen how difficult it is to enact it because,

basically, the project was tendered as an engineering project, and to make sure that we would stay involved, even though we won the competition with HUD, required a lot of active lobbying on our side to make it really clear that this was not business as usual, that in order to be successful this project really needed a different and more holistic approach. So there are possibilities, but we definitely need some successful American examples to which the public entities that organize the tendering could actually look and use as a point of reference to justify a different sort of tendering project than what they're used to.

LAV: The Dry Line and Amager Bakke are distinct for that kind of social ambition, or side effect, as you call it. Amager Bakke is distinct for reframing the relationship between the public and their waste. A next question would be, how can social ambition be implemented in projects that are smaller in scope than Amager Bakke?

BI: Actually, in Copenhagen, we're doing a project—have you seen our book *Hot to Cold*? It contains a project we

are doing in Copenhagen for a recycling facility. It looks like a peanut, or a peanut-shaped volcano. It's a classic Danish thing to have recycling stations in all cities. People drive there with their trash, not household trash, more like if they broke down a wall or they're chucking out a sofa or something else they need to get rid of. They go there, place their trash in different containers, and they are allowed to grab all the stuff they want. So it's a bit like resource pooling—like if you walk the streets of New York and see a couch someone put out, and you take it back to your place— but facilitated as a kind of marketplace for exchangeable, recyclable elements. And we designed it as efficiently as possible so people can drive in, dump their stuff, and access it from the higher levels. But we also integrated it nicely into the landscape by tucking it into a hill, to help with the noise—it can make a lot of noise when people dump stuff from their truck into a container full of steel— and incorporating other elements so it becomes a charming neighbor at a small scale, rather than a messy eyesore of a neighbor. Essentially it's Amager Bakke at the molecular level.

LAV: When adding new programs to these sorts of facilities, or when developing a unique design, inevitably this will to have a higher cost compared to ordinary facilities. How do you communicate the value of these elements to clients and the public when it may not be as evident as in the Copenhagen project?

BI: First, the projects actually have rather large costs. Often we are talking billions. So there's the facade of the WtE power plant as a facility, but the entire envelope is a 30 million dollar project, it's 3 percent of the total cost. To do it nicely doesn't cost very much. Second, I would say that if you think good architecture is expensive, try bad architecture. If you think holistic thinking costs more, it just takes more. But in the end, you use less material and therefore have lower costs by being a bit more careful. Third, with Amager Bakke, the operation of the ski slope represents a revenue model that makes it possible to maintain the public park for free. If you want to you can go there with your own skis and drag them up the hill and ski down, so you only pay for the lift card as you do on a mountain. In that sense, this has been thought out as a self-sustaining financial model. And finally, once we put the project out there, we were able to successfully secure funds from various foundations that have been excited by the project, and have resources to help make it happen.

LAV: What other design strategies did you explore in the early phases of Amager Bakke?

BI: To begin, we insisted on not just making cosmetic decisions to try and disguise an old-fashioned power plant,

but actually trying to make it look different purely because it performs differently. In addition, we wanted to try to uncover what's invisible. That's often what's interesting in architecture. Architecture has the capacity to make visible something that would otherwise remain unseen. In this case the fact that the power plant is so clean is invisible to the public, but by putting a public park on the roof it actually becomes blatantly clear to anyone passing by. And finally, we focused on the idea when designing something in a city, you can't just solve the requirements of the client. You have to resolve the concerns of the city around it. You can't make a hermetic entity that is disinterested in anything but itself. You have to make it contribute to its surroundings.

LAV: Last question. How is the day-to-day practice of an architect different when engaged in infrastructural projects as compared to other types such as museums or housing? We are very interested in the role of the architect in this sort of capacity.

BI: In my experience, it's easier to design cultural buildings because there is a genuine interest in making something exciting. There's a general understanding that the architecture is part of the public attraction of a cultural facility, and therefore it is valued as something necessary. Also the budgets per square meter are much better, and in general it's a much easier job. When working on these kind of utilitarian facilities, you need to be adamant about demonstrating the verifiable, quantifiable added value that any deviation from the norm represents. You have to be very good at explaining

that it's not more expensive, and even though it hasn't been done before it's technically fully feasible, and you have to find all of the precedents and examples that might be similar by comparison, even though they might be from different fields. Then you have to show how it will enhance the value of the core service either in terms of the public perception, in terms of making the public decision-making process more smooth, or by driving the traffic that increases public awareness. You must link the proposed extracurricular activities to something that will benefit the facility's core operation.

Amager Bakke Resource Center,
construction view

Mälarenergi AB WtE Plant, Västerås, Sweden, 2014

Design

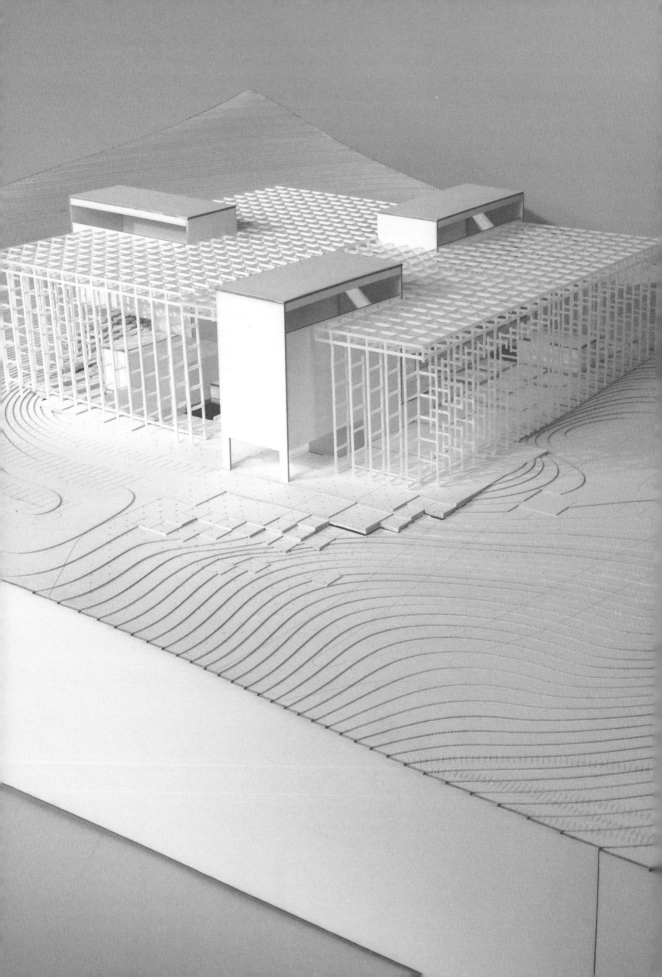

This chapter presents novel and effective strategies to rethink the relationship of architecture, waste, and energy production as they operate over different scales of space and time. The proposed design strategies focus on a range of issues associated with these infrastructures: integrating the plant with the surrounding context, improving public perception of the plants, planning for obsolescence, optimizing plant outputs, and improving the plant's internal organization. The strategies arose from the lab's study of industrial buildings' history, Waste-to-Energy (WtE) technology, architectural precedents, and interviews with designers, engineers, operators, and industry representatives. This material provided a foundation on which the lab and its associated courses developed new strategies and schemes for how these structures may be sensitively integrated within dense urban fabrics, leveraging the spatial qualities of the infrastructure, or optimizing by-products of the energy production process.

The strategies, techniques, and operations are illustrated together with design speculations produced by the WtE Design Lab's design studio, seminar, and design thesis explorations at Harvard University's Graduate School of Design. New typologies and design concepts developed by the WtE Design Lab and associated courses offer a series of solutions for WtE plants that generate clean energy, contribute to the city's social and cultural activities, and integrate proven technology with novel approaches toward the organization and design at the building, landscape, neighborhood, and/or material scales.

This chapter is organized by the three scales most highly impacted by WtE plants. Large-scale design strategies aim to sensitively integrate WtE facilities into more urban contexts. Medium-scale design strategies seek to better assimilate a plant in the context of the parcel and immediate adjacent parcels. Small-scale design strategies address individual components of a plant, attempting to add value to them or, in some cases, optimize them. Each strategy is further developed through a series of techniques and operations that address the specific strategy in different ways.

Design Opportunities

HANIF KARA, LEIRE ASENSIO VILLORIA, AND LAURA SMEAD

(Re)Planned Obsolescence studio,
site model

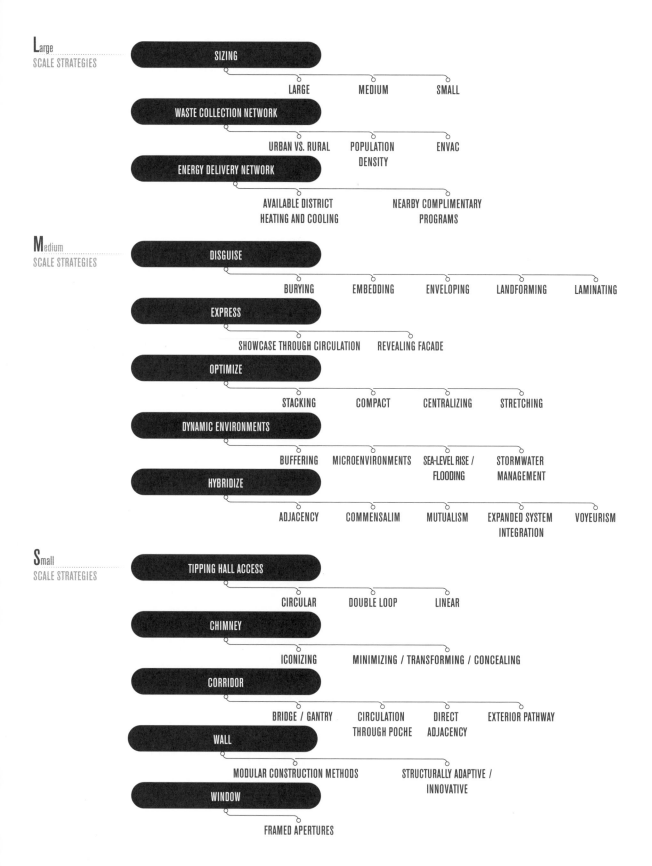

Large
SCALE STRATEGIES

SIZING
- LARGE
- MEDIUM
- SMALL

WASTE COLLECTION NETWORK
- URBAN VS. RURAL
- POPULATION DENSITY
- ENVAC

ENERGY DELIVERY NETWORK
- AVAILABLE DISTRICT HEATING AND COOLING
- NEARBY COMPLIMENTARY PROGRAMS

Medium
SCALE STRATEGIES

DISGUISE
- BURYING
- EMBEDDING
- ENVELOPING
- LANDFORMING
- LAMINATING

EXPRESS
- SHOWCASE THROUGH CIRCULATION
- REVEALING FACADE

OPTIMIZE
- STACKING
- COMPACT
- CENTRALIZING
- STRETCHING

DYNAMIC ENVIRONMENTS
- BUFFERING
- MICROENVIRONMENTS
- SEA-LEVEL RISE / FLOODING
- STORMWATER MANAGEMENT

HYBRIDIZE
- ADJACENCY
- COMMENSALIM
- MUTUALISM
- EXPANDED SYSTEM INTEGRATION
- VOYEURISM

Small
SCALE STRATEGIES

TIPPING HALL ACCESS
- CIRCULAR
- DOUBLE LOOP
- LINEAR

CHIMNEY
- ICONIZING
- MINIMIZING / TRANSFORMING / CONCEALING

CORRIDOR
- BRIDGE / GANTRY
- CIRCULATION THROUGH POCHE
- DIRECT ADJACENCY
- EXTERIOR PATHWAY

WALL
- MODULAR CONSTRUCTION METHODS
- STRUCTURALLY ADAPTIVE / INNOVATIVE

WINDOW
- FRAMED APERTURES

198

Specifically, we aim to:

Improve public perception through improving design, reducing noise and odor, increasing comfort for plant workers and neighbors by considering wind and sun exposure at the site, and providing other public uses for the site.

Plan for obsolescence by creating flexible spaces with complementary programs that have alternate uses once the plant's lifespan has finished, and planning for climate change by considering resilience of the building and surrounding landscape.

Better optimize plants by taking advantage of process outputs (such as ash, heat, electricity, water) through symbiotic hybrids, or increasing efficiencies in other ways (such as circulation of waste trucks or people).

At a large scale, these strategies involve appropriate plant sizing, siting, and programs for the surrounding waste-collection and energy-delivery networks. At a medium scale we may increase thermal comfort, reduce nuisances, and either disguise the plant or express certain features that will help improve public perception. Changing the plant's physical footprint, increasing its resilience to storms and sea-level rise, and hybridizing with complimentary programs can increase opportunities for site reuse once the power plant is no longer functional. At a small scale we can improve tipping hall circulation, public and employee circulation, and create modular or structurally adaptive walls and framed aperture windows. Finally, reimagining the appearance of the chimney may improve public perception, as this is often seen as an icon of pollution.

Following the focus of the book, all design strategies were tested in a series of sites in Sweden and the northeastern United States.

Small-, medium-, and large-scale
opportunities

199

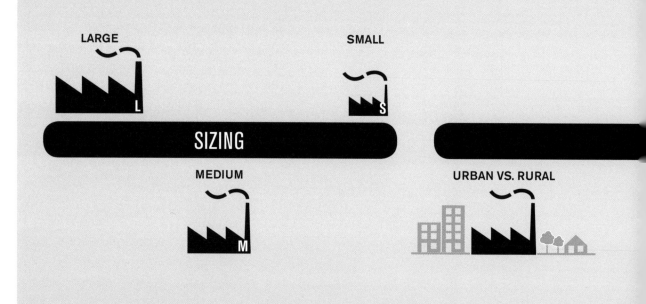

LARGE

SMALL

L

S

SIZING

MEDIUM

URBAN VS. RURAL

M

Large-Scale Strategies

ENVAC

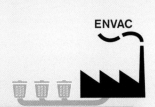

NEARBY COMPLIMENTARY
PROGRAMS

WASTE COLLECTION NETWORK

ENERGY DELIVERY NETWORK

POPULATION DENSITY

AVAILABLE DISTRICT HEATING
AND COOLING

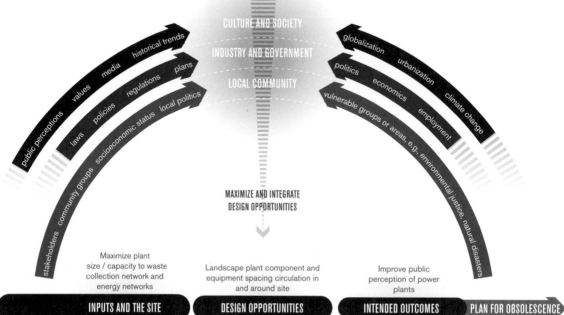

DESIGN WITH LARGER CONTEXT

CULTURE AND SOCIETY

INDUSTRY AND GOVERNMENT

LOCAL COMMUNITY

public perceptions
values
media
historical trends
plans
laws
policies
regulations
local politics
socioeconomic status
community groups
stakeholders

globalization
urbanization
politics
economics
climate change
employment
vulnerable groups or areas, e.g. environmental justice, natural disasters

MAXIMIZE AND INTEGRATE
DESIGN OPPORTUNITIES

Maximize plant
size / capacity to waste
collection network and
energy networks

Landscape plant component and
equipment spacing circulation in
and around site

Improve public
perception of power
plants

INPUTS AND THE SITE

DESIGN OPPORTUNITIES

INTENDED OUTCOMES

PLAN FOR OBSOLESCENCE

Existing topography and landscape
Existing infrastructure (WtE plant,
etc.)

Take advantage of outputs/inputs,
aesthetic expression, and visibile
hybrids

Increase efficiencies of
WtE plant space and
systems

FEEDBACK AND TRADEOFFS

Weigh risks, public perception,
time, budget, profits, feasibilty

Large-scale integration strategy

202

The relationship between WtE plants and their larger context is complex. Influencing issues often change over time and vary based on numerous factors related to a particular culture, government, and local community. Generally design opportunities at a WtE facility relate to its waste and energy networks, existing site topography and infrastructure, and larger context over time. First, the larger context of culture, industry, government, and local community affects what infrastructure, waste, and energy networks are likely available, how close the plant can be placed to denser areas, and how innovative architects can be in their plant designs. A good plant design may improve public perception of WtE plants through its visual appearance, public programming, and more efficient plant space and systems. Through careful plant siting, landscaping, technology, and design, architects can reduce noise and odor nuisances, increase resilience to industrial and natural disasters, and plan for the plant facility reuse after the WtE components become obsolete.

INTEGRATION STRATEGIES

Large-scale design opportunities seek to bring the facility closer to urban areas, which are its fuel source. WtE plants typically make more economic sense when they are located nearer to urban centers, keeping waste transportation costs down and allowing plants to charge higher tipping fees. This may also reduce traffic and pollution. The size and density of the surrounding communities impact the waste collection catchment area, the strength of the energy network, and the diversity of waste delivery transportation (such as road, train, boat, or ENVAC systems). It also impacts which plant size (physical footprint) and capacity will work best for that community. Generally speaking, plants with a smaller footprint are easier to integrate into urban areas; yet, based on our research, large-scale plants currently offer a stronger business case. This chapter, however, proposes strategies for alternative plant configurations that may allow for a variety of plant sizes to coexist with residential or other programs in an urban context, thus potentially strengthening the case for smaller WtE plants in denser areas.

MIXED-USE ORGANIZATION: DISTRICT HEATING AND COOLING VS. NEARBY COMPLIMENTARY PROGRAMS

WtE facilities are far more efficient at producing heat than electricity. Combined heat and power (CHP) plants are able to achieve much higher efficiencies and often better pollution control than only electricity-producing boilers. Therefore, where district-heating networks exist, WtE facilities offer more efficient and cost-effective sources of energy.

In a district-heating system, thermal energy is distributed to individual buildings or houses from a central plant by means of steam or hot water lines. The thermal energy is typically produced from either a boiler or a combined heat and power plant (CHP)—a plant that incinerates fuel to produce electricity and transfers excess heat through a heat exchanger to supply hot water or steam to the district-heating network. When using municipal solid waste for electricity generation alone, it can only achieve efficiencies of 20 to 30 percent. However, when used for CHP applications, WtE plants can achieve efficiencies of 85 to 90 percent. At Swedish WtE plants with cogeneration, the sale of heat for district heating can be the largest and most dependable revenue stream and provide 40 to 50 percent of total annual revenues. Gate fees and sale of electricity to the grid both typically provide the rest of the revenue stream, each representing approximately 25 percent of revenues. Sweden has a long tradition of using district heating for urban areas. The first district-heating network was introduced in 1948. The district-heating network in Sweden was expanded considerably during the late 1940s after World War II, creating an outlet for energy from waste incineration. Now, district heating can be found in every Swedish city. Currently 15 percent of the district heating production in Sweden originates from WtE production, and 90 percent is produced from renewable sources. In the United States, natural gas is the primary heating fuel (52 percent) and district heating is much less common. Furthermore, the relatively warmer climate means that most regions of the United States have lower potential revenue from district heating sales, thus making it unlikely that district heating will be a viable option in warmer parts of the United States. As a result, WtE plants in the United States are not typically used for district heating purposes. They therefore have fewer revenue streams and cannot achieve the same efficiencies that CHP plants do. As of 2008, there were 5,800 district heating/cooling systems in the United States, which provide 320,000 GWh or roughly 5 percent of US heating/cooling. Of this, approximately 14,000 GWh came from WtE energy. Of the 87 WtE plants in the United States, only 28 sell steam for district heating (21 of these cogenerate electricity and steam, while the other 7 produce steam only).[1]

District-heating networks are not nearly as common in the United States as in Sweden. However, they do exist in some areas such as Minneapolis and New York City. In order to compensate for the lack of district-heating networks, nearby complementary programs may be a solution for the US context. For example, a large energy-intensive program like a stadium, hospital, or university could create a more localized heating network and improve the plant's efficiency. In fact, many central business districts, universities, and medical centers in the United States already have some form of district-energy system (usually run on natural gas), but many take advantage of locally produced renewable fuels.[2]

SWEDEN
physical information

Area
450,295 sq. km

Population
9,747,355

WtE facilities
32

Total amount of waste
4,400,000 tonnes

Waste per capita
461.2 kg/year

RELATION OF PLANT SIZE AND ENERGY NETWORK PER A VARIETY OF URBAN DENSITIES

By categorizing the existing facilities as small, medium, or large, more productive comparisons between plants are possible. The WtE Design Lab compared the size of all existing plants in the northeastern United States and Sweden in relation to the total amount of waste (tonnes) that they process as well as the electricity and heat (both MWh) that they produce. This allowed for the identification of specific ranges of waste processing and energy production that seem to cluster around specific plant sizes. We categorized them as small (100,000 to 200,000 tonnes of waste), medium (300,000 to 400,000 tonnes of waste) and large (550,000 to 750,000 tonnes of waste).

Examining these categories relative to capital costs leads to more informed conclusions regarding the architect's key contributions in WtE facility design. It is important to note, however, the nature of larger plants: they almost always have multiple boiler lines that allow them to accommodate larger capacities and help facilitate economic efficiencies in their combustion.

Generally speaking, smaller plants currently require less emissions filtering equipment (only a baghouse filter) to meet the standards; however, this leads to higher pollutant emission rates than large-scale plants, which are required to follow more stringent filtering equipment regulations, usually leading to lower pollutant emissions rates than those specified by the standards. In addition, smaller facilities make less sense economically, as is clearly shown when charting capital cost against capacity.

INPUT/OUTPUT NETWORKS

The WtE Design Lab developed a series of associative models to help designers test various options to better integrate a WtE plant in a given context.

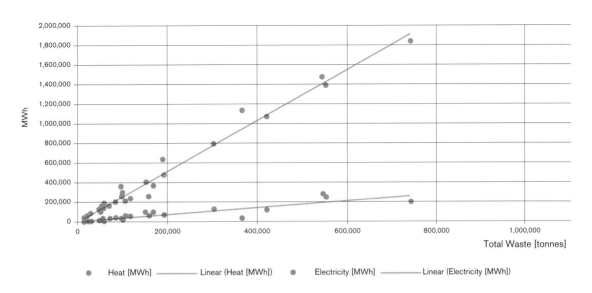

Swedish WtE facility inputs and outputs

ASSOCIATIVE MODEL I

At the scale of the city, it is possible to directly compare waste collection networks with electricity and heat distribution systems. An associative model allows designers and interested parties to estimate in real time the various scales of WtE plants' waste collection inputs and energy outputs. The platform used by the WtE Design Lab to develop this associative model is a plugin for Rhinoceros called Grasshopper.

The model accounts for a given city's population density, city fabric, urban density, parcel size, waste production, and heat and electricity consumption per capita. The model does not account for geological barriers to district heating, potential losses in electric and heat transmission, land values, transportation costs, household size, or if a vacuum system is part of the waste collection process. The model computes a series of inputs (urban density, desired WtE plant size, and programs served by the plant) inserted by the user (architect,

NORTHEASTERN US
physical information

Area
468,669 sq. km

Population
56,152,333

WtE facilities
39

Total amount of waste
53,079,297 tonnes

Waste per capita
1172 kg/year

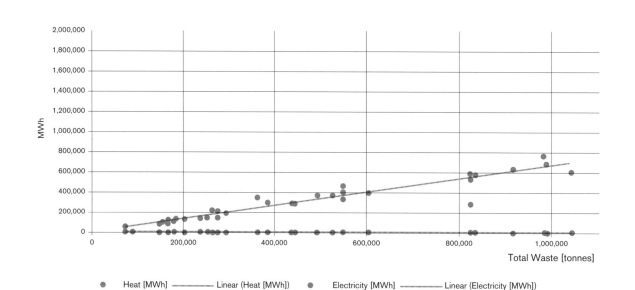

Northeast WtE facility inputs and outputs

city planner, engineer, plant operator) and returns a series of outputs such as waste collection catchment area, urban area serviced in electricity and heat by the plant, and a datum for the maximum area that could be served by a vacuum waste collection system.

There are a series of urban density input options already coded in the associative model, such as the urban densities of Barcelona's Eixample, Beijing's Chongwenmen, Boston's Back Bay, Manhattan, Phoenix's Glendale, Preston in Connecticut, and Stockholm's Södermalm, as well as three typical plant sizes—small, medium, large—and a series of programs that could be served by the plant such as residential, hospitals, swimming pools, or malls. For example, we can study how many Empire State Buildings a medium-sized plant can feed and how that affects the input and output of the urban grid. If we examine the Mall of Americas, we can see how much waste the complex is providing to the plant and how much of its energy needs are covered.

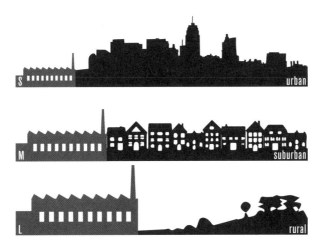

Plant size and urban fabric relationships

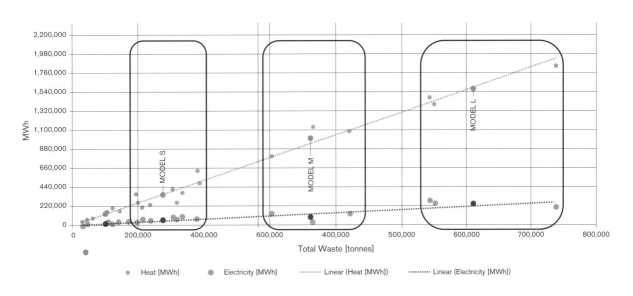

Scales of WtE Facilities

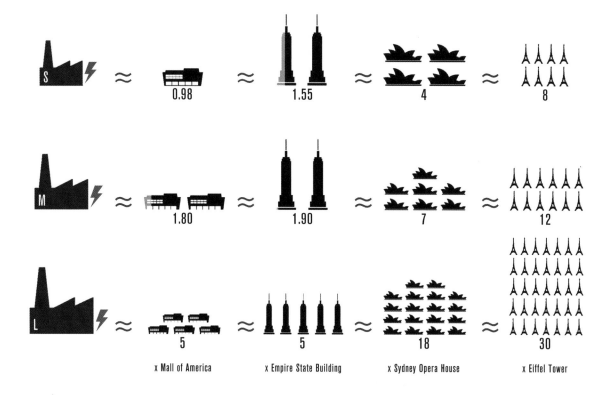

Scale comparisons

x Mall of America   x Empire State Building   x Sydney Opera House   x Eiffel Tower

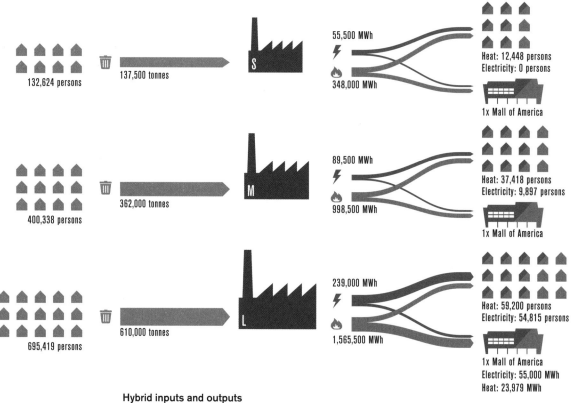

Hybrid inputs and outputs

We can also see that if we increase the number of malls to two, the energy provided by the plant is not enough, and the complex would have to seek outside sources to covers energy needs.

Furthermore, the parametric model allows us to make more complex calculations by adding two more different types of hybrid uses. With this tool, we can make realistic proposals for a complete WtE program as well as study comparatively different cases to decide the optimum size of a plant given a particular location and hybridization program.

Both the input and output information is represented using two different notation systems or diagrams. The first notation system presents the information in plan, showing the typical urban fabric, size of the WtE plant, waste collection catchment area, urban area served electricity by the plant, urban area served heat by the plant, and the potential use of vacuum waste collection system (represented by a dashed line). The second notation system presents the information in a diagram of inputs and outputs. A list showing the WtE plant size as well as the size of other programs served by the plant are linked by lines of varying thickness that represent that value of the specific input and output. The former graph translates the relationship between the city and the plant in terms of spatial ratios of inputs and outputs while the latter translates it in a quantitative way.

All the information in the associative model can be modified and updated in real time, giving the user the opportunity to efficiently test a variety of options to better integrate the plant into a given urban context. The ratios between inputs and outputs of each size are similar; however when adapting these ratios to different cities, we can see why some sizes may be more optimal than others.

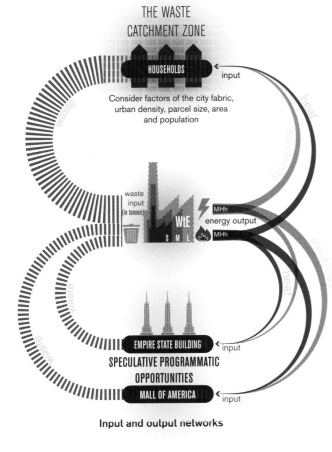

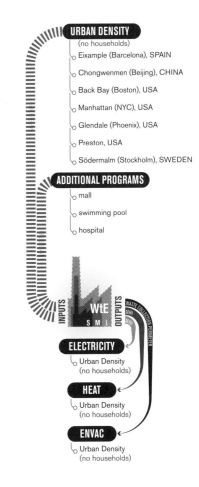

Input and output networks

WtE associative model network comparisons

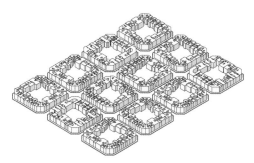

BARCELONA (EIXAMPLE)
[pop. density = 35,255/sq. km]

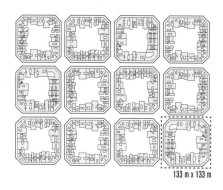

133 m x 133 m

INPUT Waste: 137,000 tonnes (176,217 persons)
OUTPUT Electricity: 55,000 MWh (16,470 persons)
Heat: 348,000 MWh (13,369 persons)

INPUT Waste: 362,000 tonnes (465,625 persons)
OUTPUT Electricity: 89,000 MWh (26,652 persons)
Heat: 998,000 MWh (38,339 persons)

INPUT Waste: 610,000 tonnes (784,616 persons)
OUTPUT Electricity: 239,000 MWh (71,570 persons)
Heat: 1,565,000 MWh (60,121 persons)

50 m

A series of urban and rural contexts such as Barcelona, Beijing, New York, Boston, Stockholm, Phoenix, and Preston, CT, each with their unique grid systems and densities, were examined and generated a number of findings.

1. In general, the input/output ratio seems to be optimal with smaller plants. On the contrary, a dense city can benefit from a larger-scale plant, since it can produce significant energy while minimizing waste transportation costs.

2. In low-density rural areas (such as Preston), the effect radius of larger plants generally surpasses the size of the city itself. Despite the fact that installing a large WtE plant in a low-density rural area is one of the most popular solutions, integration in this case is minimal. The input radius becomes significantly large while electricity and heating outputs do not correspond to an analogous ratio.

3. The impact of a WtE plant in an area with need for district heating is significantly higher than in an area that cannot support a district heating system. Heating consumption, especially in colder areas (such as Boston), surpasses the need for electricity and the area that can be covered by a WtE plant.

Note that changing the size of the plant also affects the diagram, which shows the urban grid affected by the facility, and in particular the radius of urban blocks feeding and being fed by the plant. This relationship depends not only on the size of the plant, but also on the city's density. By analyzing four different cities—Manhattan, Boston, Barcelona, and Stockholm—we see how important the urban density parameter is, which sometimes produces strikingly different results.

WtE NETWORK KEY

CATCHMENT ZONE

WASTE INPUT

ELECTRICITY OUTPUT

HEAT OUTPUT

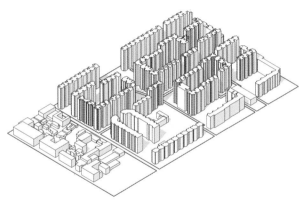

BEIJING (CHONGWENMEN)
[pop. density = 29,057/sq. km]

NEW YORK CITY (MANHATTAN)
[pop. density = 27,562/sq. km]

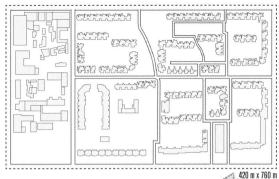

420 m x 760 m

85 m x 213 m

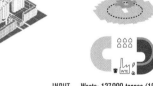

INPUT Waste: 137,000 tonnes (428,125 persons)
OUTPUT Electricity: 55,000 MWh (12,761 persons)
Heat: 348,000 MWh (53,309 persons)

INPUT Waste: 137,000 tonnes (163,008 persons)
OUTPUT Electricity: 55,000 MWh (16,470 persons)
Heat: 348,000 MWh (13,369 persons)

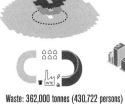

INPUT Waste: 362,000 tonnes (1,131,250 persons)
OUTPUT Electricity: 89,000 MWh (20,650 persons)
Heat: 998,000 MWh (152,880 persons)

INPUT Waste: 362,000 tonnes (430,722 persons)
OUTPUT Electricity: 89,000 MWh (26,652 persons)
Heat: 998,000 MWh (38,339 persons)

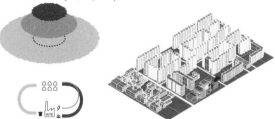

INPUT Waste: 610,000 tonnes (1,906,250 persons)
OUTPUT Electricity: 239,000 MWh (55,452 persons)
Heat: 1,565,000 MWh (239,737 persons)

INPUT Waste: 610,000 tonnes (725,803 persons)
OUTPUT Electricity: 239,000 MWh (71,570 persons)
Heat: 1,565,000 MWh (60,121 persons)

50 m

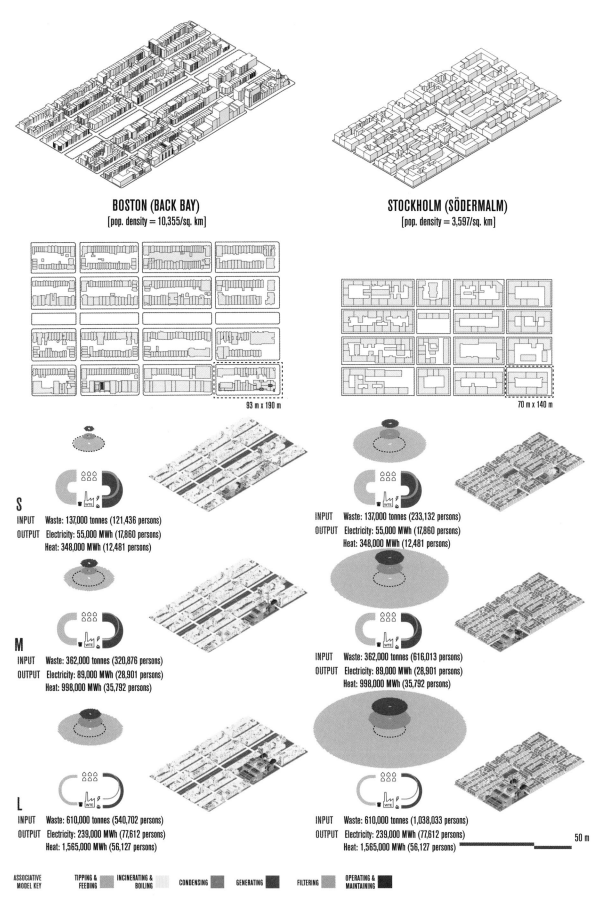

BOSTON (BACK BAY)
[pop. density = 10,355/sq. km]

STOCKHOLM (SÖDERMALM)
[pop. density = 3,597/sq. km]

93 m x 190 m

70 m x 140 m

S

INPUT   Waste: 137,000 tonnes (121,436 persons)
OUTPUT Electricity: 55,000 MWh (17,860 persons)
        Heat: 348,000 MWh (12,481 persons)

INPUT   Waste: 137,000 tonnes (233,132 persons)
OUTPUT Electricity: 55,000 MWh (17,860 persons)
        Heat: 348,000 MWh (12,481 persons)

M

INPUT   Waste: 362,000 tonnes (320,876 persons)
OUTPUT Electricity: 89,000 MWh (28,901 persons)
        Heat: 998,000 MWh (35,792 persons)

INPUT   Waste: 362,000 tonnes (616,013 persons)
OUTPUT Electricity: 89,000 MWh (28,901 persons)
        Heat: 998,000 MWh (35,792 persons)

L

INPUT   Waste: 610,000 tonnes (540,702 persons)
OUTPUT Electricity: 239,000 MWh (77,612 persons)
        Heat: 1,565,000 MWh (56,127 persons)

INPUT   Waste: 610,000 tonnes (1,038,033 persons)
OUTPUT Electricity: 239,000 MWh (77,612 persons)
        Heat: 1,565,000 MWh (56,127 persons)

50 m

ASSOCIATIVE
MODEL KEY

TIPPING &
FEEDING

INCINERATING &
BOILING

CONDENSING

GENERATING

FILTERING

OPERATING &
MAINTAINING

PHOENIX (GLENDALE SUBURB)
[pop. density = 1,570/sq. km]

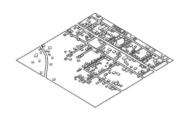

PRESTON (RURAL)
[pop. density = 57/sq. km]

804 m x 804 m

73 m x 94 m

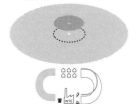

INPUT   Waste: 137,000 tonnes (104,119 persons)
OUTPUT Electricity: 55,000 MWh (10,680 persons)
        Heat: n/a

INPUT   Waste: 137,000 tonnes (135,672 persons)
OUTPUT Electricity: 55,000 MWh (18,333 persons)
        Heat: 348,000 MWh (12,481 persons)

INPUT   Waste: 362,000 tonnes (275,118 persons)
OUTPUT Electricity: 89,000 MWh (17,282 persons)
        Heat: n/a

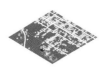

INPUT   Waste: 362,000 tonnes (358,492 persons)
OUTPUT Electricity: 89,000 MWh (29,667 persons)
        Heat: 998,000 MWh (35,792 persons)

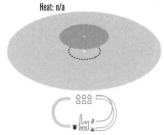

INPUT   Waste: 610,000 tonnexs (463,596 persons)
OUTPUT Electricity: 239,000 MWh (46,408 persons)
        Heat: n/a

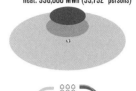

INPUT   Waste: 610,000 tonnes (604,089 persons)
OUTPUT Electricity: 239,000 MWh (79,667 persons)
        Heat: 1,565,000 MWh (56,127 persons)

100 m

213

ASSOCIATIVE MODEL II

The WtE Design Lab generated a second associative model to address a variety of possible configurations that a WtE plant could adopt to better integrate it within a given urban context and plot size. This model accounts for all the components that form a WtE plant as well as all the constraints attached to them. It allows designers to move components around to create novel WtE configurations while keeping a realistic technological outcome. Components can be moved, rotated, and stacked, and the model is able to detect problems, such as collisions, proximity constraints, and more in real time.

The basic principle behind this model is that every component of a WtE plant has connections to others; nothing works in isolation. In order to make design decisions, all the relevant connections and parameters must be taken into account and satisfied. The associative model facilitates this process by re-computing these connections at ease and noting areas of conflict so they can be quickly addressed.

With this associative model, the WtE Design Lab tested a number of strategies for better adapting WtE plants to a range of urban contexts. The strategies of compacting, stacking, fragmenting, bridging, surrounding, and burying were tested in three urban contexts—Manhattan, Boston's Back Bay, and Stockholm's Södermalm.

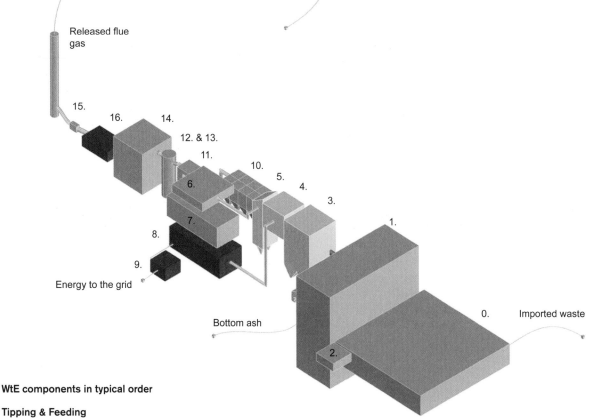

Released flue gas

15.

16. 14.

12. & 13.

11.

10.

6. 5.

4.

3.

1.

7.

8.

9.

Energy to the grid

0. Imported waste

Bottom ash

2.

WtE components in typical order

Tipping & Feeding
0. Tipping Hall
1. Bunker Hall
2. Control Room

Incinerating & Boiling
3. Incinerator
4. Superheater
5. Economizer

Condensing
6. Feed Water Tank
7. Air-Cooled Condensers

Generating
8. Turbine & Generator
9. Power Transformers

Filtering
10. Baghouse Filter
11. Wet Scrubbers
12. Water Treatment
13. Condensing Unit
14. Selective Catalytic Reduction Filter
15. Induced Draft Fan & Chimney

Monitoring
16. Emissions Control Station
17. Sampling Station

Operating & Maintaining
18. Storage Silos
19. Automation
20. Switchgear Equipment
21. Emergency Diesel
22. Lockup/Storage

	BARCELONA (EIXAMPLE)	BEIJING (CHONGWENMEN)	NEW YORK CITY (MANHATTAN)	BOSTON (BACK BAY)	STOCKHOLM (SÖDERMALM)	PHOENIX (GLENDALE)	PRESTON (RURAL)
SMALL WtE PLANT (i = 100k–200k tonnes/yr)							
EXISTING		•	+	+	+	+	+
compacting	+	+	+	+	+	+	+
stacking	+	+	+	+	+	+	+
fragmenting	+	+	+	+	+	+	+
bridging	+	+	+	+	+	+	+
surrounding	+	+	+	+	+	+	+
burying	+	+	+	O	+	+	+
MEDIUM WtE PLANT (i = 300k–450k tonnes/yr)							
EXISTING	+	+	+	+	+	+	+
compacting	+	+	+	+	+	+	+
stacking	+	+	+	+	+	+	+
fragmenting	+	+	+	+	+	+	+
bridging	+	+	+	+	+	+	+
surrounding	+	+	+	+	+	O	O
burying	+	+	O	O	+	+	+
LARGE WtE PLANT (i = 550k–750k tonnes/yr)							
EXISTING	O	+	O	O	O	+	+
compacting	+	+	+	+	+	+	+
stacking	+	+	+	+	+	+	+
fragmenting	+	+	+	+	+	+	+
bridging	+	+	+	+	+	+	+
surrounding	O	O	O	O	O	O	O
burying	+	+	O	O	+	+	+

SMALL-SCALE STRATEGIES see pgs. 258–271

MEDIUM-SCALE STRATEGIES see pgs. 223–257

LARGE-SCALE STRATEGIES see pgs. 200–222

+   compatible with urban fabric   O   incompatible with urban fabric

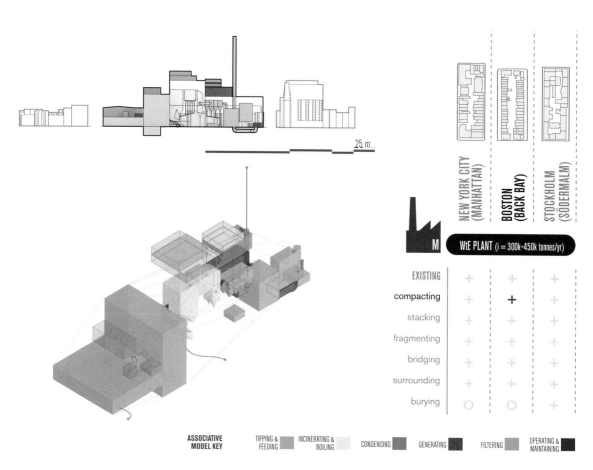

BOSTON (BACK BAY)

A notable urban development, Boston's Back Bay follows a pattern of infill and consolidation of previously unclaimed mud flats. Unlike the rest of Boston, the Back Bay was plotted in a planned grid. Like the majority of Boston, however, its narrow streets and sidewalks facilitate a pedestrian-friendly and higher-density neighborhood without the need of skyscrapers. Today it is one of the most densely populated areas in Boston, generally consisting of low- to mid-rise buildings, including a limited number of high-rise developments.

In this application, strategies aimed at reducing the building footprint and height are achieved through horizontally and vertically **compacting** the WtE components to fit and operate within the limits of a typical urban block. The various operations are linear but efficiently sequenced. An effort is made to respect existing parcel boundaries while maintaining an accessible perimeter for buffering and maintenance purposes.

25 m

	NEW YORK CITY (MANHATTAN)	BOSTON (BACK BAY)	STOCKHOLM (SÖDERMALM)
M WtE PLANT (i = 300k–450k tonnes/yr)			
EXISTING	+	+	+
compacting	+	**+**	+
stacking	+	+	+
fragmenting	+	+	+
bridging	+	+	+
surrounding	+	+	+
burying	○	○	+

ASSOCIATIVE MODEL KEY — TIPPING & FEEDING — INCINERATING & BOILING — CONDENSING — GENERATING — FILTERING — OPERATING & MAINTAINING

Medium-scale strategies per urban context

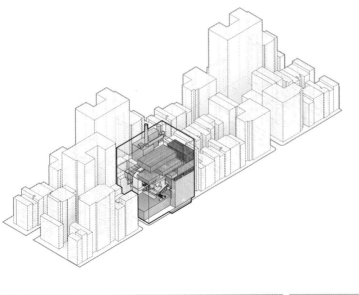

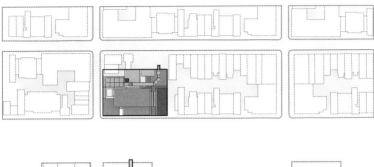

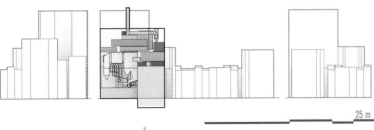

25 m

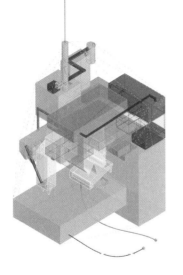

NEW YORK CITY (MANHATTAN)

Manhattan's urban fabric is notoriously compact and densely populated. High-rise development is a common practice particularly because of high land value; the primary way for a developer to make a profit is to build tall. Such dense, high-rise laden conditions pose a serious challenge for typical industrial applications, whereas such restrictions are rare in the rural context in which WtE plants are commonly placed.

A significant reduction of the building footprint and of the overall organization of WtE processes is required for the **stacking** strategy. Proper access and means of waste delivery to the tipping hall are paramount. When organized on site, a stacking strategy that superimposes the various components within a limited area can be conceived. This creates new spatial relationships by rethinking the way space, heat, and enclosure can operate dynamically in section.

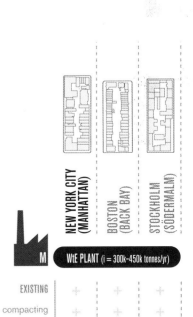

	NEW YORK CITY (MANHATTAN)	BOSTON (BACK BAY)	STOCKHOLM (SÖDERMALM)
M	**WtE PLANT** (i = 300k–450k tonnes/yr)		
EXISTING	+	+	+
compacting	+	+	+
stacking	+	**+**	+
fragmenting	+	+	+
bridging	+	+	+
surrounding	+	+	+
burying	○	○	+

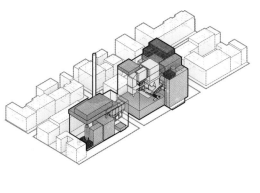

Södermalm is the largest and one of the most densely populated boroughs in Stockholm. A historic settlement, the area's origins trace to a period in which roads were narrow and a sporadic tapestry of networked open spaces peppered the city. While pressure for development is now high, opportunities for building are scarce and developers must forge creative strategies to develop wherever and however they can.

Fragmentation is one such strategy to achieve flexible integration into the urban context. It can allow for the zoning of certain WtE components in association with particular processes to produce thermally like-minded ecosystems. For instance, WtE components linked with incineration and heat generation could be housed alongside other heat-related programs and functions. The same could be true in terms of the filtering and monitoring/operating components, which could be linked with more temperate programs. Within this context fragmentation similarly aids in providing increased accessibility for all maintenance and industrial processes.

25 m

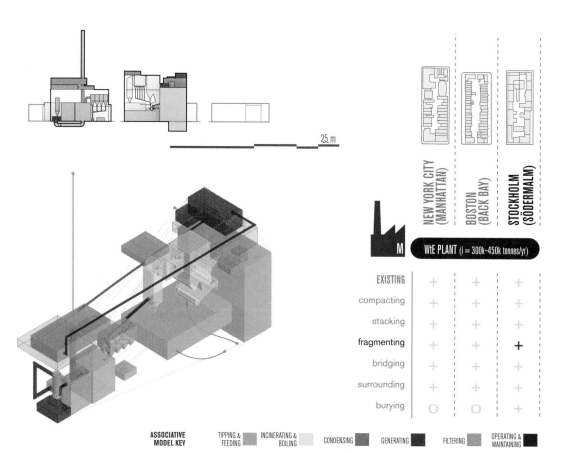

	NEW YORK CITY (MANHATTAN)	BOSTON (BACK BAY)	STOCKHOLM (SÖDERMALM)
WtE PLANT (i = 300k–450k tonnes/yr)			
EXISTING	+	+	+
compacting	+	+	+
stacking	+	+	+
fragmenting	+	+	**+**
bridging	+	+	+
surrounding	+	+	+
burying	○	○	+

ASSOCIATIVE MODEL KEY   TIPPING & FEEDING   INCINERATING & BOILING   CONDENSING   GENERATING   FILTERING   OPERATING & MAINTAINING

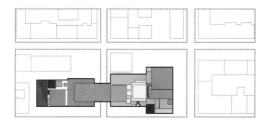

STOCKHOLM (SÖDERMALM)

Building on the idea of fragmentation, the **bridging** of these subdivided components can physically reconnect several of the spatial and thermal exchanges lost during the dividing process. Designers must define quantitatively and qualitatively how much and to what degree such bridging is allowed to occur.

For example, the illustration shows the air-cooled condensers as the bridging element that links the incinerating and filtering components. This is particularly noteworthy in this application because not only must the air condensers function as an intermediary between the boilers and the generator, but they must also be exposed to the outdoors to allow airflow for cooling. Spatially, this bridging moment allows the opportunity to associatively designate certain programs, users, and functions that may be linked with the specific microclimate of the inhabited space. One can imagine an elevated network of pedestrian bridging that spans the industrial exchanges taking place on the ground level.

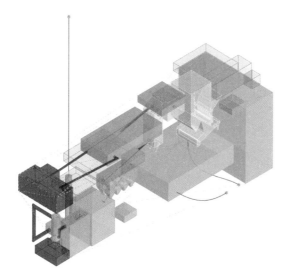

25 m

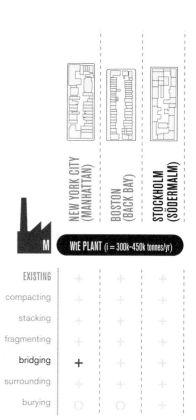

	NEW YORK CITY (MANHATTAN)	BOSTON (BACK BAY)	STOCKHOLM (SÖDERMALM)
M WtE PLANT (ï = 300k–450k tonnes/yr)			
EXISTING	+	+	+
compacting	+	+	+
stacking	+	+	+
fragmenting	+	+	+
bridging	**+**	+	+
surrounding	+	+	+
burying	○	○	+

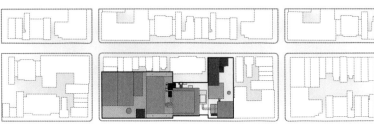

NEW YORK CITY (MANHATTAN)

Surrounding does not assume, where stacking did, that land speculation is a factor or a rarity in Manhattan. Rather, this is a speculative proposal venturing how a more conventional horizontal assembly of WtE components could be integrated into this densely packed urban fabric. The layout follows the allotted footprint of the city property parcels, allowing the opportunity to weave in and around adjacent urban structures, whether they are buildings or existing infrastructure. The strategy of surrounding demonstrates a scheme in which the generating components are placed across the New York city block, connecting opposite sides of the street. This not only offers increased access to the energy generating components for maintenance opportunities, but also to the remainder of the WtE facility, which is bordered by three extremely busy urban streets.

25 m

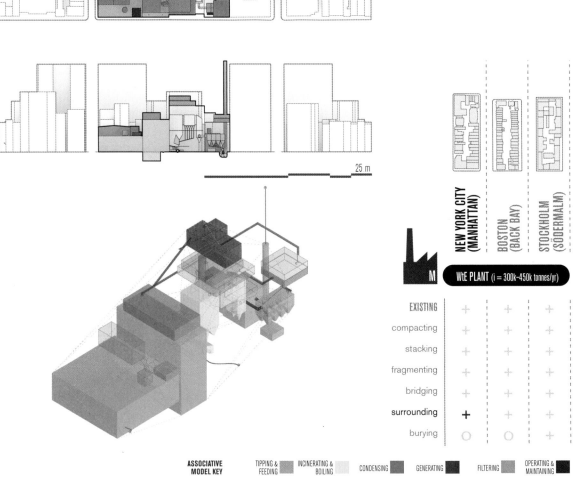

	NEW YORK CITY (MANHATTAN)	BOSTON (BACK BAY)	STOCKHOLM (SÖDERMALM)
M	WtE PLANT (i = 300k–450k tonnes/yr)		
EXISTING	+	+	+
compacting	+	+	+
stacking	+	+	+
fragmenting	+	+	+
bridging	+	+	+
surrounding	**+**	+	+
burying	○	○	+

ASSOCIATIVE MODEL KEY

TIPPING & FEEDING — INCINERATING & BOILING — CONDENSING — GENERATING — FILTERING — OPERATING & MAINTAINING

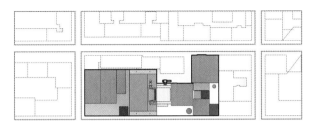

STOCKHOLM (SÖDERMALM)

In this circumstance, the strategy of **surrounding** similarly explores the potential of a conventional horizontal assembly of WtE components. Unlike Manhattan, Södermalm's urban fabric is not as dense. Its courtyard typology offers its inhabitants a patchwork of networked green spaces accessible from the ground level. Although vehicles are allowed, vehicular traffic is generally low and sporadic, and its narrow streets offer a pedestrian-friendly experience.

This speculative proposal plays on Södermalm's urban conventions by elevating crucial WtE processes and components, further opening the ground plane to pedestrian traffic. Necessary portions of the facility are allowed to weave, partially surrounding adjacent building parcels. However, it weaves in such a way as to maintain open passages across the ground plane. This is a complete reversal of conventional industrial practices, because it invites public pedestrian interaction with the WtE facility without actually exposing the public to the potentially hazardous industrial processes, which are primarily elevated and separated from the general public.

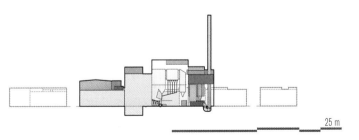

25 m

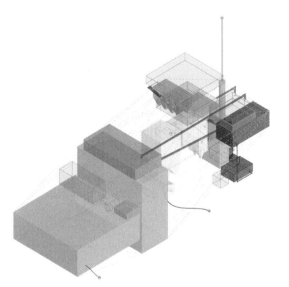

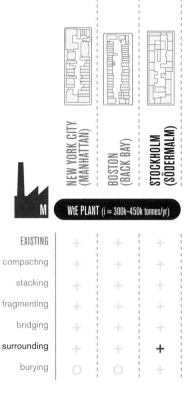

	NEW YORK CITY (MANHATTAN)	BOSTON (BACK BAY)	STOCKHOLM (SÖDERMALM)
M WtE PLANT (i = 300k–450k tonnes/yr)			
EXISTING	+	+	+
compacting	+	+	+
stacking	+	+	+
fragmenting	+	+	+
bridging	+	+	+
surrounding	+	+	**+**
burying	○	○	+

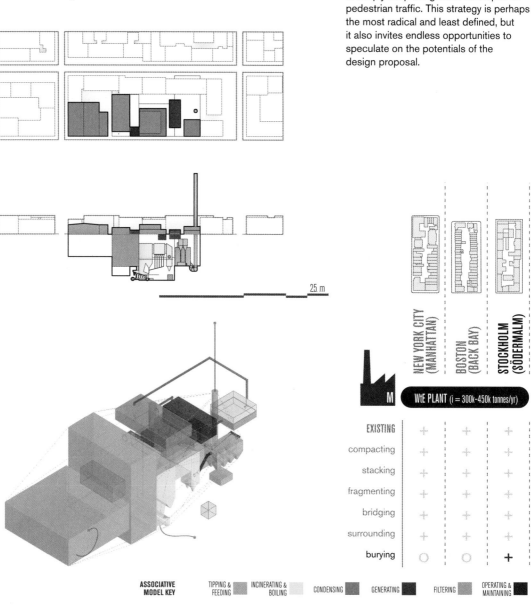

STOCKHOLM (SÖDERMALM)

The near **burial** of the entire WtE facility is one such scheme that exploits the potential of minimizing the physical impact on the urban fabric. Certain technical requisites restrict the degree to which the WtE facility may be hidden. For example, access to the tipping hall must be maintained, and hence visible, from the ground level. Several other components require access to outside air and should to some respect remain visible. These include the air-cooling condensers, generator, automation, and chimney.

The design opportunities with this scheme involve further developing architectural strategies to engage with the public. Perhaps the solution could be to simply keep the ground level open to pedestrian traffic. This strategy is perhaps the most radical and least defined, but it also invites endless opportunities to speculate on the potentials of the design proposal.

25 m

	NEW YORK CITY (MANHATTAN)	BOSTON (BACK BAY)	STOCKHOLM (SÖDERMALM)
M WtE PLANT (i = 300k–450k tonnes/yr)			
EXISTING	+	+	+
compacting	+	+	+
stacking	+	+	+
fragmenting	+	+	+
bridging	+	+	+
surrounding	+	+	+
burying	○	○	+

ASSOCIATIVE MODEL KEY — TIPPING & FEEDING — INCINERATING & BOILING — CONDENSING — GENERATING — FILTERING — OPERATING & MAINTAINING

NOTES

1. Matt Williams, "Waste-to-Energy Success Factors in Sweden and the United States" (George Washington University School of Business, 2011), http://www.acore.org/wp-content /uploads/2012/04/WTEWTEWTE-in -Sweden-and-the-US-Matt-Williams.pdf.

2. Environmental and Energy Study Institute (ESSI), *Fact Sheet: What is District Energy*? (2011), http://www.districtenergy.org /assets/pdfs/White-Papers/What -IsDistrictEnergyEESI092311.pdf; Dan Henning and Alemayehu Gebremedhin, "District Heating and Cooling Enable Efficient Energy Resource Utilisation," in *Sustainable Energy: Recent Studies* (INTECH Open Science, 2012),

http://www.intechopen.com/books /sustainable-energy-recent-studies /district-heating-and-cooling-enable -efficient-energy-resource-utilisation; and Priscilla Ulloa, "Potential for Combined Heat and Power and District Heating and Cooling from Waste-to- Energy Facilities in the US–Learning from the Danish Experience" (thesis, Columbia University, 2007).

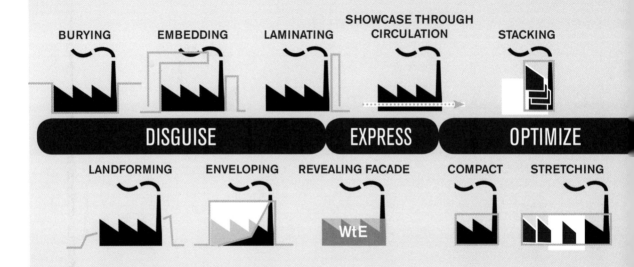

BURYING

EMBEDDING

LAMINATING

SHOWCASE THROUGH
CIRCULATION

STACKING

DISGUISE

EXPRESS

OPTIMIZE

LANDFORMING

ENVELOPING

REVEALING FACADE

WtE

COMPACT

STRETCHING

Medium-Scale Strategies

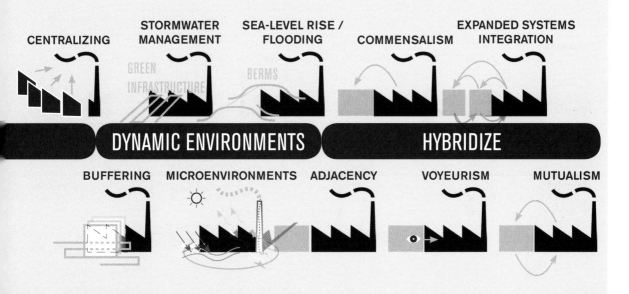

CENTRALIZING

STORMWATER MANAGEMENT

GREEN INFRASTRUCTURE

SEA-LEVEL RISE / FLOODING

BERMS

COMMENSALISM

EXPANDED SYSTEMS INTEGRATION

DYNAMIC ENVIRONMENTS

HYBRIDIZE

BUFFERING

MICROENVIRONMENTS

ADJACENCY

VOYEURISM

MUTUALISM

Mosque   Madrasa

Progressive Purification, see pg. 276
David Hamm and Snoweria Zhang

Greenhouse   Wellness
Center

Wellness, Climate, Atmosphere,
see pg. 296
Nastaran Arfaei and Jana Masset

Anaerobic   Multimodal
Treatment   Transit Station

Catalytic Currents, see pg. 318
Michael Haggerty and Dana McKinney

Hedonism   Hospitality

5H Hybrid, see pg. 340
Alberto Embriz de Salvatierra

Recycling/   Parkspace
Market

Pittsfield Thermal Baths
Nancy Nichols and Joshua Feldman

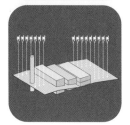

Research   Greenhouse
Center

Adjacency | Wildlife Refuge
Lee Ann Bobrowski, Clementine Jiang, and Ivy Pan

Recycling   Parkspace
Center

Waste, Reuse, and the PARKSpace,
see pg. 286
Felipe Oropeza Jr.

Biomass   Trails

The (Re)creational Park, see pg. 306
Taehyun Jeon

Thermal   Culinary
Grove   Program

Thermal Grove, see pg. 330
Michael Clapp and Mike Johnson

Stadium   E-Transit

Show/Flow, see pg. 352
Andrew Keating and Scott Smith

Ferry   Nightclub

Wast(ed)
**Larissa Belcic, Elizabeth Biney-Amissah,
and Clementine Jang**

Aquaponics   Green Roof

STACK^x
**Alberto Embriz de Salvatierra, Jennifer Hiser,
and Larisa Ovalles**

Housing   Chute
Gardens

Heterotic Architecture: Stacks, Chimneys, and Shoots
Joshua Feldman

Medium-scale design strategies seek to better integrate a WtE plant in the context of the parcel and immediate adjacent parcels. The WtE Design Lab has developed strategies that help address public perception by reducing nuisances and negative visual impact, promoting resilience, and adding educational or other components that allow the public to better understand the processes that take place in the plant.

One of the strategies developed in the WtE Design Lab is that of hybridization. Hybrid buildings go beyond mixed-use development, as hybrids are a pre-engineered exchange of building functions, often codependent on one other, whereas mixed-use developments involve adjacent uses (most often commercial and housing) sharing the same land or building. The hybridization strategy tries to address all of the aims above, but also attempts to make the issue of obsolescence more robust while minimizing the loss of energy, making the plant more efficient in its inputs/outputs. Hybridization strategies were strongly investigated in the context of the seminar and option studio offered by the Lab.

There are a number of medium-scale strategies such as disguise, express, optimize, dynamic environments, and hybridize that are explained in detail in this part of the chapter. Each strategy will be accompanied by a number of techniques and operations that could be applied to existing plant organizations in order to shift the way they are situated, perceived by the public, or engaged with a number of adjacent or intertwined programs. Each operation is followed by a number of examples that test the specific strategy, technique, and operation. These examples were developed in the context of the design studio, seminar, and thesis advising activity offered by the WtE Design Lab at the Harvard University Graduate School of Design. These projects are further explained in the Design Speculations section.

WtE Design Lab speculation catalog

DISGUISE

The architectural act of **burying** in these examples minimizes both the facility's exterior volume and its perceptual presence in the landscape. It closely approximates an attempt of erasure as less of the elevation and WtE processes are made externally visible. This strategy shifts the focus away from the actual building itself and onto its surrounding rural and/or urban context(s). In a **fully buried** scheme, the depth of burial depends on the required height of the bunker hall. Most, if not all, evidence of the WtE facility is hidden from view. Preference is given to intervention with minimal impact on the surrounding landscape.

A **significantly buried** scheme may involve the full or partial burial of main processes within the operations chain. At first glance it may not be apparent that a significant industrial operation is taking place, and the partially exposed portion of the facility can be used to either mask or reveal the true nature of the operation. In a partially buried scheme, the tipping hall, for example, could be buried to avoid nuisance odors. This would be ideal in a densely populated urban context where space is limited and the ability to **partially bury** the WtE operations is not only convenient but necessary.

BURYING

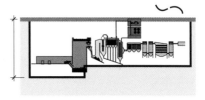

FULLY BURIED

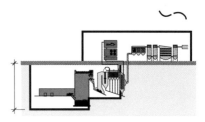

SIGNIFICANTLY BURIED

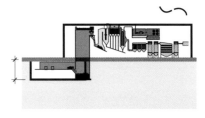

PARTIALLY BURIED

MEDIUM-SCALE STRATEGIES — DISGUISE

- BURYING
- EMBEDDING
- ENVELOPING
- LANDFORMING
- LAMINATING

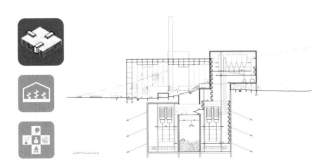

Image A

Wellness, Climate, Atmosphere, see pg. 296
Nastaran Arfaei and Jana Masset

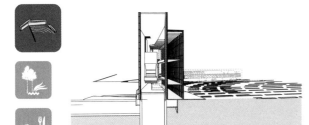

Image B

Thermal Grove, see pg. 330
Michael Clapp and Mike Johnson

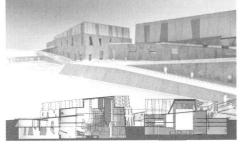

Image C

Waste, Reuse, and the PARKSpace, see pg. 286
Felipe Oropeza Jr.

Image A
In this example, the delivery, bunker hall, and incineration processes are buried below grade, allowing the earth to act as a heat sink while using portions of waste heat to facilitate hybrid programs above.

Image B
Portions of the program and plant operations are pushed below grade to reduce the plant's visual impact.

Image C
The tipping hall and bunker hall are buried underground to establish a minimal, monolithic appearance in the form of a clean, stark bar form.

DISGUISE

Whereas burial is the physical minimization of a volume within the landscape, **embedding** is an attempt at integration with its rural or urban landscape. Both the architectural and operational functions of the WtE facility are strategized with respect to current and future considerations of context. Some schemes exhibit conditions of **building up** supplementary programs, which facilitate a beneficial exchange in close proximity to its end use. In others the **surrounding** of context and facilities is used to nest the plant within other programming that may make use of its beneficial outputs.

The envelope offers the opportunity to work with or without regard for its specific setting. **Enveloping** can either emphasize or de-emphasize the physical impact of the enclosure through a negotiation of both practical and aesthetic nuances. **Camouflaging** is a technique used to obscure the visual impact and perception of a plant in the landscape or its urban context. **Wrapping** of the plant itself helps to soften the impact of industrial infrastructure on its immediate surroundings.

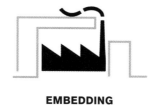

EMBEDDING

BUILDING UP

SURROUNDING

ENVELOPING

CAMOUFLAGING

WRAPPING

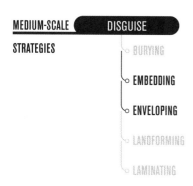

MEDIUM-SCALE   DISGUISE

STRATEGIES

- BURYING
- EMBEDDING
- ENVELOPING
- LANDFORMING
- LAMINATING

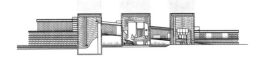

Catalytic Currents, see pg. 318   **Image A**
Michael Haggerty and Dana McKinney

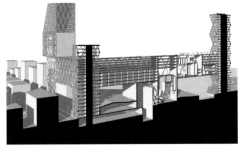

5H Hybrid, see pg. 340   **Image B**
Alberto Embriz de Salvatierra

The (Re)creational Park, see pg. 306   **Image C**
Taehyun Jeon

Progressive Purification, see pg. 276   **Image D**
David Hamm and Snoweria Zhang

Image A
The WtE volumes are wrapped in a concrete brise-soleil that affords views into the internal components from the various surrounding public concourses.

Image B
Sited in a rural industrial area, this scheme anticipates a future urban condition in which urban sprawl has enveloped the lakeside towers and its parks.

Image C
The building form is encompassed with its surrounding natural landscape to zone the various programs and processes of the WtE facility while also facilitating various levels of interconnected space between its built and landscaped environment.

Image D
This proposal capitalizes on the existing site topography to embed the facility within its surrounding landscape. To relate the processes of purification to cleanliness, the building is divided and wrapped sequentially into various distinct "lung" spaces that may also serve as volumetric butters, atriums, and circulation areas.

DISGUISE

In **landforming**, various landform grading techniques, technologies, and construction methods either highlight or diminish certain WtE processes within a global treatment that engages with the greater landscape and ecological environment. Often strategies take advantage of a **fully bermed** condition to the extent that only the entrance emerges from the built-up mound. This complements the rural context in which a WtE facility may exist with near-seemless integration into the surrounding landscape. A **partially bermed** strategy may have built-up mounds on each side for a portion of its overall height. This allows for the integration into a more urban context, perhaps alongside a major waterway where berming offers a means of protection against flooding. A **ha-ha's** primary function is to utilize a lowered landform to remove visual distractions or blights from the privileged view of the surrounding landscape.

LANDFORMING

FULLY BERMED

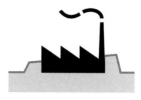

PARTIALLY BERMED

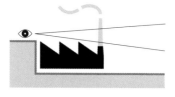

HA-HA

The (Re)creational Park, see pg. 306
Taehyun Jeon

Image A

Catalytic Currents, see pg. 318
Michael Haggerty and Dana McKinney

Image B

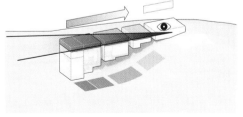

Progressive Purification, see pg. 276
David Hamm and Snoweria Zhang

Image C

Image A
The (Re)creational Park is fully bermed with entrances to the plant and covered program emerging as cuts through the mounded earth around the central circulation.

Image B
Catalytic Currents proposes that the structure be integrated with a plinth-like berm intending to act as a barrier against storm surge, which has affected the site in the past.

Image C
A ha-ha is adapted to this site by using the vantage point of the hill on which it rests to raise the hybrid programming of recreational spaces above the sightlines of the plant, allowing unobstructed views of the urban landscape beyond.

DISGUISE

Often strategies take advantage of a **terracing** technique to creating a stepped landform, provide open views, facilitate programmatic functions, and better integrate within a sloped topography. **Shoring** refers to the process of supporting a building or trench with proper structural bracing. For this industrial application shoring may be used as a thermal tempering agent or to reduce the visual impact of the plant on its surroundings.

The process of **laminating** adds an additional layer of program and visual disconnection to the industrial process. It may be used to supplement the functionality of the laminated elements, or as a visual mechanism and/or physical barrier to certain external forces.

LANDFORMING CONT'D

TERRACING

SHORING

LAMINATING

MEDIUM-SCALE DISGUISE

STRATEGIES

- BURYING
- EMBEDDING
- ENVELOPING
- LANDFORMING
- LAMINATING

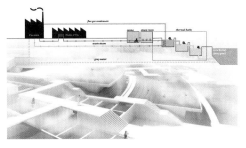

Pittsfield Thermal Baths
Nancy Nichols and Joshua Feldman

Image A

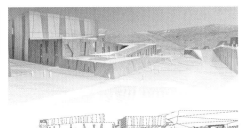

Waste, Reuse, and the PARKSpace, see pg. 286
Felipe Oropeza Jr.

Image B

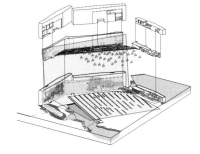

Thermal Grove, see pg. 330
Michael Clapp and Mike Johnson

Image C

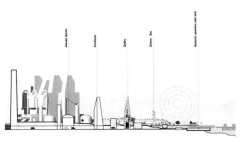

STACKˣ
Alberto Embriz de Salvatierra, Jennifer Hiser, and Larisa Ovalles

Image D

Image A
A range of pool types provide visitors with varying thermal conditions and terraced levels of privacy. From the first large recreational pool, swimmers proceed to a series of more intimate pools that gradually step down to a series of larger pools.

Image B
Material and energy flows are facilitated through a gradual stepping up of the various aquaculture/water storage tanks that also complement the gently sloped topography of the seaside facility.

Image C
The programmed spaces of PARKSpace have been shored up by earth berms to hide the scale of the plant itself while allowing ramping access to portions situated on the main structure's roof.

Image D
A vegetated lamination of vertical greenhouses uses the heat from the plant to supplement its temperature control mechanisms.

DISGUISE

The ability to sequentially choreograph a series of industrial processes and operations using a **showcase through circulation** for the purpose of providing both spectacle and educational value is a powerful organizational strategy for various projects. These moments can be arranged along a predetermined thoroughfare of circulation. Likewise, a predetermined organization of spaces can determine the circulation. The facade may be used as a tool or indicator to locate certain operational or spatial moments of interest that may otherwise be hidden from view. Various methods of **revealing** (the) **facade** including formal, material, and operational strategies may be implemented.

SHOWCASE THROUGH CIRCULATION / EDUCATIONAL TOOL

MAJOR AXIAL PROCESSION

DEGREES OF INTERFACE INTENDED

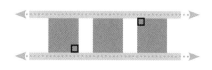

PERIPHERAL (INCIDENTAL)

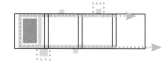

PUNCTUATED / INTERMITTENT

REVEALING FACADE

Image A
The main axes running through the programmed areas of this proposal are lined with glazed enclosures to expose the interior organization.

Image B
The WtE plant processes are showcased here for visitors to the hybrid programs as well as those visiting to learn about the plant itself.

Image C
Though obscured from view from the exterior, the plant processes are largely on display as visitors circulate between the vertical greenhouse component and the plant within.

Image D
Tangential experiences are choreographed in this proposal by exposing plant components as visual showpieces in areas of vertical circulation.

MEDIUM-SCALE STRATEGIES — EXPRESS
- SHOWCASE THROUGH CIRCULATION
- REVEALING FACADE

The (Re)creational Park, see pg. 306
Taehyun Jeon

Image A

Waste, Reuse, and the PARKSpace, see pg. 286
Felipe Oropeza Jr.

Image B

Thermal Grove, see pg. 330
Michael Clapp and Mike Johnson

Image C

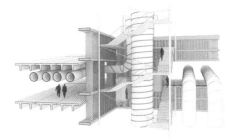

Catalytic Currents, see pg. 318
Michael Haggerty and Dana McKinney

Image D

Progressive Purification, see pg. 276
David Hamm and Snoweria Zhang

Image E

Thermal Grove, see pg. 330
Michael Clapp and Mike Johnson

Image F

5H Hybrid, see pg. 340
Alberto Embriz de Salvatierra

Image G

Image E
The peripheral circulation inherent to this scheme is provides privileged views of the plant at specific nodes when circulating in and out of the exterior shell wrapping.

Image F
Large exterior operable glazed apertures expose glimpses of the massive infrastructure concealed within the massive, heavy shell exteriors of the bars.

Image G
Portions of the exterior facade are exposed by largely glazed apertures that reveal the industrial functions within.

OPTIMIZE

Optimization refers to an operationally optimized design. The standard linear sequence of WtE components may be rethought in many ways, thus allowing new spatial and organizational sequences. The **stacking** or vertical **aggregation** of WtE components is conducive for strategies with limited site area, as these operations tend to free space at ground level, allowing for the components' insertion into tight, restricted urban fabrics. The horizontal **consolidation** or **compacting** of WtE components is similarly geared toward reducing the building footprint, potentially economizing final construction costs in terms of material and labor.

Centralizing WtE components around a strategic focal node of interest draws previously untapped allowances in terms of efficiencies and other interrelation exchanges. This can aid in reducing redundancy in elements that can serve multiple lines of waste processing. **Focusing** the components around a central location to increase efficiency in the use of shared facilities is a useful organizational method in relation to specific elements such as the bunker hall.

STACKING

AGGREGATION

COMPACTING

CONSOLIDATION

CENTRALIZING

FOCUSING

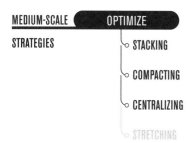

MEDIUM-SCALE STRATEGIES — OPTIMIZE
- STACKING
- COMPACTING
- CENTRALIZING
- STRETCHING

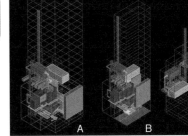

Thermal Grove, see pg. 330
Michael Clapp and Mike Johnson

Image A

5H Hybrid, see pg. 340
Alberto Embriz de Salvatierra

Image E

Wellness, Climate, Atmosphere, see pg. 296
Nastaran Arfaei and Jana Masset

Image B

Wellness, Climate, Atmosphere, see pg. 296
Nastaran Arfaei and Jana Masset

Image C

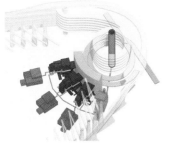

Show/Flow, see pg. 352
Andrew Keating and Scott Smith

Image D

Image A
The stacking of multiple boilers is an attempt to increase the density of processing within a slender shell envelope.

Image B
Efforts were made here to centralize the bunker hall pit, so that delivery could be more timely and efficient while allowing a radial organization of incineration lines.

Image C
Placing shared facilities for portions of the WtE process within a compact form allowed this scheme to then be surrounded with filtration components sharing a common flue gas stack.

Image D
The forms rotating about a common center aid this proposal in creating a variety of compartmentalized spaces around the perimeter to facilitate diverse uses.

Image E
Formalistically studying the stacking of various components of the process was an exercise developed in proposal A. Proposals B and C are compacted formal studies seeking to reduce the plant's footprint and organize its components for efficiency of space.

OPTIMIZE

The act of **stretching** makes use of what would otherwise be an inefficient strategy to exploit certain benefits related to the transfer of thermal energy and spatial fluidity associated with WtE delivery processes. While these allowances are limited with respect to the engineering requisites for essential operability between each particular component, the potential spatial, programmatic, and ecological benefits are considerable.

Component stretching involves the elongation of the plant components themselves, often within an extended form of enclosure. **Separating delivery / processing** from the remainder of plant operations is often seen as beneficial for removing the presence of any associated nuisance noises and odors. **Fragmentation/compartmentalization** of certain groups of components can facilitate various functions for the mutual benefit of the plant and any augmenting hybrid programs.

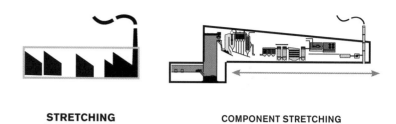

STRETCHING   **COMPONENT STRETCHING**

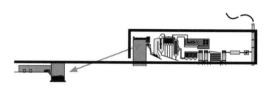

SEPARATING DELIVERY / PROCESSING

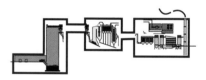

FRAGMENTING / COMPARTMENTALIZING

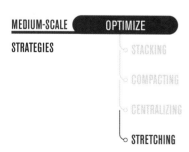

MEDIUM-SCALE — OPTIMIZE

STRATEGIES
- STACKING
- COMPACTING
- CENTRALIZING
- STRETCHING

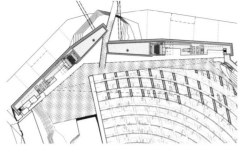

Image A

Thermal Grove, see pg. 330
Michael Clapp and Mike Johnson

Image B

Wellness, Climate, Atmosphere, see pg. 296
Nastaran Arfaei and Jana Masset

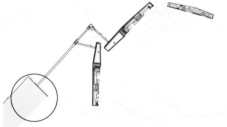

Image C

Thermal Grove, see pg. 330
Michael Clapp and Mike Johnson

Image D

Catalytic Currents, see pg. 318
Michael Haggerty and Dana McKinney

Image A
Because of the slenderness desired in the form of the overall structure, this proposal stretched the components of the WtE plant to elongate the heavy industrial typology.

Image B
Many proposals make an effort to displace the delivery of waste to the site in order to remove the immediacy of odors that may be associated with this type of fuel.

Image C
A vacuum propulsion system is used to transfer the waste from a separate and distant delivery facility into the bunker hall.

Image D
This proposal displays a stretching of the compartmentalized processes of delivery, incineration, and flue gas cleaning. The extension of the three core areas breaks down the scale of the overall WtE facility, allowing the latent heat to be distributed more evenly throughout the occupied spaces.

245

DYNAMIC ENVIRONMENTS

The use of physical separators in the form of **buffering** zones in the built or natural environment may shield or restrict access to certain hazardous aspects of the WtE processes. Likewise, as with the use of pavement and/or vegetated groundcover softscapes, these may be implemented to invite communal congregations of people. Hardscapes as a **hard buffer** may be implemented to separate public areas from the less desirable aspects of industrial landscapes. A **soft buffer**, through the use of softscaping elements, provides a subtler means of providing separation of adjacencies. Vegetation may be used to provide filtered sunlight, mitigate industrial noise and air pollution, and protect against the extremes of drastic temperature changes.

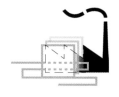

BUFFERING

HARD BUFFER

SOFT BUFFER

MEDIUM-SCALE DYNAMIC ENVIRONMENTS

STRATEGIES

BUFFERING
HARD/SOFT

MICROENVIRONMENTS

SEA-LEVEL RISE /
FLOODING

STORMWATER
MANAGEMENT

Thermal Grove, see pg. 330
Michael Clapp and Mike Johnson

Image A

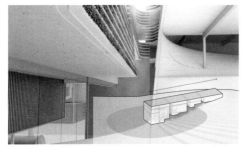

Progressive Purification, see pg. 276
David Hamm and Snoweria Zhang

Image B

5H Hybrid, see pg. 340
Alberto Embriz de Salvatierra

Image C

Thermal Grove, see pg. 330
Michael Clapp and Mike Johnson

Image D

Image A
The stretched, wall-like forms of the WtE facility provide a shield and a buffer between the traditionally gritty and unsightly industrial landscape and the isolated Thermal Grove.

Image B
The vegetated "lungs" of the Progressive Purification proposal facilitate a softening of the transition from industrial production to spaces of quietude and reflection. These green buffers further imbue those spaces with a sense of well-being.

Image C
Buffering may take the form of planned recreation spaces and small parks strategically placed to ease the perception of the industrial presence on site.

Image D
The vertical greenhouse program that wraps the facade of the WtE plant and pushes into its volume provides a natural buffer between the decidedly man-made and the idyllic realm of the exterior.

DYNAMIC ENVIRONMENTS

The designation of certain microenvironments in association with hybridized functions can work both for and against the static ecological base condition of the WtE facility. Passive and nonpassive strategies enhanced by the guiding principles of thermodynamics can provide dynamically innovative spatial arrangements and interrelationships.

The building form has the potential to serve various functions related to prevailing winds on the site. **Wind analysis / shielding / directing** are strategies that can provide a protective barrier and direct crosscurrents into interior courtyards for tempering. Solar orientation has an impact on how these plants are organized, especially with future design considerations in mind to avoid the typical "industrial shed" typology. Proper **sun analysis / shading** strategies must be implemented to avoid concentrations of sunlight on occupied locations or on areas where odors might be worsened. **Operable apertures** provide the occupants a greater degree of control over the microenvironment. This allows a more seasonally specific treatment of variable spaces in the overall scheme. **Building orientation with respect to stationary openings** has an impact on localized wind patterns at the microsite scale. Openings between and through buildings have the capacity to induce pleasant airflows across the site.

MICROENVIRONMENTS

WIND ANALYSIS / SHIELDING / DIRECTING

SUN ANALYSIS / SHADING

OPERABLE APERTURES

MEDIUM-SCALE **DYNAMIC ENVIRONMENTS**

STRATEGIES

- BUFFERING HARD/SOFT
- **MICROENVIRONMENTS**
- SEA-LEVEL RISE / FLOODING
- STORMWATER MANAGEMENT

BUILDING ORIENTATION / STATIONARY OPENINGS

Thermal Grove, see pg.330
Michael Clapp and Mike Johnson

Image A

Heteroritc Architecture: Stacks, Chimneys, & Shoots
Joshua Feldman

Image E

W

E

S

Waste, Reuse, and PARKSpace, see pg. 286
Felipe Oropeza Jr.

Image B

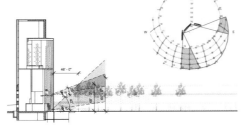

Thermal Grove, see pg.330
Michael Clapp and Mike Johnson

Image C

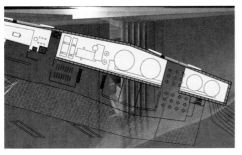

Thermal Grove, see pg.330
Michael Clapp and Mike Johnsun

Image D

Image A
The orientation of the massive vertical structures enclosing the WtE lines act as wind shields, protecting the artificially created landscape within the Thermal Grove.

Image B
The WtE plant was carefully nestled at the base and collusion of two of the three hills existing in the landscape to funnel airflows through the site.

Image C
Solar orientation was vital to the functionality of the vertical greenhouses' hybrid program; a balance of environmental factors informed the ultimate location of the industrial "bars" on site.

Image D
Operable glazing components within the building envelope shell that were developed to provide access to maintenance equipment for also provide cross ventilation through public portions of the culinary program.

Image E
To provide ample airflow across the housing and gardening spaces, this project utilizes the modular structural grid of chimney and chutes to disperse heat and any residual gaseous emissions.

DYNAMIC ENVIRONMENTS

The **stack effect** is a time-tested historic method of producing a passively tempered space by inducing a natural convection of hot air into a vertical shaft, such as a chimney, to pull cooler air into occupied spaces. **Evaporative cooling** utilizes on-site water for cooling via the process of evaporation, entailing the removal of latent heat from the surface on which evaporation takes place.

With projections of significant coastal **sea-level rise / flooding** by the end of the century, there is an urgency to consider this issue when thinking about obsolescence and future use. WtE facilities can and should play a role in this discussion, particularly those that receive waste via busy shipping thoroughfares. Such strategies have the opportunity to integrate **earth berms** as an architectural element that function as a physical stationary and or raised barrier. As barriers, berms both anchor and soften the visible impact on the environment, potentially blending into existing infrastructure.

STACK EFFECT

EVAPORATIVE COOLING

SEA-LEVEL RISE / FLOODING /
EARTH BERMS

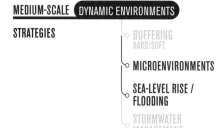

MEDIUM-SCALE DYNAMIC ENVIRONMENTS

STRATEGIES

BUFFERING
HARD/SOFT

MICROENVIRONMENTS

SEA-LEVEL RISE /
FLOODING

STORMWATER
MANAGEMENT

Image A

Heteroritc Architecture: Stacks, Chimneys, & Shoots
Joshua Feldman

Image B

Progressive Purification, see pg. 276
David Hamm and Snoweria Zhang

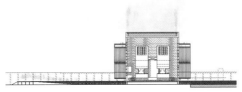

Image C

Catalytic Currents, see pg. 318
Michael Haggerty and Dana McKinney

Image A
Making use of the residual heat of the chimney stack, passively tempered gardening spaces are allocated along the vertical extents of the shaft.

Image B

The open vertical wells connecting to the spiraling floor plates of the shared and outdoor spaces of this proposal aid by inducing the stack effect of vertical airflow.

Image C
Integrated with its landmass plinth, the proposal for Catalytic Currents establishes a constructed berm in response to coastal floodplain regulations that require dedicated means of access above a certain height.

DYNAMIC ENVIRONMENTS

Proper **stormwater management** practices for industrial operations are critical in reducing the amount of heavy metals, vehicular fluids, and other known pollutants in storm-drain runoff that flows into the natural environment. Ideally rainwater runoff is prevented from coming into contact with contaminated areas, but if this cannot be avoided, measures to remove pollutants to meet water quality discharge requirements must be implemented.

Planted zones and natural vegetation aid in integrating the WtE plant process with its immediate surroundings, and often mitigate stormwater runoff in beneficial ways. In locations where large quantities of rainwater need to be treated, onsite wetlands can be designed to either slow or contain contaminants through a process of phytoremediation until the wetland vegetation removes pollutants.

STORMWATER MANAGEMENT / GREEN INFRASTRUCTURE

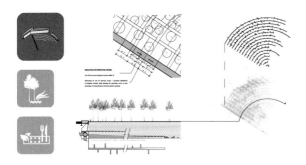

Thermal Grove, see pg. 330
Michael Clapp and Mike Johnson

Image A

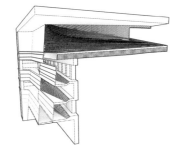

Progressive Purification, see pg. 276
David Hamm and Snoweria Zhang

Image B

LARGE PARTICLES ARE FILTERED, REMOVED FROM REMAINING RUNOFF

SEDIMENTS AND POLLUTANTS SETTLE

THEY ARE BROKEN DOWN AND HELD BY PLANTS/SOIL

INFILTRATION   TREATMENT   COLLECTION

Adjacency | Wildlife Refuge
Lee Ann Bobrowski, Clementine Jiang, and Ivy Pan

Image C

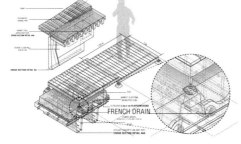

FRENCH DRAIN

Waste, Reuse, and the PARKSpace, see pg. 286
Felipe Oropeza Jr.

Image D

Image A
The Thermal Grove elements of this proposal work to manage and reutilize runoff water from the site as irrigation and as recreational facilities. Integral channels direct the water along orchestrated paths to ensure the vitality of the grove.

Image B
Captured rainwater runoff is directed to storage wells after absorbing heat from industrial processing, subsequently tempering rising air, which serves occupied park areas.

Image C
The existing flat topography presented an opportunity to regrade the site, to a more undulating landform that will better manage runoff by increasing infiltration and collection opportunities.

Image D
The implementation of integrated systems such as French drains work to channel stormwater runoff from the structured landscaped surface into a centralized location for both filtration and on-site graywater use.

HYBRIDIZE

Linking mutually beneficial functions and programs dynamically amplifies the physical and metaphysical perception of the hybridized space. An **adjacency** is the most basic relationship of a hybrid typology. It denotes a proximity to, and identity with, the WtE plant with little to no physical interface. As part of the concept of symbiosis, **commensalism** describes a situation in which only one of the participants benefits from the relationship while the other is not significantly affected. **Mutualism**, however, describes a form of symbiosis in which both parties benefit from the relationship. This hybrid type often uses the outputs from the WtE process stream and further contributes to its ongoing operations by creating additional or more efficient inputs.

HIERARCHY OF HETEROSIS

CREATING A GRADIENT OF INCREASINGLY INTEGRAL AND DEPENDENT SYSTEMS

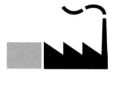

ADJACENCY

COMMENSALISM

MUTUALISM

Image A
The Thermal Grove creates an adjacency between a man-made landscape installation and the industry-based structures surrounding and protecting it from prevailing environmental factors.

Image B
The hybrid envisioned in this proposal establishes an unexpected adjacency between a mosque and a WtE plant.

Image C
The WtE plant embedded within the stepping form of the mosque and its supplemental facilities and outdoor spaces provides great benefits in the way of heat exchanges, which produce comfortable meeting spaces.

MEDIUM-SCALE STRATEGIES — HYBRIDIZE
- ADJACENCY
- COMMENSALISM
- MUTUALISM
- EXPANDED SYSTEM INTEGRATION
- VOYEURISM

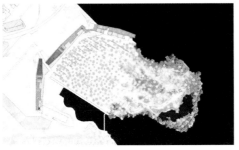

Thermal Grove, see pg. 330
Michael Clapp and Mike Johnson

Image A

"Waste, Reuse, and the PARKSpace" see pg. 286
Felipe Oropeza Jr.

Image E

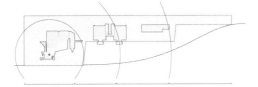

Progressive Purification, see pg. 276
David Hamm and Snoweria Zhang

Image B

Show/Flow, see pg. 352
Andrew Keating and Scott Smith

Image F

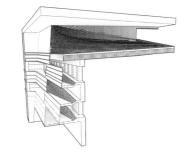

Progressive Purification, see pg. 276
David Hamm and Snoweria Zhang

Image C

Image D
Many of the Wellness Center's spaces are specifically designed to take advantage of the latent heat by-product of the WtE process, and further utilize the energy generated by the plant to cater light therapies and thermal qualities of spa spaces for the benefit of visitors and its exotic plant species.

Image E
This scheme provides for hybrid programs that create mutually beneficial components for the plant and the newly established uses. Waste that remains after recycling has been maximized passes back to the WtE stream, while by-products of the plant's production facilitate ongoing operations of the public programs.

Image F
The entertainment component of this program is meant to generate an ample supply of fuel for the WtE process, while using the outputs to provide energy for operations as well as facilitating the additional program of electric transit hub.

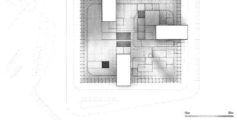

Wellness, Climate, Atmosphere, see pg. 296
Nastaran Arfaei and Jana Masset

Image D

255

HYBRIDIZE

In the moment of **expanded systems integration**, the systems and processes involved in the WtE process are enhanced and synergies are created to aid in tying the plant and hybrid into a larger infrastructural network. **Voyeurism**, an extension of the adjacency principle, allows the imagery of the industrial infrastructure to provide an engaging backdrop to program components of the hybrid.

EXPANDED SYSTEMS INTEGRATION

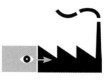

VOYEURISM

MEDIUM-SCALE STRATEGIES

HYBRIDIZE

ADJACENCY

COMMENSALISM

MUTUALISM

EXPANDED SYSTEM INTEGRATION

VOYEURISM

Image A
Not only does the Thermal Grove act as a heat sink for the tempering of hot process water to aid in district heating, but the additional hybrids proposed in the culinary programs provide new inputs to greenhouse operations while expanding the capacity of the WtE system to accept organic waste.

Image B
After examining the historical, physical, and legislative context in which the Wheelabrator plant in Baltimore currently exists, this project links the material and energy flows of the combustion plant with that of the aquaculture tanks in an approach that celebrates and expresses the synergistic operations.

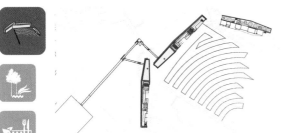

Thermal Grove, see pg. 330
Michael Clapp and Mike Johnson

Image A

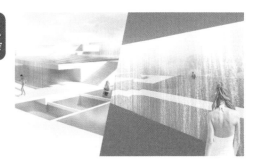

Pittsfield Thermal Baths
Nancy Nichols and Joshua Feldman

Image E

GREENHOU
RESIDUAL STR
ORGANIC STR
AQUAPON
Watellnk
Plants, Fish, Mushroom Pr
ANAEROI
DIGESTI

STACKˣ
Alberto Embriz de Salvatierra, Jennifer Hiser, and Larisa Ovalles

Image B

The (Re)creational Park, see pg. 306
Taehyun Jeon

Image F

Wast(ed)
Larissa Belcic, Elizabeth Biney-Amissah, and Clementine Jiang

Image C

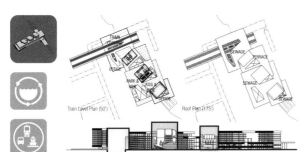

Train Cover Plan (50')   Roof Plan (175')

Catalytic Currents, see pg. 318
Michael Haggerty and Dana McKinney

Image D

Image C
A three-level glass-and-steel nightclub is proposed with direct viewing access into the bunker of the WtE facility.

Image D
Adjacent programming here involves the organization of a multimodal transit hub and a WtE plant.

Image E
Terracing along the sloped topography provides a gradation of private thermal baths.

Image F
This approach to creating hybridization facilitates engaging views of the industrial activities within while limiting physical access.

257

CIRCUMFERENCE OF PLANT

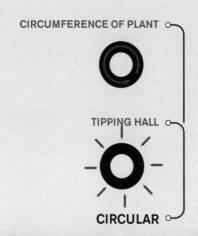

TIPPING HALL

CIRCULAR

ICONIZING

FRAMING
OPERATIONS

TIPPING HALL ACCESS

CHIMNEY

WINDOW

LINEAR

DIRECT ACCESS

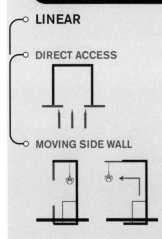

MOVING SIDE WALL

DOUBLE LOOP

BUNKER HALL

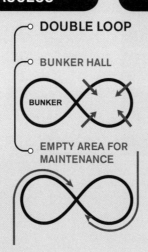

EMPTY AREA FOR
MAINTENANCE

CONCEALING

Small-Scale Strategies

CIRCULATION THROUGH POCHE

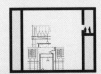

EXTERIOR PATHWAY

STRUCTURALLY ADAPTIVE

CORRIDOR

WALL

BRIDGE / GANTRY

DIRECT ADJACENCY

MODULAR CONSTRUCTION

Small-scale design strategies address individual components of a plant, attempting to add value to or optimize them. The WtE Design Lab identified a series of easily recognizable components that are typically associated with WtE plants, such as the chimney, stack, or tipping hall, and developed strategies to address their negative public perception or other nuisances that they may generate.

In some cases, such as the tipping hall, alternative organizations may make the process of arrival, weighing, tipping, and departing faster and more enclosed, thus reducing odors. In other cases, a specific tectonic system such the window or corridor may allow visitors to see the plant in operation, therefore making the processes more transparent to the general public.

Similar to the medium-scale strategies, each small strategy is accompanied by a number of techniques and operations that can be applied to an existing plant. Each operation is followed by examples where the specific strategy, technique, and operation has been tested in the option studio, seminar, and thesis advising offered by the WtE Design Lab.

(Re)Planned Obsolescence studio, site model

Prefabricated modular structural wall with aperture assembly

TIPPING HALL ACCESS AND CIRCULATION

Alongside the technical requirements, the layout of WtE plants is subject to certain local and project-specific boundary conditions. This has significant influence on the subsequent functionality and operation of the plant and any associated programs. Obtaining proper access to the tipping hall is one of the most critical aspects for proper operations.

Access granted in a **circular** manner via the circumference of the plant begins to define a strategy that breaks with the conventional linear processes of the typical WtE facility. This allows the opportunity to rethink the operations process as disseminating from the center out. The tipping hall may be placed at the center of the overall operations, with the potential to radiate the remaining operations outward in a much less restricted manner.

Access granted via a **double loop** from opposing entry points of the plant offers the chance to fragment the conventional **linear** WtE facility arrangement. Limited by technical restrictions imposed by the components themselves, the plant may potentially be dispersed over the site. The incinerator, for example, may not have to be located directly adjacent to the filter, just as the tipping may not have to be directly adjacent to the bunker. However, they must all be located within reasonably close proximity.

**CIRCULAR ACCESS
VIA CIRCUMFERENCE OF PLANT**

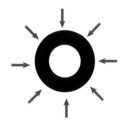

CIRCULAR ACCESS INTO TIPPING HALL

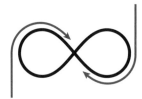

**DOUBLE LOOP ACCESS VIA
OPPOSING ENTRY POINTS OF PLANT**

**DOUBLE LOOP ACCESS
INTO TIPPING HALL**

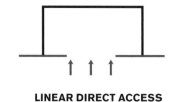

LINEAR DIRECT ACCESS

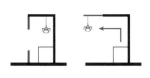

LINEAR MOVING SIDE WALL

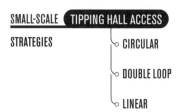

SMALL-SCALE **TIPPING HALL ACCESS**

STRATEGIES
- CIRCULAR
- DOUBLE LOOP
- LINEAR

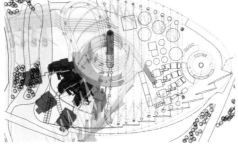

Show/Flow, see pg. 352
Andrew Keating and Scott Smith

Image A

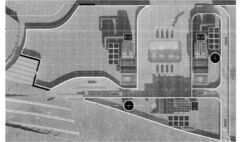

Heteroritc Architecture: Stacks, Chimneys, & Shoots
Joshua Feldman

Image B

Image A

In an attempt to create a more efficient traffic pattern for WtE plants, this proposal designed a helical delivery system for waste trucks to avoid congestion.

Image B

Note the fragmentation of the various WtE processes with respect to tipping hall access and circulation.

CHIMNEY

The chimney stack has long been a recognizable element of the industrial typology. Emblematic of a movement that began in the 18th century in which machinery and industry as a whole fundamentally changed a person's way of life, propositions for contemporary renditions of WtE plants seek to readapt this withstanding industrial element by **iconizing** it into more publicly engaging manifestations.

Other proposals, however, attempt to conceal or obscure the typical vertically extruded form of the chimney through strategic operations of **minimizing / concealing / transforming**. This facilitates integration into the urban or rural context. Technological advancements in industrial flue filtering technologies and delivery methods have made the need for such structures obsolete.

ICONIZING

MINIMIZING / TRANSFORMING / CONCEALING

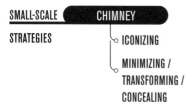

264

STACKˣ
Alberto Embriz de Salvatierra, Jennifer Hiser, and Larisa Ovalles

Image A

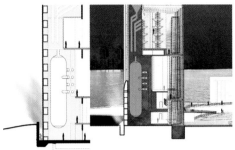

Thermal Grove, see pg. 330
Michael Clapp and Mike Johnson

Image E

Heteroritc Architecture: Stacks, Chimneys, & Shoots
Joshua Feldman

Image B

Waste, Reuse, and the PARKSpace, see pg. 286
Felipe Oropeza Jr.

Image C

Show/Flow, see pg. 352
Andrew Keating and Scott Smith

Image D

Image A
The smokestack's verticality is used to transform the negative perception of this industrial element by expressing the functions of the program and highlighting the material flows of the industrial ecology.

Image B
The multiplicity of vertical smokestack elements blends in with downtown Johannesburg's existing city skyline.

Image C
The visual impact of the chimney has been eliminated within the overall landscaped tectonics of the parklike topography.

Image D
The chimney stack has been developed as an integral part of the structure and function of the hybrid connections designed around the WtE plant. It is concealed from the exterior, however, by the draped roof structure.

Image E
In a small number of plants, reduced height stacks have been explored as an option for reducing visual impact of the plants in urban realms. This proposal has transformed the typical high-rising cylindrical stack with a linear diffusing well at the perimeter of the building, reinforcing its aesthetic design intentions.

WINDOW

Treatment of the facade can take many forms, with the window being one method of showcasing certain features of the WtE process. Windows, glazed or unglazed, may be implemented to not only allow in air and light, but to specify certain **framed apertures** both into and out of the plant. The desire to highlight the landscape comes with an inherent need to withhold views when necessary. This method of not exposing the whole view of the landscape initially engages our curiosities, which then allows us to question the space itself.

FRAMED APERTURES
INTERMITTENT OPENINGS
[PIXELATED] / ENSHROUDING
[DISSOLUTION] / SPECTACLE

Image A
The level of transparency, based on opening size and depth of the aperture, indicates to the visitor which spaces are accessibly visible to the public and which are reserved for private functions of the facility.

Image B
Operable glazed apertures are placed at strategic locations in the facade to serve dual functions: exposing the industrial workings within, and acting as maintenance access for regularly removing and repairing equipment.

Image C
A large glazed aperture over the bunker allows visitors to observe the waste feeding process from a unique perspective.

Image D
The modular diagrid allows plant components to be seen from the exterior. Specific interior moments provide educational viewing portals into the hydroponic and heat programs.

Image E
A continuous glazed surface exposes the internal working of the landformed roofscape structure.

Image F
Glazed pathways showcase the various phases of WtE processes for viewing and educational purposes.

Image G
The structural shell's large glazed skylight provides much needed southerly sun into the transit hall.

SMALL-SCALE   WINDOW
STRATEGIES   └○ FRAMED APERTURES

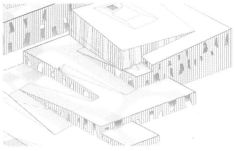

Image A

Waste, Reuse, and the PARKSpace, see pg. 286
Felipe Oropeza Jr.

Image E

The (Re)creational Park, see pg. 306
Taehyun Jeon

Image B

Thermal Grove, see pg. 330
Michael Clapp and Mike Johnson

Image F

The Architecture of Waste
Mariana Llano and Ivan Ruhle

Image C

Wellness, Climate, Atmosphere, see pg. 296
Nastaran Arfaei and Jana Masset

Image G

Show/Flow, see pg. 352
Andrew Keating and Scott Smith

Image D

5H Hybrid, see pg. 340
Alberto Embriz de Salvatierra

CORRIDOR

Coordination in terms of movement through and throughout a plant influences the organization of spaces within the building. A suspended or separated **bridge / gantry** walkway with a privileged view into the plant is one unique way of creating an educational procession, or otherwise facilitate circulation adjacent to the industrial components. **Circulation through poche**—or the infill spaces—of a structure can provide protected bounded corridors acting as subtle buffers between the harshness of the industry within and world outside. At times, the only way to experience and appreciate the impact of the technology serving the WtE process is to do so up close. A **direct adjacency** of circulation can help teach a skeptical public about WtE's progressive technology.

Locating unique vantage points from which to view the obscured internal workings via **exterior pathways** can be a way of engaging the greater public realm at a safe and protected distance. These pathways may be planned and integrated within a holistic urban and landscaping concept, developing strategies that ingrain the industrial processes of WtE within a larger masterplan.

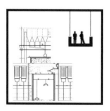

BRIDGE / GANTRY

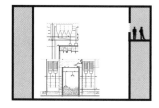

CIRCULATION THROUGH POCHE

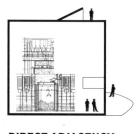

DIRECT ADJACENCY

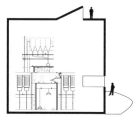

EXTERIOR PATHWAY

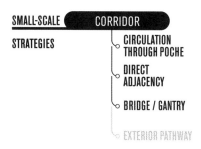

SMALL-SCALE STRATEGIES — CORRIDOR
- CIRCULATION THROUGH POCHE
- DIRECT ADJACENCY
- BRIDGE / GANTRY
- EXTERIOR PATHWAY

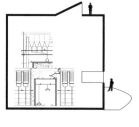

INTERIOR PATHWAY

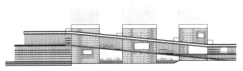

Catalytic Currents, see pg. 318
Michael Haggerty and Dana McKinney

Image A

Image E

The (Re)creational Park, see pg. 306
Taehyun Jeon

Progressive Purification, see pg. 276
David Hamm and Snoweria Zhang

Image B

Pedestrian

Waste, Reuse, and the PARKSpace, see pg. 286
Felipe Oropeza Jr.

Image F

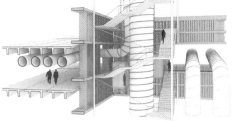

Catalytic Currents, see pg. 318
Michael Haggerty and Dana McKinney

Image C

Waste, Reuse, and the PARKSpace, see pg. 286
Felipe Oropeza Jr.

Image D

Image A
The use of elevated gantry-style walkways creates a sense of protection and separation from the plant's inner workings.

Image B
Passing through the poche space of the envelope creates a filtered experience of inside and out.

Image C
Exposure to the massive industrial elements occurs in areas of vertical circulation as service space and corridors become one.

Image D
In some schemes, a curated experience is developed to educate the public on the technology embedded in the WtE process.

Image E
Carefully placed apertures line the facility in this proposal to provide unobtrusive glimpses into the plant below.

Image F
The operations of carving slices through a man-made mound and articulating the adjacent facades as if the ground plane had been peeled up create a unique experience.

WALL

In a **structurally adaptive/innovative** proposal, the wall is no longer simply an architectural component used to define an area, carry a load, or provide enclosure from the elements. Such proposals rethink conventional construction methods to achieve an architectural proposition that negotiates between the required components and sequence of processes involved with the WtE facility and the hybrid.

Whether considered for immediate or a pre-planned future use, an endless tabulation of **modular construction methods** would provide an expandable catalog of interchangeable parts to facilitate a range of functional and structurally contingent apertures.

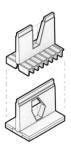

STRUCTURALLY ADAPTIVE / INNOVATIVE

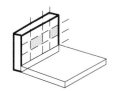

MODULAR CONSTRUCTION METHODS

Image A
Planning for the plant's afterlife, the structural envelope has modular openings to facilitate a variety of future programs such as residential or commercial use.

Image B
The diagrid structural system frees the interior for a variety of spatial organizations and uses.

Image C
Fabric-formed columns accept the vertical and trust forces of a draped structural shell, facilitating a unique sequence of free-flowing spaces.

SMALL-SCALE STRATEGIES — WALL
└ STRUCTURALLY ADAPTIVE / INNOVATIVE
└ MODULAR CONTRUCTION METHODS

270

Waste, Reuse, and the PARKSpace, see pg. 286
Felipe Oropeza Jr.

Image A

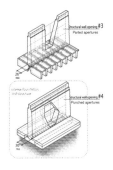

Waste, Reuse, and the PARKSpace, see pg. 286
Felipe Oropeza Jr.

Image E

5H Hybrid, see pg. 340
Alberto Embriz de Salvatierra

Image B

Catalytic Currents, see pg. 318
Michael Haggerty and Dana McKinney

Image F

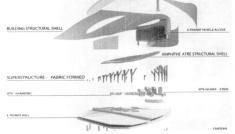

Show/Flow, see pg. 352
Andrew Keating and Scott Smith

Image C

Image D
Embedding the WtE facility within the cable-suspended megaslab creates opportunities to maximize internal spatial and organizational flows that would have been partially by conventional load bearing elements.

Image E
A catalog of modularly interchangeable precast structural components allows for a diverse range of programmatic and industrial uses while providing a varied visual expression of the facade.

Image F
The brise-soleil registers the pace of pedestrian circulation within the building and offers views into the WtE facility, offering a different composition on ovory face.

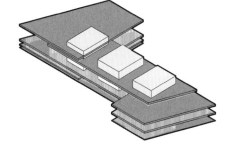

Catalytic Currents, see pg. 318
Michael Haggerty and Dana McKinney

Image D

Design Speculations

HANIF KARA AND LEIRE ASENSIO VILLORIA

STOCKHOLM	BRIDGEPORT	VÄSTERÅS	PRESTON

As part of the Waste-to-Energy (WtE) Design Lab's research, a design option studio was conducted at the Harvard University Graduate School of Design in spring 2016. The studio was led by Hanif Kara and Leire Asensio Villoria, with participating students from the Graduate School of Design's Departments of Architecture and Landscape Architecture. The studio focused on the development of architectural designs that outline both the strategy and feasibility for initiating hybrid combinations between the industrial infrastructures associated with the WtE process and other potential public or private programs, as well as functions that may benefit from this synergistic relationship.

Despite the recent emergence of a number of novel industrial buildings, the role of the designer, and specifically the architect, has been largely absent from this field of design inquiry. This can, in part, be due to the perceived absence of clearly defined roles for architecture to play in the formulation of these complex and predominantly technical buildings. The rare engagement by the design field with the technical and economic constraints as well as ecological challenges surrounding these building types can be explained by a general perception of a lack of scope for design innovation.

The studio addressed how these often very large, blank buildings may be integrated both physically and programmatically within their urban or suburban contexts, and how the generally negative perception of industrial buildings may be strategically challenged by design. As a result of the projected need for integration within existing neighborhoods and environments, the students were expected to produce design solutions to develop hybrid WtE facility types that adopt a new role for these buildings in communicating or connecting with the wider public. There was also a focus on exploring the possibility of weaving new public or institutional programs into the energy production chain that could be mutually beneficial for the operational practices of these facilities and the wider public constituencies and stakeholders. The new typologies and design concepts developed in the studio offer hybrid WtE building solutions that generate clean energy, contribute to the city's social and cultural activities, and integrate proven technology solutions with novel approaches toward the organization and design at the building, landscape, neighborhood, and/or material scales.

Our primary field of investigation was in Sweden and the northeastern United States, two countries with differing stages of engagement with WtE technologies. More specifically, the sites were located in Bridgeport and Preston, in Connecticut, and Mälarenergi Västerås and Högdalen, in Sweden. Each of these sites currently has a WtE plant in operation, which in some cases has reached the end of its life. The students were tasked with developing new schemes as alternatives that would replace the existing WtE facilities. Building on the current master plans for these sites, the students found opportunities to systematically and conceptually define novel urban qualities, performances, and experiences through the hybridization of the WtE infrastructures.

(Re)Planned Obsolescence, studio final review

Project Högdalenverket CHP-Plant

Date 1970

Owner Fortum Värme and the City of Stockhom

Operator Fortum Värme

Status operating

Technology mass burn

Capacity approx. 1,752 tonnes per day

No. of boilers 7 (4 use household waste)

Gross electric capacity 422 MW (69,205 households)

Full-time employees 840

Customers served 11,700 (from 17 municipalities)

20,000	40,000	60,000	80,000	100,000	120,000	140,000	160,000	180,000	200,000

site area (sq. m) — **62,124**

5,000	10,000	15,000	20,000	25,000	30,000	35,000	40,000	45,000	50,000

building footprint (sq. m) — **20,256**

75,000	150,000	225,000	300,000	375,000	450,000	525,000	600,000	675,000	750,000

waste input (tonnes/year) — **613,200**

10,000	20,000	30,000	40,000	50,000	60,000	70,000	80,000	90,000	100,000

electric output (households) — **69,205**

Högdalen is a suburban district of Stockholm, located about 7 km south of Stockholm's city center. It is bordered by the districts of Bandhagen, Fagersjö, Gubbängen Örby, and Rågsved. Högdalen itself was originally planned around the metro station. Near the metro in the city center, it is roughly divided into distinct residential and commercial areas, with an industrial area and landfill further east.

As of 2011, the population of Högdalen was 7,862 people. When distributed over an area of 2.01 sq. km, this result in an average density of about 3.911 per sq. km. Like much of Stockholm, Högdalen is growing and there is a projected increase in demand for new homes. The area around the plant is currently slated for residential housing development. In the area south of Stockholm's city center, upwards of forty thousand new homes are planned for construction by 2030.

HÖGDALEN DISTRICT, STOCKHOLM, SWEDEN

Progressive Purification

DAVID HAMM
SNOWERIA ZHANG

Politically and geographically situated in the context of the ongoing humanitarian refugee crisis in Europe, and Sweden's tensions concerning their pro-migrant stance within growing isolationist sentiment from neighboring countries, this project seeks to provide a refuge that would alleviate the inevitable isolation and anxiety experienced by these migrating people when settling in a foreign country with a different language, culture, climate, and religious affiliation.

A suburb of Stockholm, Högdalen has rapidly become a center for immigrants, with growing communities of Muslims inhabiting what is projected to become some of the most residentially sought-after properties in Stockholm. Municipal projections exceeding upward of forty thousand new homes are to be developed in the Stockholm suburbs within the next several decades.

Considering the high concentration of Muslim immigrants and the fact that the site is also situated on a man-made hill overlooking one of Stockholm's highest points, this project proposes a mutually dynamic WtE/mosque hybrid. This hybrid condition links the WtE processes with those that fulfill the hill's sacred role in Islam. The hill plays an important part in symbolically collapsing the city by visually linking peripheral residential areas with the city center.

As many obsolete industrial sites are being absorbed by expanding city centers, this project explores the role of architecture in reconciling both the perceived and physical dualism of an industrial and spiritually endearing place of refuge.

View of roof park with city of Stockholm beyond

ADJACENCY

Islam is about purification. The organization of the project relates this process of purification to cleanliness. The building is divided into four distinct units with interstitial spaces in between. These "lungs" serve climatic and pragmatic roles by directing air and stormwater flows as well as creating volumetric buffers, atriums, and circulation spaces.

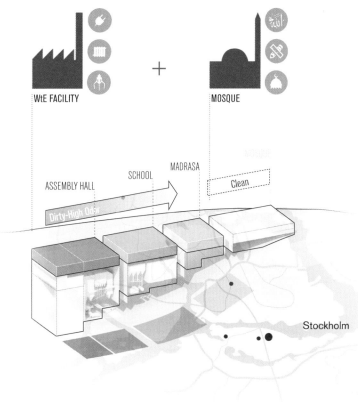

WtE FACILITY

+

MOSQUE

ASSEMBLY HALL   SCHOOL   MADRASA   Clean

Dirty-High Odor

Stockholm

Program diagram

 Högdalen WtE

EFFICIENT LOCALIZED ENERGY NETWORK

The WtE process itself involves a
progressive purification beginning
with high-odor waste. Resources flow
between the process components and
the urban networks of waste, electricity,
and heat.

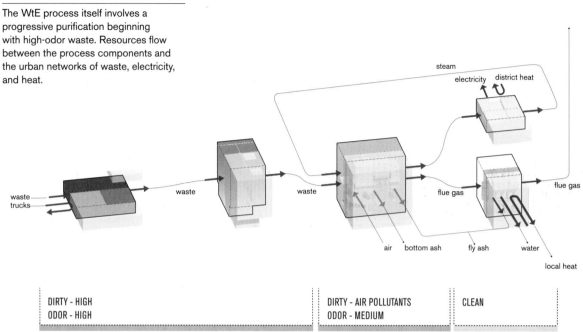

waste
trucks

waste

waste

flue gas

steam

electricity   district heat

flue gas

air   bottom ash   fly ash   water

local heat

DIRTY - HIGH	DIRTY - AIR POLLUTANTS	CLEAN
ODOR - HIGH	ODOR - MEDIUM	

WtE operations

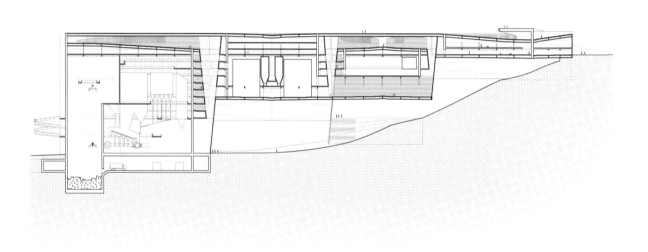

MUTUALISM

Each spatially distinct program shares climatic, structural, and accessibility resources with the others.

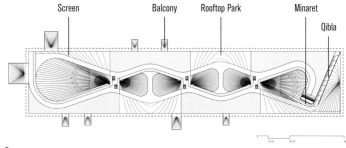

Screen · Balcony · Rooftop Park · Minaret · Qibla

Roof plan

EMBEDDING/BUILDING UP

The project capitalizes the existing site topography, embedding the facility in its surrounding landscape.

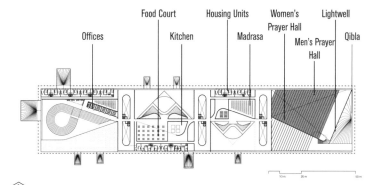

Offices · Food Court · Kitchen · Housing Units · Madrasa · Women's Prayer Hall · Men's Prayer Hall · Lightwell · Qibla

Mosque level plan

HA-HA

From the top of the existing hill and the new roof park, the form of the building visually obscures the WtE facility.

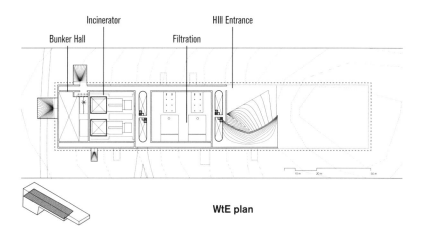

Bunker Hall · Incinerator · Filtration · Hill Entrance

WtE plan

Compressed city section

The diagram below demonstrates the relative height of the WtE facility and mosque in comparison to Stockholm's city center.

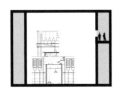

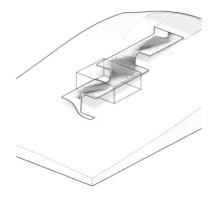

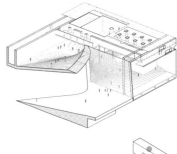

CIRCULATION THROUGH POCHE

The WtE plant and the hill deal with height
in a significant way, so vertical circulation
becomes very important.

In order to address both accessibility and
continuity of spaces, the design adopts a
surface topology that begins with a stair
and extends to a ramp on the exterior,
with semi-occupiable park space on the
interior. This system is applied at three
different scales within the project: the large
scale, in which a park is created; medium
scale, within the lungs, to provide service
access and to delay the air flow; and small
scale, as a part of the plant circulation for
workers and visitors.

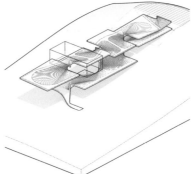

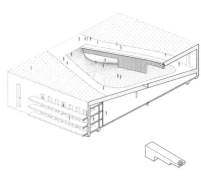

Rooftop park

REVEALING FACADE

The WtE zone of the building is contained
within shear walls on either side, creating
a single span toward the top of the hill. All
of the facades are clad with screens that
provide varying levels of privacy for the
interiors, with the greatest level of opacity
concentrated around the industrial
equipment.

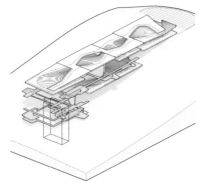

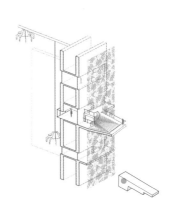

Circulation

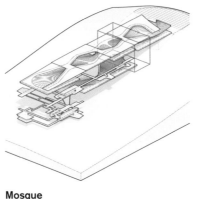

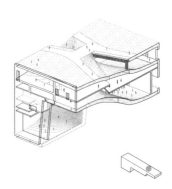

Mosque

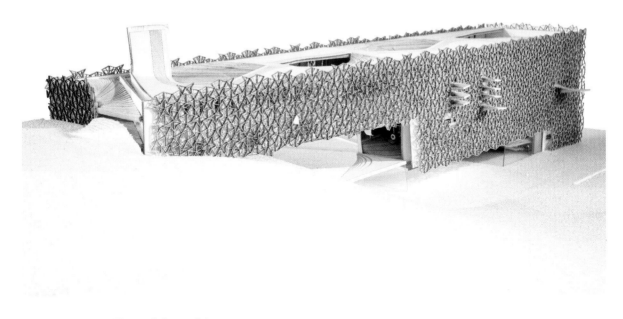

Views of site model

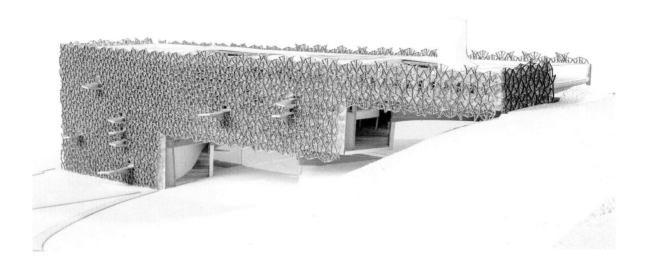

STORMWATER MANAGEMENT

Stormwater is utilized as part of a heat exchange system to mediate the air temperature between different public spaces, providing irrigation for plants within the project lungs.

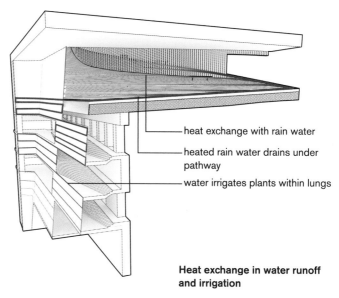

heat exchange with rain water

heated rain water drains under pathway

water irrigates plants within lungs

Heat exchange in water runoff and irrigation

STACK EFFECT

The building's form passively controls air temperature, slowing the upward rise of warm air from the lungs. This results in a warm rooftop park space that mediates the climatic differences between Sweden and the Middle East.

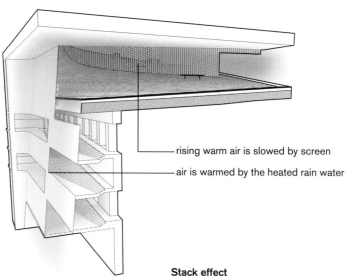

rising warm air is slowed by screen

air is warmed by the heated rain water

Stack effect

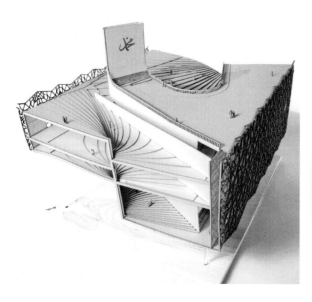

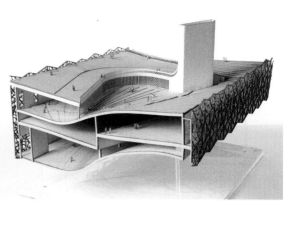

Views of sectional model

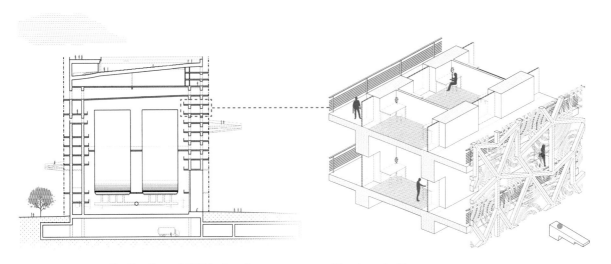

Section through WtE incinerator

Structure of offices

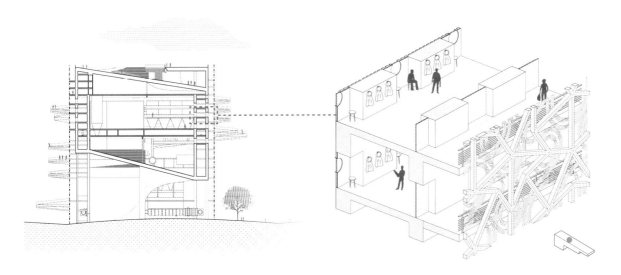

Section through WtE filters

Structure of staging area

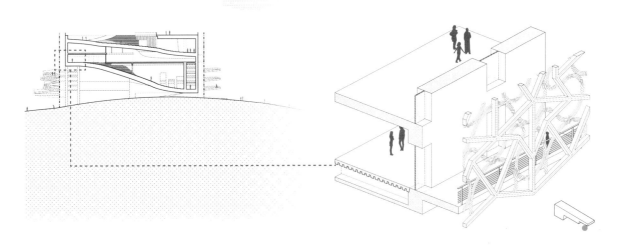

Section through mosque

Mosque structure

283

View of men's prayer hall

View of Stockholm from within mosque

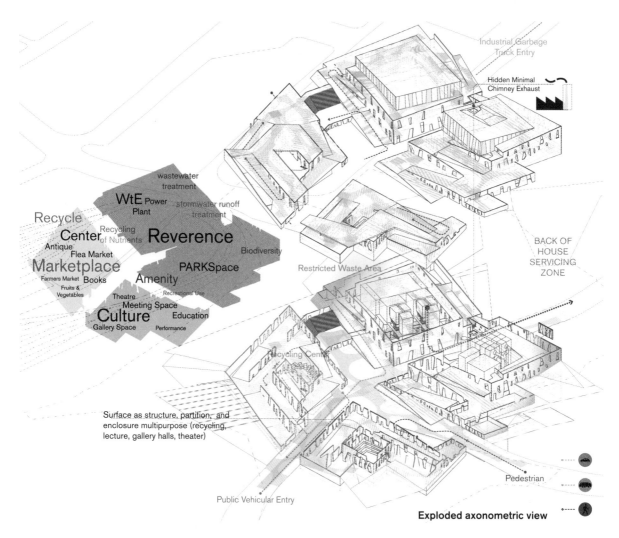

Industrial Garbage Truck Entry

Hidden Minimal Chimney Exhaust

wastewater treatment

WtE Power Plant

stormwater runoff treatment

Recycle

Center Recycling of Nutrients

Reverence

Antique

Flea Market

Biodiversity

Marketplace

PARKSpace

BACK OF HOUSE SERVICING ZONE

Farmers Market Books

Amenity

Restricted Waste Area

Fruits & Vegetables

Theatre

Recreational Use

Meeting Space

Culture Education

Gallery Space Performance

Recycling Center

Surface as structure, partition, and enclosure multipurpose (recycling, lecture, gallery halls, theater)

Pedestrian

Public Vehicular Entry

Exploded axonometric view

Waste, Reuse, and the PARKspace

FELIPE OROPEZA JR.

Forecasts indicate a 25 percent projected increase in Stockholm's population by 2030, and Högdalen is no exception. This proposal seeks to integrate a design strategy for a future WtE power station, landscape park, community recycling center, and marketplace that facilitates the notion of reuse as a critical practice within its localized industrial waste management ecosystem.

Inspired by a scaled-down version of Stockholm's Green Wedge approach to urban planning, which implements a region-wide system of interlinked park and open spaces that preserve natural areas for ecological and human health, this strategy considers such factors as networks of flows, circulation, and accessibly within the greater landscape, proposing three distinct zones of culture, marketplace, and industry.

The notion of the parkspace as the canvas on which to integrate via burying and land-forming the WtE processes thus becomes integral to the project. A 20 x 20 m grid, derived from a car-parking module, governs the underlying organizational fabric that ultimately provides the means to hybridize and bring a synergy to all programmatic, circulatory, and structural components.

SITE STRATEGY

1. Adaptively Interlink
The primary arteries of transportation appropriate existing paths across the site to facilitate new linkages between the current and future proposed housing developments. Flows related to waste are separately maintained from those of the general public

2. Resituate
The preliminary extents of the proposed facility and its necessary components are situated within the new schematic network of paths

3. Calibrate Sprawl
The various required WtE components, programs, and overall formal arrangement are negotiated in relation to the topography, the proposed network of flows, and any additional considerations regarding the public communal space

4. Accentuate and Populate
The widening of the primary communal axes of transportation and establishment of secondary linkages emphasizes the importance of accessing the public realm

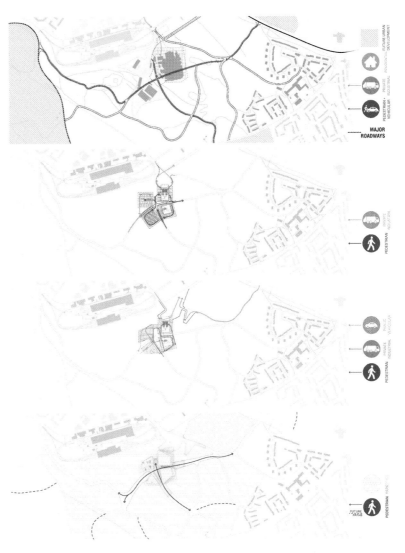

Waste management hierarchy of Högdalen
Considering that approximately 100,000 new homes are projected to be built, enabling more people to live and work in the same area, this project streamlines the waste management process via an emphasis on prevention.

The inclusion of a marketplace-type function, such as a flea market, speaks to the aspect of prevention and reuse currently lacking at the site; prevention and reuse are the two main strategies in the waste management hierarchy.

Proposed waste management

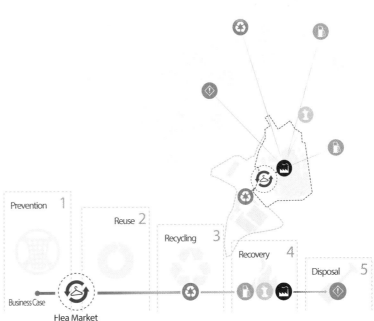

EFFICIENT LOCALIZED
ENERGY NETWORK

The production and distribution of energy will coordinate with the surrounding urban development to maximize an efficient network of energy flows.

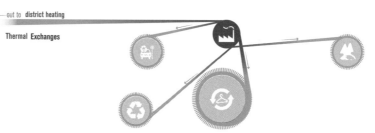

EXPANDED SYSTEM BOUNDARIES

Interconnected flows and exchanges of recyclable material and waste occur between the various actors and public visitors on site. Every actor contributes to the prevention and reuse of waste, but what makes this possible is the active participation of the general public.

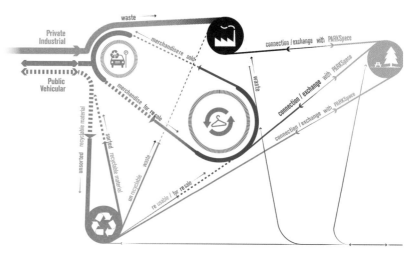

User and resource flows

SUN ANALYSIS / SHADING +
WIND ANALYSIS / SHIELDING / DIRECTING

A consistently south, southwesterly annual prevailing wind and solar exposure are critical considerations concerning the orientation and eventual placement of the project on site.

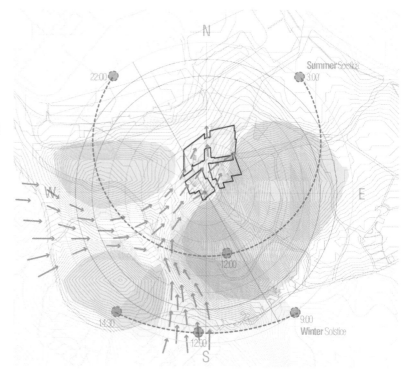

Path of sun and annual prevailing wind

288

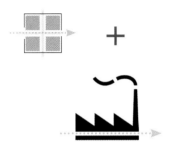

SHOWCASE THROUGH CIRCULATION /
MAJOR AXIAL PROCESSION

Major thoroughfares of public space provide the interstitial space that allows the variously programmed zones room to breathe, both figuratively and literally, underscoring the distinction between each zone. The thoroughfares act as a pedestrian-oriented public piazza, paved to approximate human-scaled outdoor rooms surrounded on all sides by buildings and additional passageways, facilitating the activity of people watching.

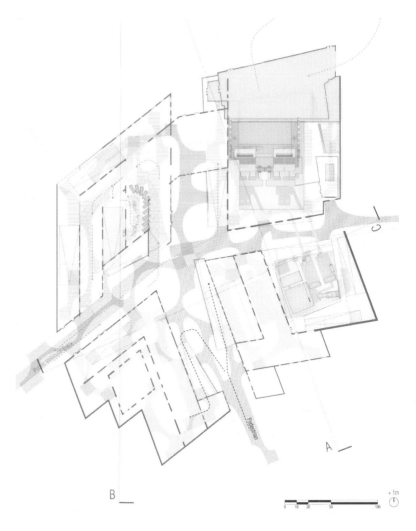

FRAGMENTATION

Fragmentation of the incinerating and filtering components allows each to exist as a separate piece of the larger whole. Each component highlights the perception of being a polluter versus the reality of having low emissions.

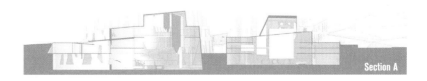

Section A

BURIAL / LANDFORMING

Burial and landforming of the WtE components are techniques undertaken to reduce the facility's prominence while camouflaging its true scale. This plays to the aspect of the spectacle when the hidden is revealed.

Section B

Section C

MODULAR + STRUCTURALLY ADAPTIVE
CONSTRUCTION METHODS

Considerations for post-occupancy use at the moment of obsolescence include adapting the site for a future mixed-use housing development. Implementations of modular and structurally adaptive construction methods would facilitate this transition while minimizing waste and labor costs.

EXTERIOR PATHWAY WITH FRAMED VIEWS
EDUCATIONAL TOOL

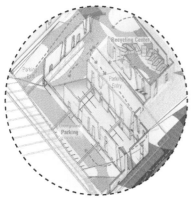

Underground parking

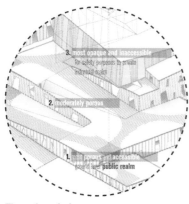

Three facade layers

Calibrated Transparency

This project highlights the nuances of the dynamic multilayered sequence of operations via an architectural exploration of the wall ground, roof, and roof surface. This offers the opportunity to seamlessly integrate the WtE components in their landscape context.

Framed opportunities occur within and throughout providing the spectator unique vantage points that both showcase and educate the public about various critical operations within the complex.

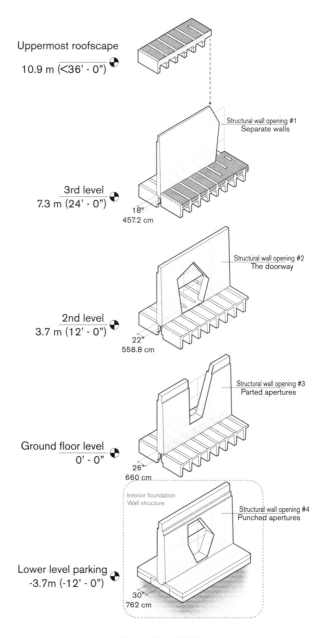

Concrete wall hierarchy

290

View from within the marketplace zone overlooking the recycling center's daily operations

View from within the WtE power plant observing–but also learning about–the Waste-to-Energy operations of the power station

View from roofscape overlooking the public interior courtyard

OBSOLESCENCE AND POST OCCUPANCY

Phase 1
Clear site of WtE components. Recycle steel frame enclosure and prepare the now-empty structural concrete shell for development.

Phase 2
Implement housing development plans prepared in advance of the planned obsolescence. These include plans for new underground parking, mixed-use, and residential development. The marketplace and culture zones of amenities will continue to exist and function on site.

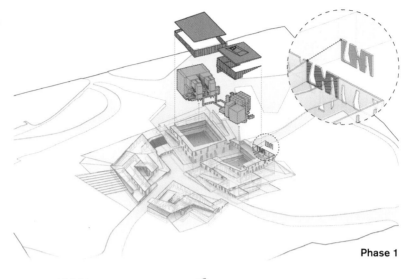

Phase 1

Multi-Bedroom Flat
102-129 sq. m two story flat (several special case unit will be larger).

Housing Units
A selection of various housing types ranging from studio to two-to-three-bedroom units. Working with both the local Högdalen and greater Stockholm governmental agencies in conjunction with a few private collaborators, emphasis will be placed on providing low- to middle-income affordable units to the area.

Marketplace (retail) *existing*
marketplace zone flea market, farmers market small locally managed retail establishments

Mixed-Use (culture zone) *existing*
cultural, recreational, institutional

Basic Studio Flat
76 sq. m flat, featuring a public entry garden and a small private terrace

Residential *proposed*

Mixed-Use *proposed*
commercial, cultural, institutional, or industrial

Underground Parking
proposed multilevel car park

Phase 2

Phase 3
This will be a 300- to 350-unit housing development around a central courtyard and in relative proximity to a variety of amenities offered for private residential and greater public use.

Additional considerations in terms of accessibility, proposed use, and climate in the absence of the former power station will need to be carefully reconsidered at various stages of the facility's life and obsolescence.

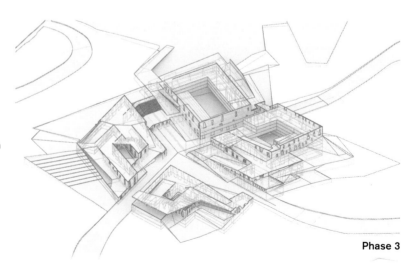

Phase 3

Phases of obsolescence

View from marketplace roofscape
overlooking the public interior
courtyard space

View from the zone of reverence /
marketplace roofscape overlooking
public interior areas of performance
and spectacle

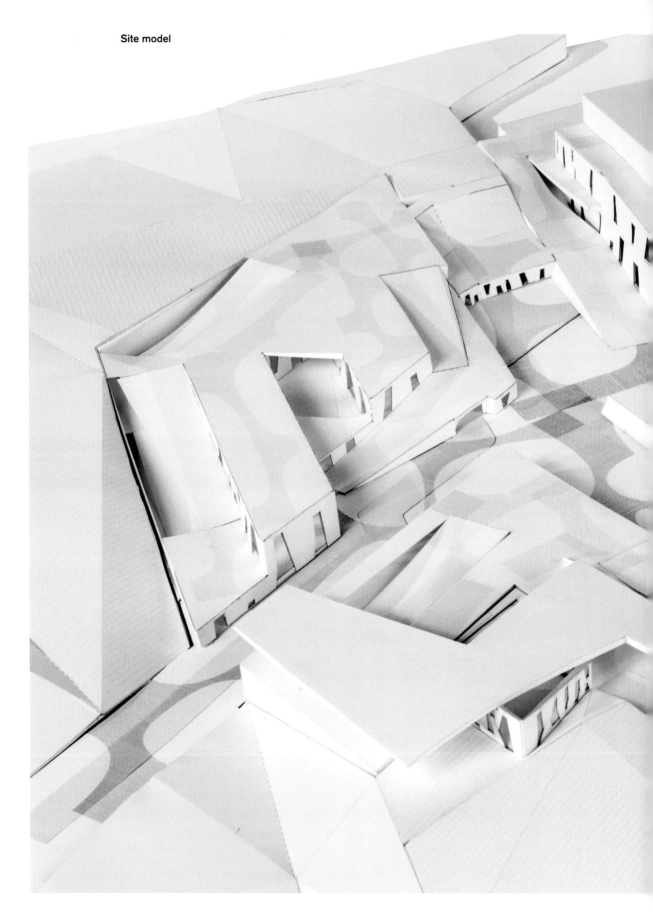

Site model

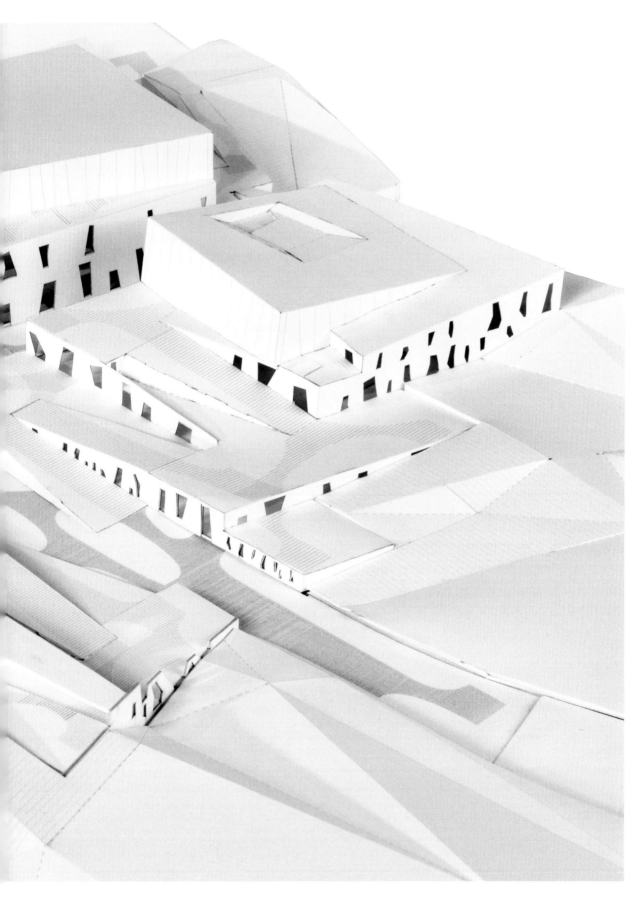

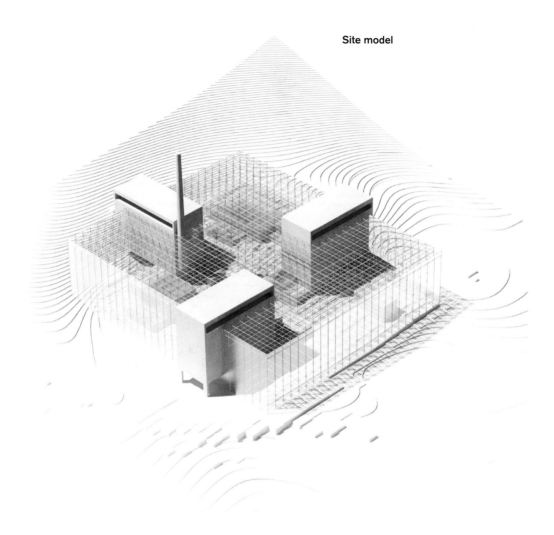

Wellness, Climate, Atmosphere

NASTARAN ARFAEI
JANA MASSET

The Högdalen WtE facility is located in suburban Stockholm, within a 15-minute walk from several residential neighborhoods, recreation facilities, commercial and industrial properties, and two subway stations. The building scale and program hybrids were developed in response to both these immediate and broader contexts.

Generally speaking, the goal of WtE technology is to conserve resources through minimizing energy loss. If considered through the lens of emergy—"an expression of all the energy used in the work processes that generate a product or service"—as described by Howard Odum, aside from information, human services require the greatest energy investment.[1] This hybrid proposal therefore minimizes energy loss in two distinct ways: by using resources such

as excess heat from the WtE facility to support other programs, and by promoting human wellness in support of social and economic productivity. The programmatic proposal includes guest lodging, a wellness program including therapeutic and spa spaces, and biofuel greenhouses.[2]

Theses:
1. Resource conservation can be achieved through symbiotic relationships between programs.
2. Human wellness is not only economically valuable through the conservation of emergy, but is also supported by Swedish cultural values.
3. Encountering a sublime industrial space in a suburban context can promote visitors' wellness by providing an escape from everyday routine and generating collective curiosity.

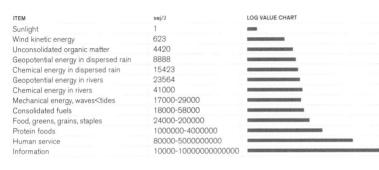

ITEM	sej/J	LOG VALUE CHART
Sunlight	1	
Wind kinetic energy	623	
Unconsolidated organic matter	4420	
Geopotential energy in dispersed rain	8888	
Chemical energy in dispersed rain	15423	
Geopotential energy in rivers	23564	
Chemical energy in rivers	41000	
Mechanical energy, waves<tides	17000-29000	
Consolidated fuels	18000-58000	
Food, greens, grains, staples	24000-200000	
Protein foods	1000000-4000000	
Human service	80000-5000000000	
Information	10000-10000000000000	

← Typical solar transformities (solar emjoules per joule)

↙ Prevalence of Seasonal Affective Disorder (SAD) in Sweden

↓ Site plan

↓ Waste collection network
We propose collecting waste from the city of Stockholm though a network of remote sorting and shredding stations placed along the extensive rail lines. The waste would be delivered by train to a tipping point adjacent to the facility.

800,000
people in Sweden suffer from SAD

300,000
report severe or disabling symptoms [2]

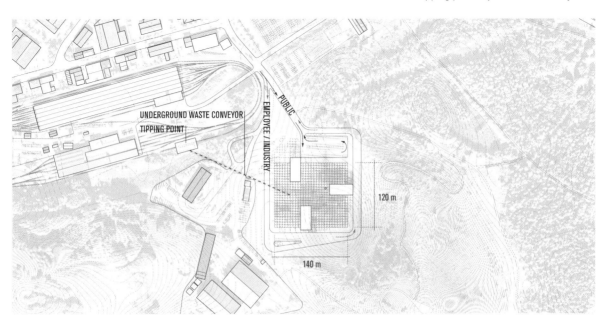

UNDERGROUND WASTE CONVEYOR
TIPPING POINT
PUBLIC
EMPLOYEE / INDUSTRY
120 m
140 m

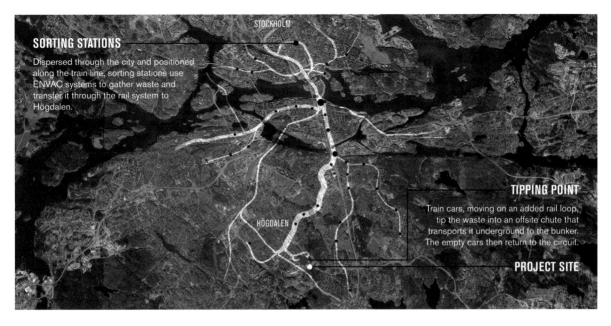

STOCKHOLM

SORTING STATIONS
Dispersed through the city and positioned along the train line, sorting stations use ENVAC systems to gather waste and transfer it through the rail system to Högdalen.

HÖGDALEN

TIPPING POINT
Train cars, moving on an added rail loop, tip the waste into an offsite chute that transports it underground to the bunker. The empty cars then return to the circuit.

PROJECT SITE

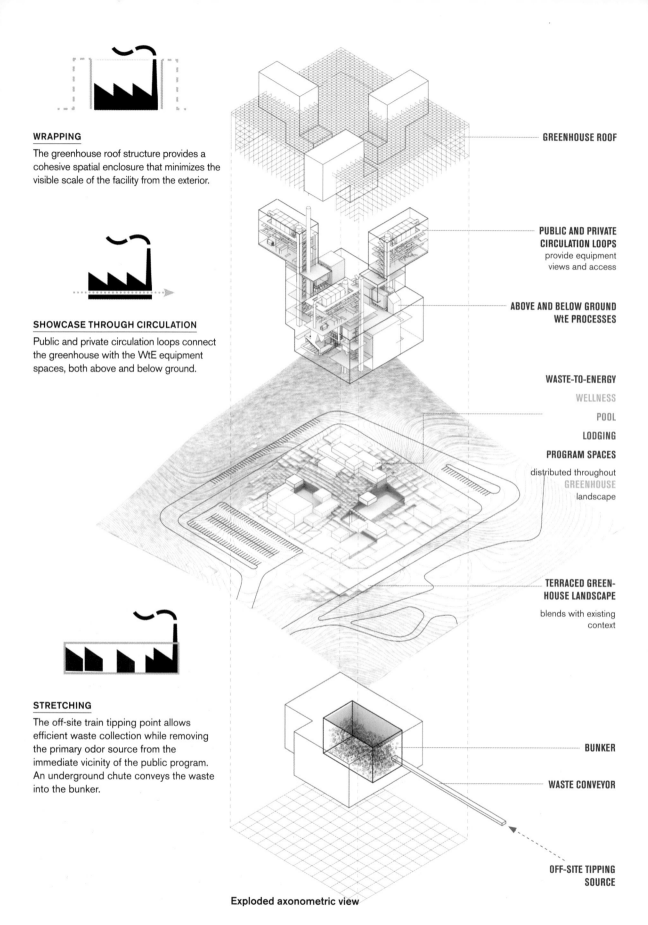

WRAPPING

The greenhouse roof structure provides a cohesive spatial enclosure that minimizes the visible scale of the facility from the exterior.

SHOWCASE THROUGH CIRCULATION

Public and private circulation loops connect the greenhouse with the WtE equipment spaces, both above and below ground.

STRETCHING

The off-site train tipping point allows efficient waste collection while removing the primary odor source from the immediate vicinity of the public program. An underground chute conveys the waste into the bunker.

GREENHOUSE ROOF

PUBLIC AND PRIVATE CIRCULATION LOOPS provide equipment views and access

ABOVE AND BELOW GROUND WtE PROCESSES

WASTE-TO-ENERGY WELLNESS POOL LODGING **PROGRAM SPACES**

distributed throughout GREENHOUSE landscape

TERRACED GREEN-HOUSE LANDSCAPE

blends with existing context

BUNKER

WASTE CONVEYOR

OFF-SITE TIPPING SOURCE

Exploded axonometric view

COMMENSALISM

MUTUALISM

Program resource flow
The WtE, wellness, and greenhouse programs have a network of resource sharing that embodies both commensalism and mutualism in different cases.

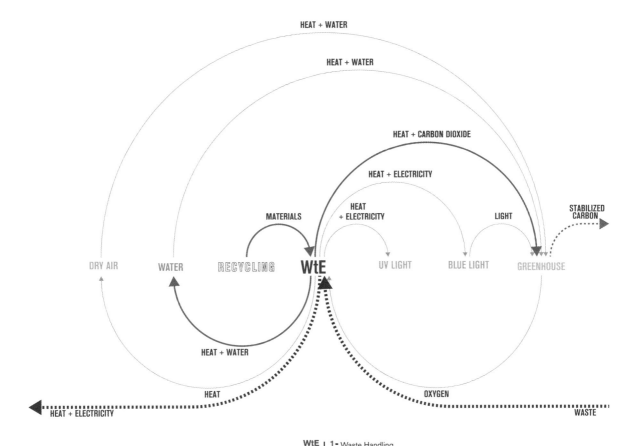

HEAT + WATER

HEAT + WATER

HEAT + CARBON DIOXIDE

HEAT + ELECTRICITY

HEAT + ELECTRICITY

MATERIALS

HEAT + ELECTRICITY

LIGHT

STABILIZED CARBON

DRY AIR   WATER   RECYCLING   WtE   UV LIGHT   BLUE LIGHT   GREENHOUSE

HEAT + WATER

HEAT

OXYGEN

HEAT + ELECTRICITY

WASTE

WtE
1 - Waste Handling
2 - Incineration
3 - Filtering
4 - Super Heater
5 - Economizer
6 - Monitoring
7 - Chimney
8 - Auxilary Equipment

Greenhouse
9 - Hot Greenhouse
10 - Warm Greenhouse
11 - Cool Greenhouse

Therapy
12 - Consulting
13 - UV Therapy
14 - Blue Light Therapy
15 - Warm Water
16 - Dry Air

Light intensity

Light Intensity

Humidity

Humidity

Temperature

Temperature

Environmental condition requirements
The WtE equipment operates at a range of temperatures. Each of the wellness programs requires a specific climatic environment for effective treatment as well as human comfort. The biofuel plants grown in the greenhouse require three different climate zones. The ideal climatic conditions of light intensity, temperature, and humidity were plotted for each of our program spaces. This becomes an organizational tool to understand either the adjacencies between different spaces or the type of material barrier required between them. In this sense, the distance between programs in each axis translates to a material barrier related to that climatic condition or physical distance between the programs.

Program organization and evaluation

Following the development of multiple options for the organization of the WtE core, climatic and more pragmatic requirements were used to develop a set of rules to guide the process of placing program spaces around these cores. For example, the greenhouses were distributed based on heat flow analysis, and their climates were used to mediate between different programs' required conditions. The resulting options were evaluated based on the criteria listed in this table, with their scores interpolated to a scale of 1 through 5. Higher scores were assigned to those with greater independence of entrances, less distance between WtE lines, smaller volumes of above-ground WtE enclosures, less displaced earth due to excavation, and greater shared area between the wellness and WtE programs.

Independence of Entrances
Distance Between WtE Lines
Maximum volume of WtE Enclosure
Volume of Displaced Earth
Interface Between Therapy and WtE
SUM

Preliminary massing model

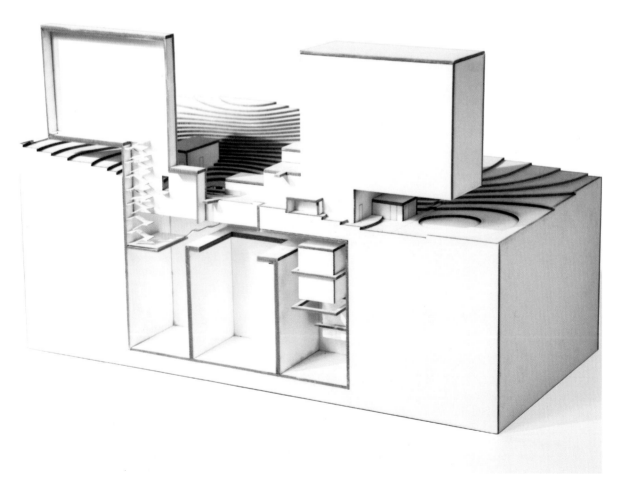

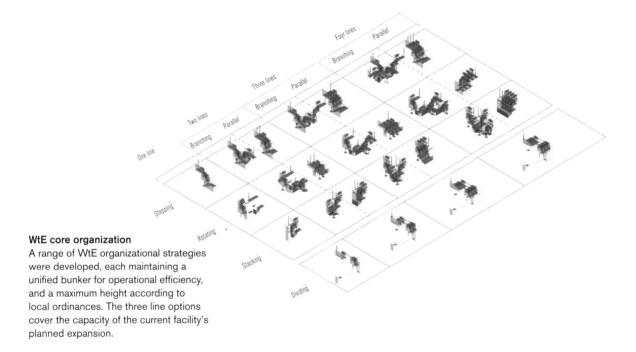

2	3	3	4	5	5
5	5	5	2	2	1
2	2	2	5	4	4
2	4	5	5	3	1
4	4	1	5	2	3
15	18	16	**21**	16	14

WtE core organization

A range of WtE organizational strategies were developed, each maintaining a unified bunker for operational efficiency, and a maximum height according to local ordinances. The three line options cover the capacity of the current facility's planned expansion.

Site Model

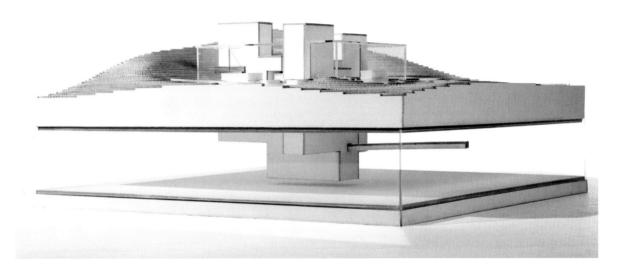

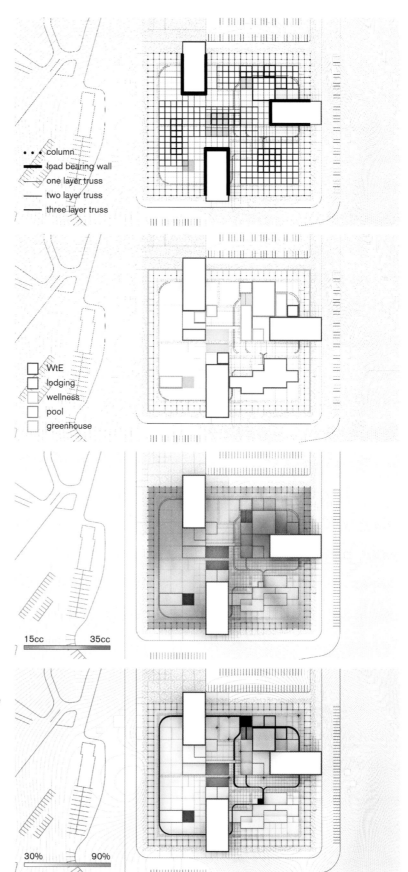

Greenhouse enclosure

Supported by the three WtE concrete cores, as well as vertical elements along the outer walls, the greenhouse is enclosed by a Vierendeel truss. The roof depth increases with greater distance from the supports. Its thin structural members, with a reflective chrome finish, maximize access to natural light within the greenhouse. Glare is minimized by using treated glass for the enclosure.

- • • column
- ▬ load bearing wall
- ⟋ one layer truss
- — two layer truss
- — three layer truss

Program distribution

The WtE processes are contained underground and in three cores above ground. Each of the wellness and lodging spaces are distributed throughout the varying greenhouse environments.

- ☐ WtE
- ☐ lodging
- ☐ wellness
- ☐ pool
- ☐ greenhouse

Temperature distribution

Heat is generated by two independent sources. First, the chimney insulation is reduced to provide heat to the adjacent space. Second, a network of open water channels, heated through a closed loop system, run throughout the project and are concentrated according to heat requirements.

15cc   35cc

Humidity distribution

Humidity is provided through the open water channel network, pool spaces in the spa program, and supplemental misting fixtures placed within the landscape.

30%   90%

1

BURYING

Burying is used as a strategy to not only minimize the visual impact of the plant from the exterior, but also to encourage visitor curiosity and further exploration by creating an unexpected encounter with this sublime industrial equipment within the space.

2

VOYEURISM

A large opening in the landscape and an accessible glass ceiling over the bunker allow visitors to observe the waste-feeding process from a unique perspective.

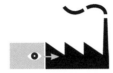

3

BRIDGE / GANTRY

Public and private service walkways provide access to the above- and below-ground WtE equipment spaces.

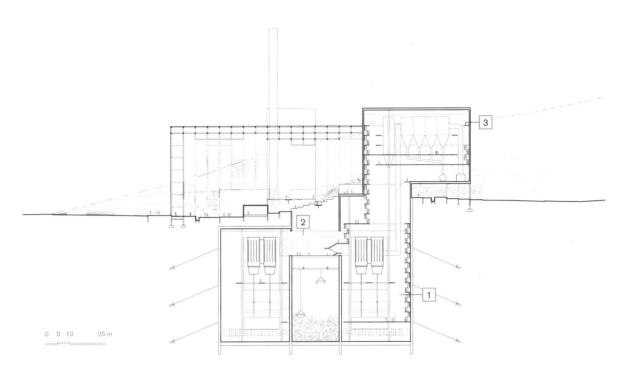

0 5 10   25 m

3

2

1

Section

Atmospheric concept

While producing dramatically varying atmospheric qualities throughout the project, planned adjacencies allow barriers to have minimal presence within the space.

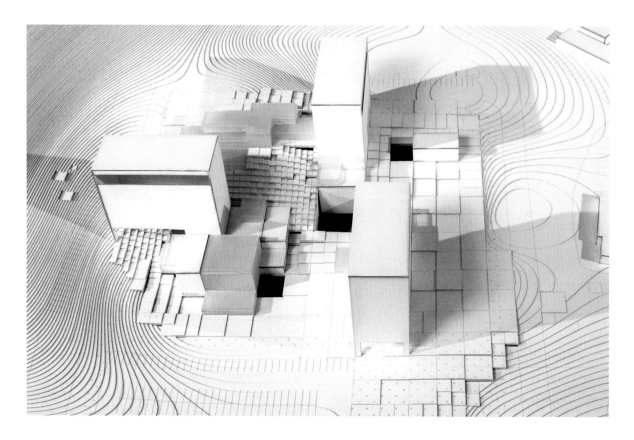

Site model

SOFT BUFFER

The varied greenhouse climates act as a buffer to minimize the necessity for climate control of each program space within the project.

NOTES

1. Emergy, defined by Wikipedia, https://en.wikipedia.org/wiki/Emergy; and Howard T. Odum, "Self-Organization, Transformity, and Information," *Science 242*, no. 4882 (Nov. 25, 1988): 1132–39.

2. C. Rastad, P. O. Sjödén, and J. Ulfberg, "High Prevalence of Self-reported Winter Depression in a Swedish County," *Psychiatry and Clinical Neurosciences*, no. 59, vol. 6 (2005): 666–75.

Interior view

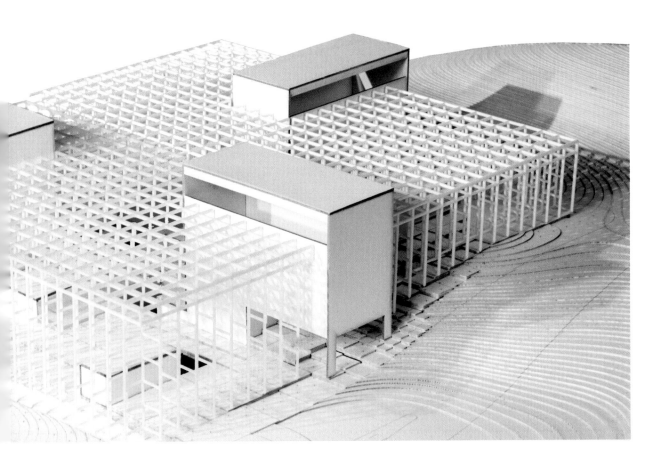

305

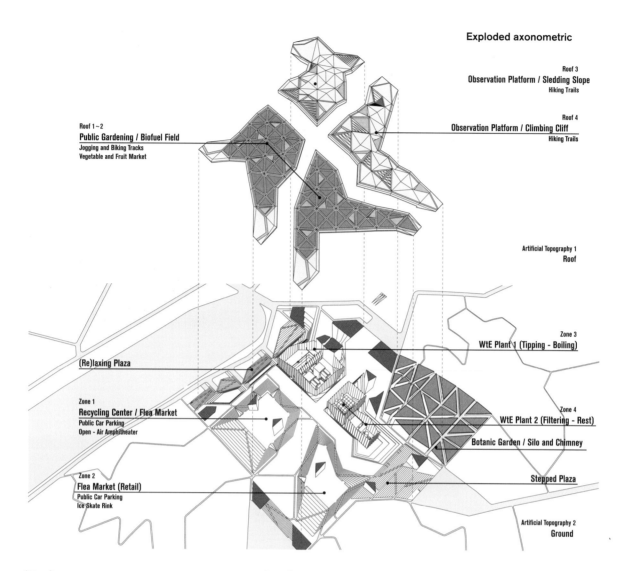

Exploded axonometric

Roof 3
Observation Platform / Sledding Slope
Hiking Trails

Roof 4
Observation Platform / Climbing Cliff
Hiking Trails

Roof 1~2
Public Gardening / Biofuel Field
Jogging and Biking Tracks
Vegetable and Fruit Market

Artificial Topography 1
Roof

(Re)laxing Plaza

Zone 3
WtE Plant 1 (Tipping - Boiling)

Zone 1
Recycling Center / Flea Market
Public Car Parking
Open - Air Amphitheater

Zone 4
WtE Plant 2 (Filtering - Rest)

Botanic Garden / Silo and Chimney

Zone 2
Flea Market (Retail)
Public Car Parking
Ice Skate Rink

Stepped Plaza

Artificial Topography 2
Ground

(Re)creational Park, Waste to (Re)source, and (Re)use-Scape

TAEHYUN JEON

The title "The (Re)creational Park, Waste to (Re)source, and (Re)use-Scape" indicates that this proposal explores public activities as a means to reconsider WtE processes, associated building typologies, and cultural activities as resources for hybridization, and then employs these elements to create unprecedented values and relationships in terms of sustainability and community.

To handle the projected population boom, Stockholm municipality's vision for future growth involves creating a walkable city by infill development. Under this condition, intensifying usability of public parks and open spaces is highly recommended. As a response to those circumstances, this project focuses on extending the previous WtE processes to form a better integrated and self-sufficient part of a new urban network, on top of creating a

WtE plant as a public park situated on the urban network system. Moreover, the introduction of flea market and public gardening programmatic elements, both sustained by public participation, could promote the reduction and reuse of waste, strategies suggested at the top of the waste management pyramid hierarchy. In addition, recreational activities loved by Swedish people designate special uses throughout the project. As for spatial uses, a set of hybrid strategies creates interchangeable methods, responding to a time schedule. Thus, the project is an infrastructural platform, a hybrid WtE plant, that offers Swedes a sustainable and community-oriented area in which to spend their leisure time.

306

Design concept

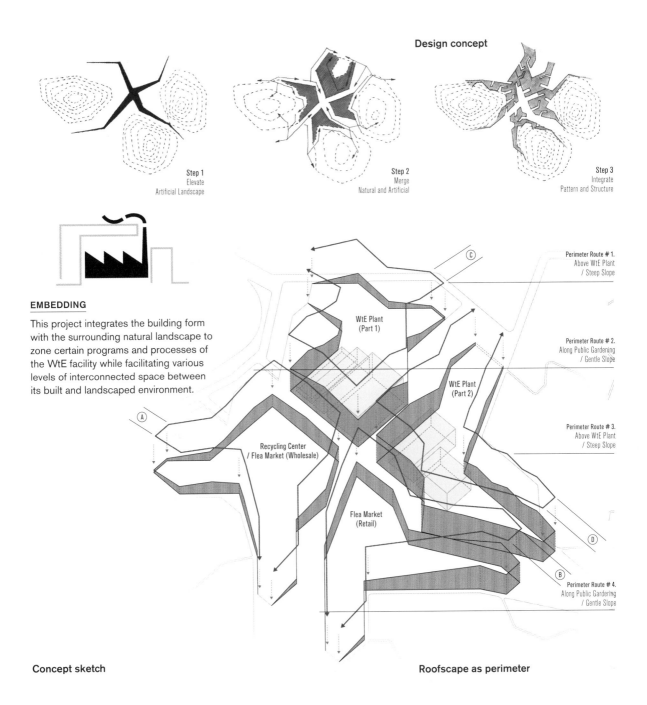

Step 1
Elevate
Artificial Landscape

Step 2
Merge
Natural and Artificial

Step 3
Integrate
Pattern and Structure

EMBEDDING

This project integrates the building form with the surrounding natural landscape to zone certain programs and processes of the WtE facility while facilitating various levels of interconnected space between its built and landscaped environment.

Ⓒ

Perimeter Route # 1.
Above WtE Plant
/ Steep Slope

WtE Plant
(Part 1)

WtE Plant
(Part 2)

Perimeter Route # 2.
Along Public Gardening
/ Gentle Slope

Ⓐ

Recycling Center
/ Flea Market (Wholesale)

Perimeter Route # 3.
Above WtE Plant
/ Steep Slope

Flea Market
(Retail)

Ⓓ

Ⓑ

Perimeter Route # 4.
Along Public Gardening
/ Gentle Slope

Concept sketch

Roofscape as perimeter

SUN ANALYSIS / SHADING

The parcels of biofuel grasses on the roof are positioned to maximize annual daylight exposure. Conversely, the width of the glazed canyon-like pathways minimize solar exposure, providing a filtered day-lit experience.

ADJACENCY

Functional and recreational activities are positioned alongside the WtE processes.

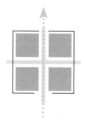

MAJOR AXIAL PROCESSION

The positioning of major thoroughfares for both pedestrian and vehicular traffic is determined by the directionality of prominent annual winds.

SHORING

An undulating topographical frame allows the roofscaped canopy to integrate with the surrounding hilly topography.

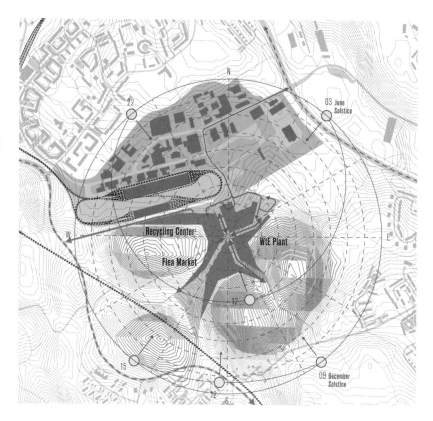

Phase 4. Redefine topography. Elevate artificial landscape in response to the surrounding hills to receive stable natural day light in summer, and integrate with the existing landscape.

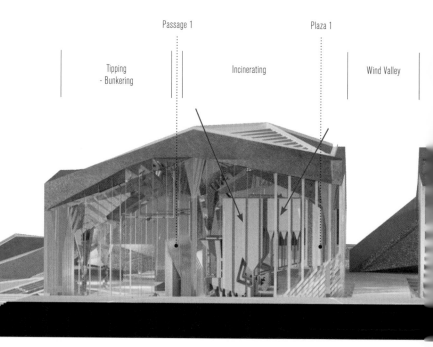

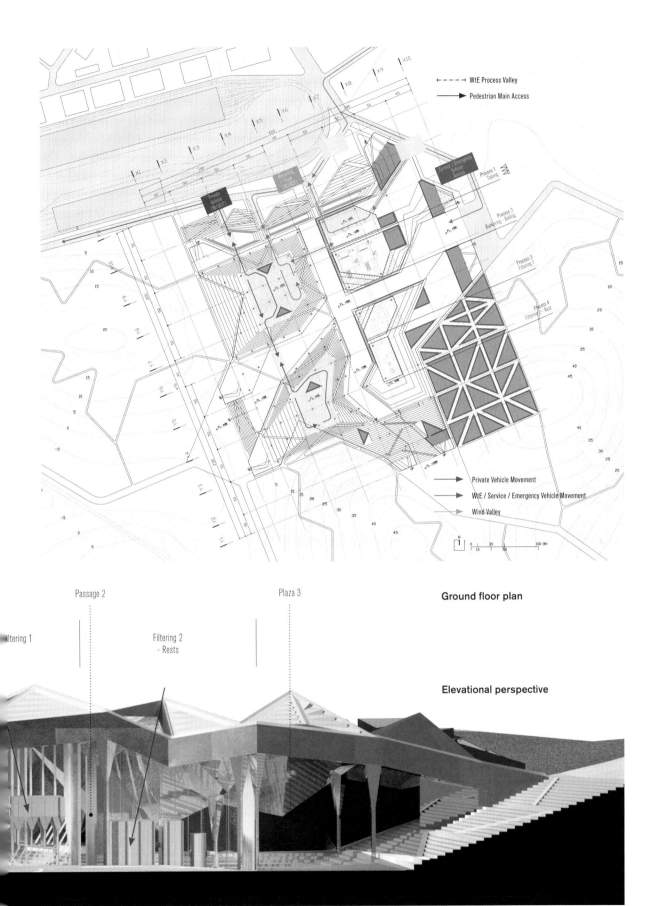

WtE Process Valley ⊢ – – – ⊣

Pedestrian Main Access →

Process 1
Tipping

Process 2
Bunkering - Boiling

Process 3
Filtering 1

Process 4
Filtering - Rest

Private Vehicle
(IN/OUT)

Receiving Truck
(IN/OUT)

Survey / Emergency
Vehicle Access

Private Vehicle Movement →

WtE / Service / Emergency Vehicle Movement →

Wind Valley →

Ground floor plan

Passage 2

Plaza 3

Filtering 1

Filtering 2
- Rests

Elevational perspective

WIND ANALYSIS / SHIELDING / DIRECTING

Prominent winds, which for the most part originate annually from a south to southwesterly direction, channel fresh air into the variously programmed interior and industrial spaces. The canyon-like corridors in conjunction with the placement of inlets and outlets on opposite faces induce a passive cross-ventilation breeze.

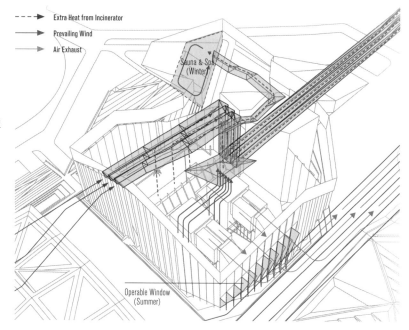

- - - ➤ Extra Heat from Incinerator
──➤ Prevailing Wind
──➤ Air Exhaust

Sauna & Spa (Winter)

Operable Window (Summer)

Natural ventilation and heat transfer

HARD / SOFT BUFFER

The treatment of the landscaped surface, whether with plants or concrete, provides transitions from space to space.

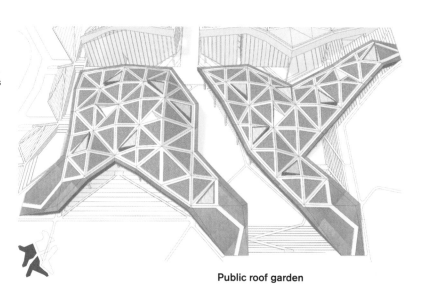

Public roof garden

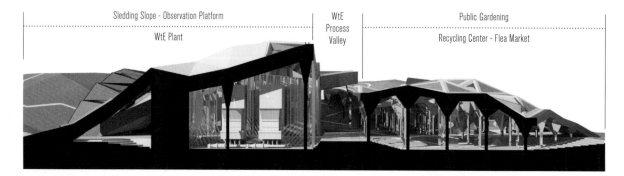

Sledding Slope - Observation Platform   WtE Process Valley   Public Gardening

WtE Plant   Recycling Center - Flea Market

Sectional perspective

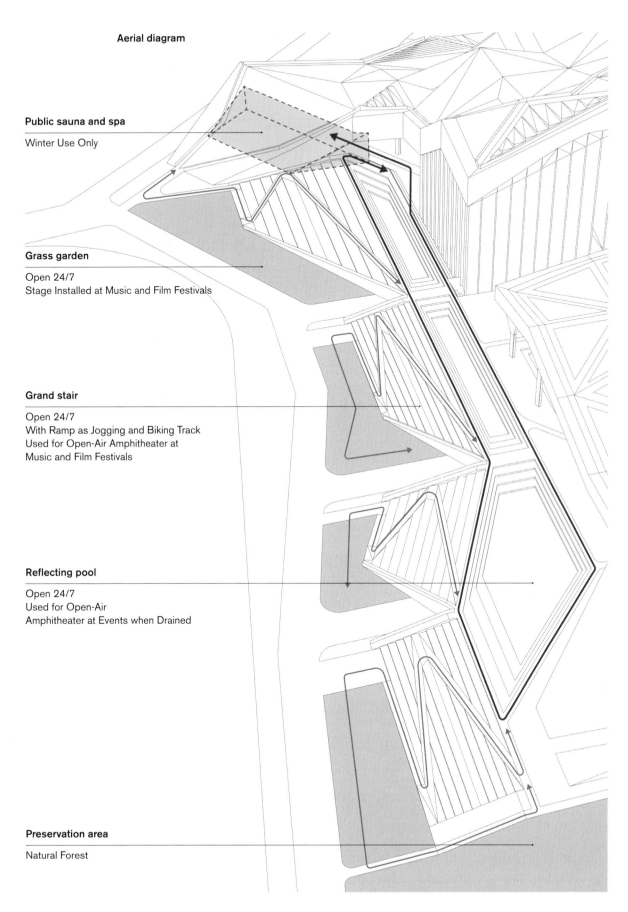

Aerial diagram

Public sauna and spa

Winter Use Only

Grass garden

Open 24/7
Stage Installed at Music and Film Festivals

Grand stair

Open 24/7
With Ramp as Jogging and Biking Track
Used for Open-Air Amphitheater at
Music and Film Festivals

Reflecting pool

Open 24/7
Used for Open-Air
Amphitheater at Events when Drained

Preservation area

Natural Forest

Reflective skin as cladding of structure

Celling

Hunch

Post

Vertical Core

Structural Module Type 1
Flea Market / Roof Public Gradering
(Soil and Planting Loads)

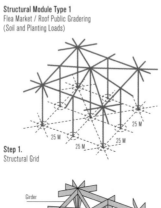

Step 1.
Structural Grid

25 M 25 M 25 M 25 M

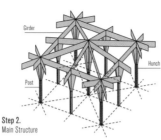

Girder

Hunch

Post

Step 2.
Main Structure

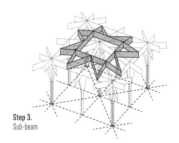

Step 3.
Sub-beam

Structural Module Type 2
WtE Plant
(Long Span)

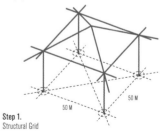

Step 1.
Structural Grid

50 M 50 M

Girder

Hunch

Post

Step 2.
Main Structure

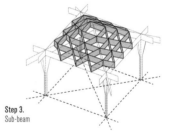

Step 3.
Sub-beam

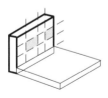

MODULAR CONSTRUCTION METHODS

The implementation of conventional modular construction methods informed decisions such as the adoption of the 25 m and 50 m column grids.

Structural system

View of interior spatial quality with reflective finish

View from axial approach

Site model

Site model

Project Wheelabrator Bridgeport

Date 1988

Owner Wheelabrator Bridgeport LP

Operator Wheelabrator Bridgeport LP

Status operating

Technology mass burn

Capacity approx. 2,250 tonnes per day

No. of boilers 3

Gross electric capacity 67 MW (10, 988 households)

Full-time employees 74

Customers served 815,807

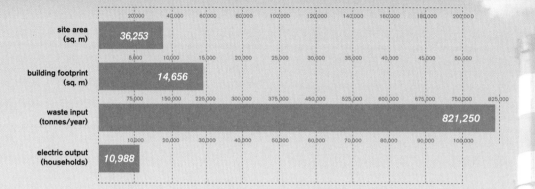

	20,000	40,000	60,000	80,000	100,000	120,000	140,000	160,000	180,000	200,000
site area (sq. m)	36,253									

	5,000	10,000	15,000	20,000	25,000	30,000	35,000	40,000	45,000	50,000
building footprint (sq. m)		14,656								

	75,000	150,000	225,000	300,000	375,000	450,000	525,000	600,000	675,000	750,000	825,000
waste input (tonnes/year)										821,250	

	10,000	20,000	30,000	40,000	50,000	60,000	70,000	80,000	90,000	100,000
electric output (households)	10,988									

Bridgeport is the most populated city in Connecticut as well as the fifth largest city in New England. As of 2013, Bridgeport's population was 147,216, numbers which reveal a slight decline in inhabitants over time. The industrial site of Wheelabrator is on the southernmost end of the West Side/West End neighborhood of Bridgeport. The site is zoned light industrial, and is adjacent to other light and heavy industrial areas as well as residential and mixed-use developments. Nearby development includes both industrial businesses, tourist and entertainment areas, shipyards, marinas, and a large park.

There are several noteworthy locations less than a km south directly across the Cedar Creek; this includes the 1.4 sq. km Seaside Park, a vast sanctuary adjacent to the nearby industrial landscape designed by Frederick Law Olmsted. Near the WtE plant is the city's water treatment facility. Roughly a km southwest is the Captain's Cove Seaport complex, which includes a restaurant, amusement center, and full-service marina.

BRIDGEPORT, CONNECTICUT

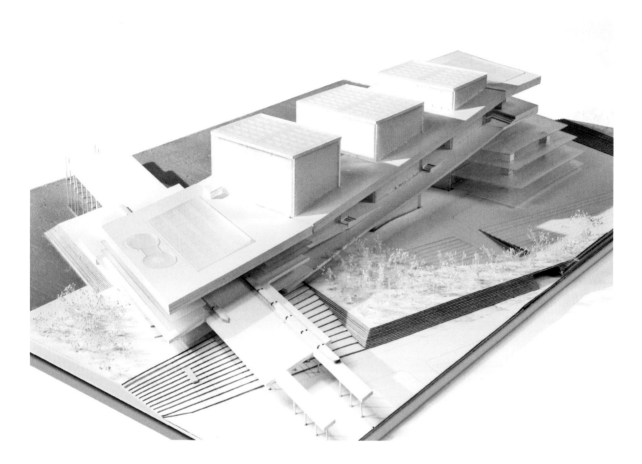

Catalytic Currents

Site model

MICHAEL HAGGERTY
DANA MCKINNEY

Catalytic Currents takes the position that WtE facilities have a role in achieving environmental justice in urban areas. The hybridization of WtE, and the extension of its life cycle, three to four times the typical 25 years, offers alternatives to other forms of obsolescence in places like Bridgeport, Connecticut. In this city, industrial lands and neighborhoods have been divested by the market, existing energy infrastructure results in health impacts, and the waterfront is at risk of inundation through storm surge and rising sea levels. Catalytic Currents claims the waterfront and regenerates Bridgeport's South End neighborhood by bringing energy, transportation, and wastewater infrastructure to the harbor and integrating these systems with storm surge barriers.

This WtE facility features the syncopation of several built systems and physical flows. Together, this bundling of systems and flows activate public space across three levels—the ground plane, an elevated public concourse, and the building roof. This project aims to reconnect and revitalize the formerly polluted coastline, isolated low-income neighborhoods, and energy-production facilities by combining infrastructure and regenerating the coal plant site on the waterfront. Doing so improves connectivity to the harbor and local rivers in both the South End and downtown, thereby supporting city development and creating three new waterfronts. At the regional scale, utilizing Long Island Sound for barging reduces the health impacts of trucking municipal waste through Connecticut neighborhoods.

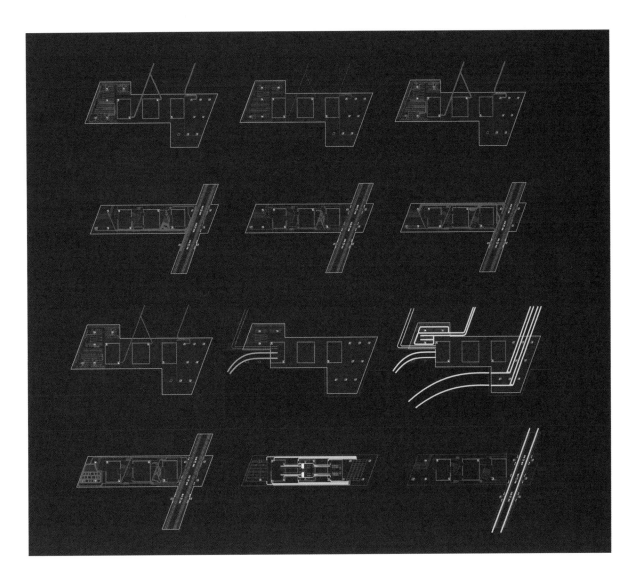

The hybridization of WtE with other urban infrastructures prompts architectural thinking across scales, from site to neighborhood to waterfront, and long-term planning that sees obsolescence as the adversary of resilience. Moreover, through hybridization, WtE catalyzes currents of all kinds, those of energy, water, people, and cities.

Program and circulation diagrams

View of multimodal access concourse

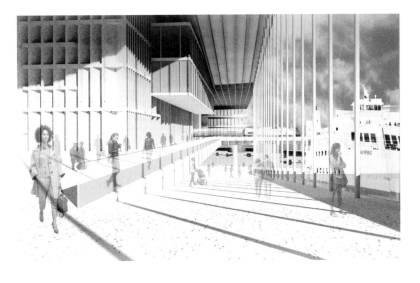

REVEALING FACADE

A brise-soleil with public circulation wraps the building cores. This feature, animated by the daily flow of pedestrians, allows curated views of the WtE structures within.

STRETCHING

Breaking the WtE process into three separate cores minimizes the perceived scale of this expansive proposal on the edge of an urban center.

VOYEURISM

The flowing plans of public program throughout the building offer occasional glimpses into the industrial WtE facilities and processes.

SHOWCASE THROUGH CIRCULATION / EDUCATIONAL TOOL

Publicly accessible spaces are allocated for educational programs, providing an opportunity to engage children and local residents.

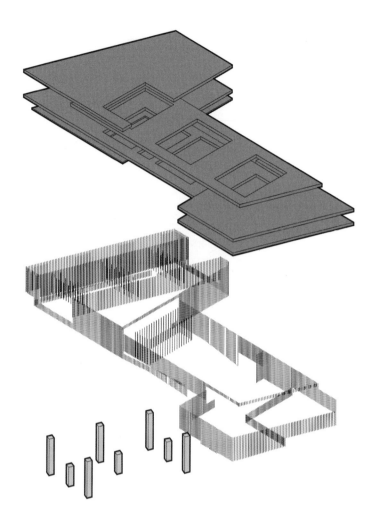

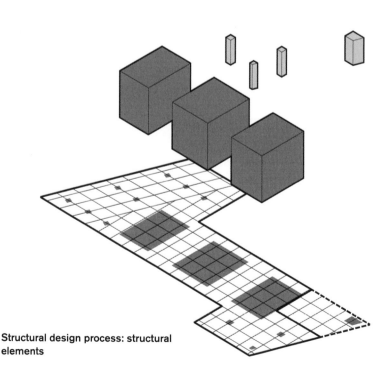

Structural design process: structural elements

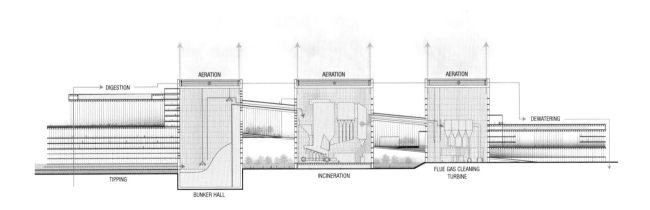

DIGESTION → | AERATION | AERATION | AERATION | → DEWATERING

TIPPING

BUNKER HALL

INCINERATION

FLUE GAS CLEANING
TURBINE

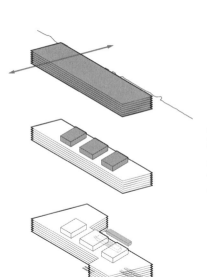

WRAPPING

The WtE volumes are wrapped in a concrete brise-soleil that affords views into the interior and directs the gaze at specific educational moments.

EVAPORATIVE COOLING

The roof is used as an elevated surface for aeration pools that direct evaporation and odors upward, away from the ground level.

PARTIALLY BERMED

Portions of the building are disguised from public view by the build up of land-forms within the site. Subsequently, these berms serve as a protective measure for future flood risk and create active outdoor public gathering spaces.

SUN SHADING

The overall network of tensile cables in the building's perimeter is uniquely tuned as a filtering filigree that shades from sunlight.

Structural design process: initial operations

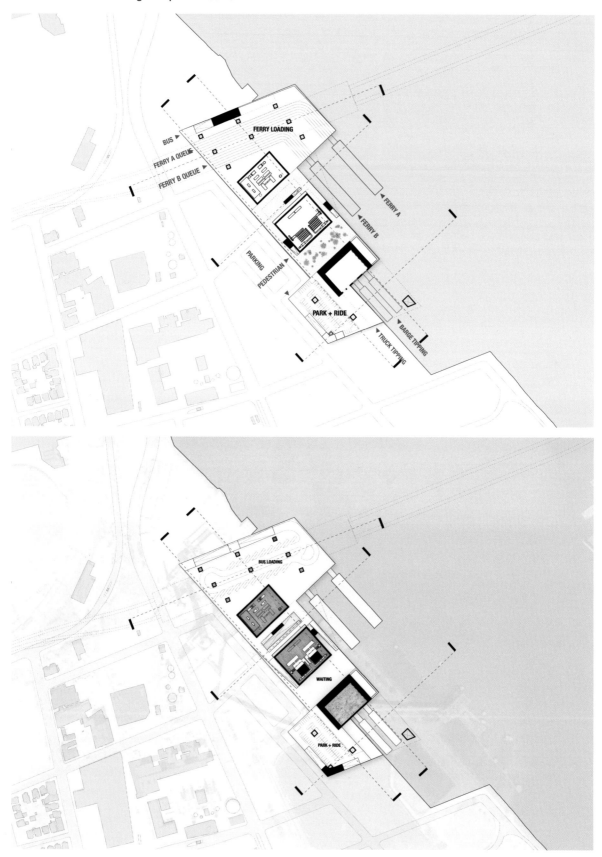

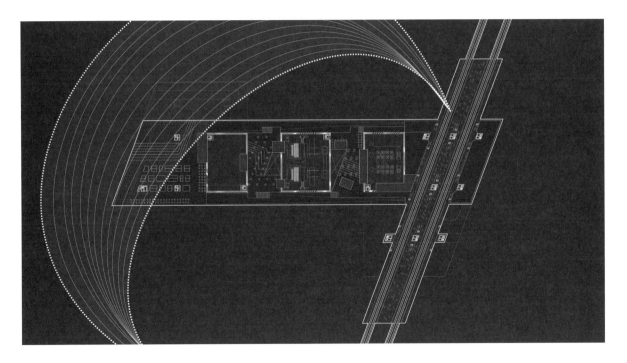

Diagram of public spaces' district heating

  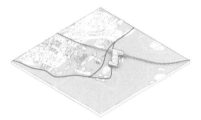

Flood protection scenarios for the site
Three scenarios are illustrated: 1. present, 2. short term, and 3. long term conditions, including a protective berm.

The syncopation of system hierarchies allows for sharing excess heat and exhaust from the WtE process with sewage treatment. Waste heat is also used to warm and cool public spaces in the transportation terminal. In addition, circulation to and within the facility is linked with the surrounding natural and urban landscape. Waste inputs and outputs are primarily barged to and from the facility, utilizing the harbor as a transport asset. Pedestrian circulation offers access to the waterfront and, on the elevated concourse, views of the harbor. These flows of inputs and outputs cycle south to north and south again through the building. Lastly, the WtE facility itself is located in three concrete bunkers that are wrapped in a brise-soleil. These envelopes afford views of the WtE plant from the public concourse and, from the waterfront at night, an illuminated structure. The WtE facility therefore catalyzes the public spaces around it, connecting the visual experience of the building with the dynamism of movement around the harbor.

Views of section model

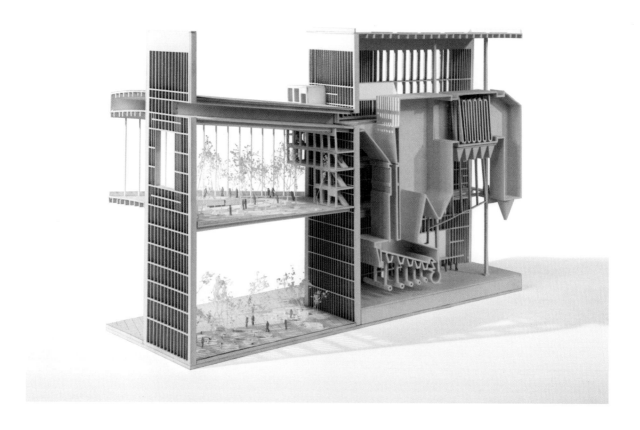

Rendered nighttime view

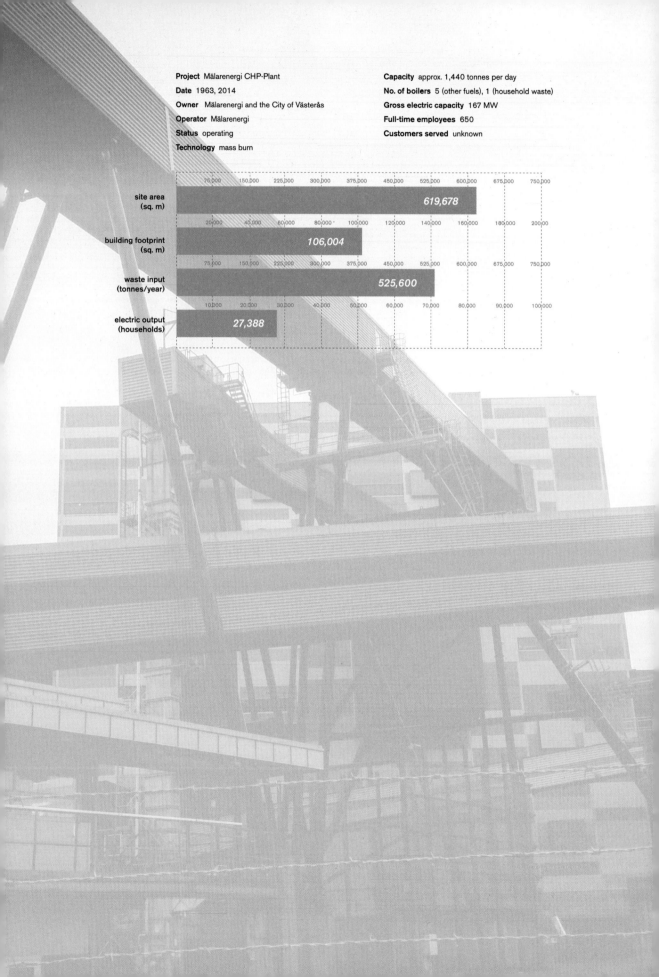

Project Mälarenergi CHP-Plant
Date 1963, 2014
Owner Mälarenergi and the City of Västerås
Operator Mälarenergi
Status operating
Technology mass burn

Capacity approx. 1,440 tonnes per day
No. of boilers 5 (other fuels), 1 (household waste)
Gross electric capacity 167 MW
Full-time employees 650
Customers served unknown

	75,000	150,000	225,000	300,000	375,000	450,000	525,000	600,000	675,000	750,000

site area
(sq. m)
619,678

	20,000	40,000	60,000	80,000	100,000	120,000	140,000	160,000	180,000	200,000

building footprint
(sq. m)
106,004

	75,000	150,000	225,000	300,000	375,000	450,000	525,000	600,000	675,000	750,000

waste input
(tonnes/year)
525,600

	10,000	20,000	30,000	40,000	50,000	60,000	70,000	80,000	90,000	100,000

electric output
(households)
27,388

Located in central Sweden roughly 100 km west of Stockholm's city center, Västerås is Sweden's sixth biggest city and capital of the province of Västmanland. While known as one of the oldest cities in Sweden and Northern Europe, Västerås boasts a very international feel, with immigrants comprising more than 7 percent of its inhabitants. Predominantly identified as an industrial city, Västerås is most known for the Asea Brown Boveri (ABB) electrical industries that are based there. It is the second largest city on the shores of Lake Mälaren, Sweden's third largest lake, and it will be home to new residential housing developments and various sporting and cultural facilities that are currently in the works. As of 2015, Västerås and its surrounding suburbs had a combined population of 145,840.

VÄSTERÅS, SWEDEN

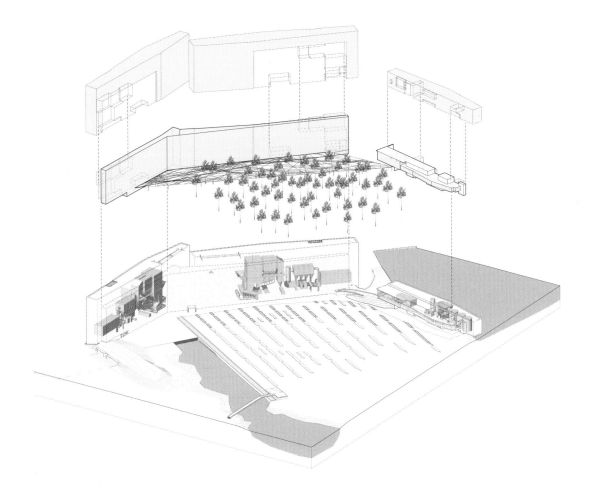

Thermal Grove

MICHAEL CLAPP
MIKE JOHNSON

The Thermal Grove is a direct response to the perceptual stigma harbored by the public for WtE facilities and their inherent place within the urban realm they inhabit. How does one approach the stigma of the barren wasteland? These zones of service and industry were once peripheral blights on the cusp of the city proper, but urban growth and expansion threaten to overtake them, creating an uncomfortable tension between their necessary evils and the idyllic urban realm. What shift in paradigms must occur to alter their perception in the public eye? One response is the creation of an equally poignant corporeal reality in the Thermal Grove. This project proposes that the byproducts of the WtE process become

the tangible instigators of this radical landscape, an otherworldly experience—one that is both alluring and aloof. What if it provoked questions of creation and destruction simultaneously?

The industrial process of production embodies an incredible amount of energy. The grove initiates a symbiotic relationship whereby the typical process of waste removal producing heat and electricity is amplified by transforming the fuel into atmospheric potential. It becomes an environment for growth.

View of the Thermal Grove

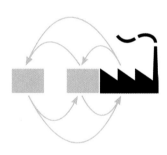

EXPANDED SYSTEMS INTEGRATION

The formal manifestations of these concepts begin to take shape as they wrap themselves around the centrally located Thermal Grove. This creates a buffer between the existing industry and the subliminal atmosphere within. A dichotomy emerges as one considers whether the entity of the grove is overtaking and reclaiming its rightful ownership of the environment in spite of the imposition of industry, or whether the greenhouse is a mutualistic product of the clean energy being produced in this highly technical process, melding into the metaphorical benefits of the grove itself.

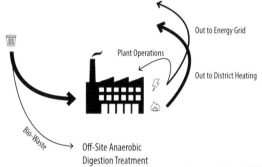

Conventional WtE sequence

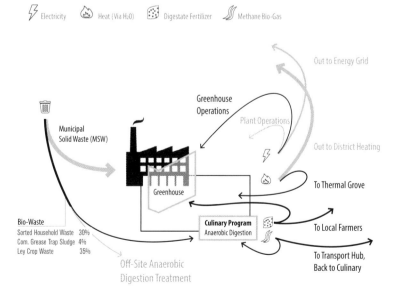

Proposed WtE / Thermal Grove hybrid

WIND ANALYSIS / SHIELDING / DIRECTING

The ultimate location of vertical program and its optimal orientation on the site was the result of a careful balance of site factors.

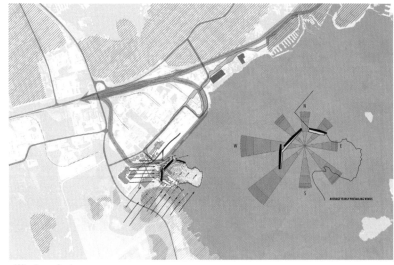

Wind analysis

SUN ANALYSIS / SHADING

When considering orientation of the volumes of the buildings, solar exposure was a contributing factor to the feasibility of the vertical greenhouse components. A number of times throughout the year natural sunlight is sufficient for a majority of the plantings within the vertical structure.

Sun analysis

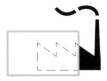

HARD BUFFER

Not only were natural processes considered, but design intention relating to approach and access from the city contributed to creating an architecture that is sustainable in that it considers the reality of the building in human experience.

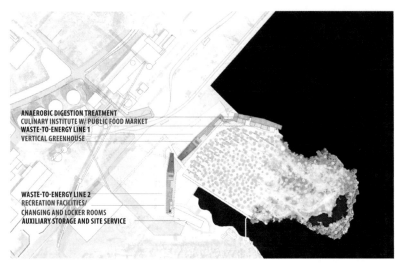

ANAEROBIC DIGESTION TREATMENT
CULINARY INSTITUTE W/ PUBLIC FOOD MARKET
WASTE-TO-ENERGY LINE 1
VERTICAL GREENHOUSE

WASTE-TO-ENERGY LINE 2
RECREATION FACILITIES/
CHANGING AND LOCKER ROOMS
AUXILIARY STORAGE AND SITE SERVICE

Context plan

OPERABLE BUILDING OPENINGS

Operable openings provide ventilation in addition to access as required for equipment maintenance.

Entryway to the grove

Aperture operation

333

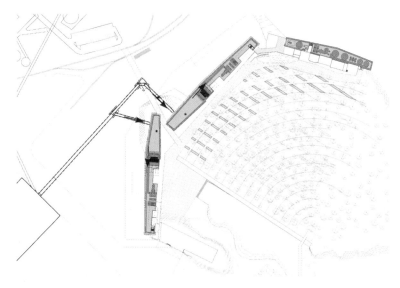

Site plan

Section through grove

View inside grove

STORMWATER MANAGEMENT

The Thermal Grove is designed as a gradient, with formalized and highly planned infrastructure feathering toward a more naturally occurring environment as it radiates away from the main axis of the freshwater irrigation well.

STRETCHING

Two WtE lines operate independently within separate structures. This complete independence allows for uninterrupted operation of one line while the other undergoes maintenance.

ADJACENCY

The culinary program takes full advantage of the products being produced within the vertical greenhouse as well as the garden planters of the Thermal Grove, which are radiantly heated with heat generated from the WtE processes.

SOFT BUFFER

The elements that comprise the organizing structure of the Thermal Grove include a curated arrangement of birch trees, raised planters with integral bench seating, stand–alone benches, plinth steam channels, an irrigation channel system, and a radiant–, heated concrete ground plane throughout. The combination of these elements provides an atmosphere that is both pleasant and mysterious.

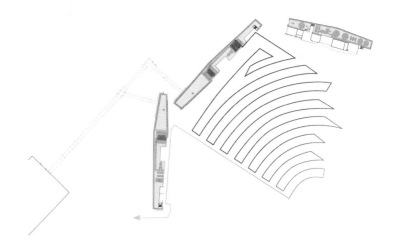

Irrigation concept

Grove tempering of district heating

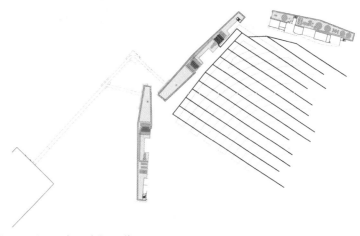

Stream atmosphere integration

Site section

ICONIZING

A steam well along the base of the building replaces the typical chimney form. Its steam contributes to the visual and physical layering experienced through the site approach.

LAMINATING

Monolithic masses contain the WtE processes, creating a strong formal barrier between the urban context and the thermal grove.

SHOWCASE THROUGH CIRCULATION / EDUCATIONAL TOOL

Subtractive voids facilitate visual interaction between public/culinary institute programs and anaerobic processes.

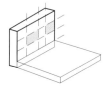

MODULAR CONSTRUCTION METHODS

The modularization of the building panels lends itself to locations that would quickly convert to use as other typologies in the project's obsolescent afterlife.

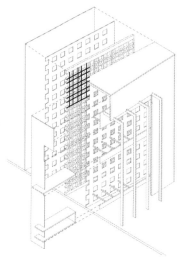

Exploded axon of building structure
Using a CLT structural system with intermittent shear walls, the building as a whole acts as a wall structure with diaphragm walls composed of CLT with a charred exterior finish.

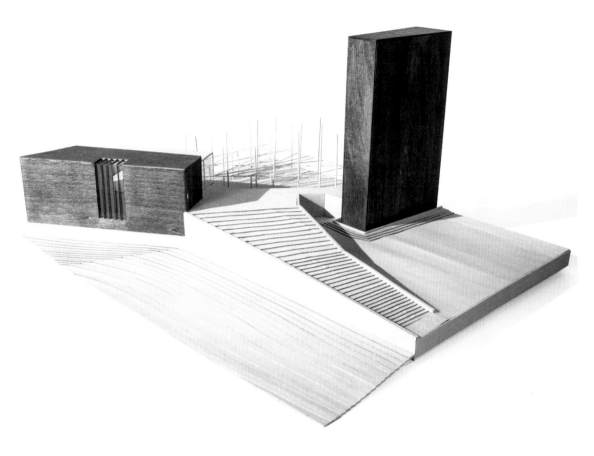

Views of sectional model

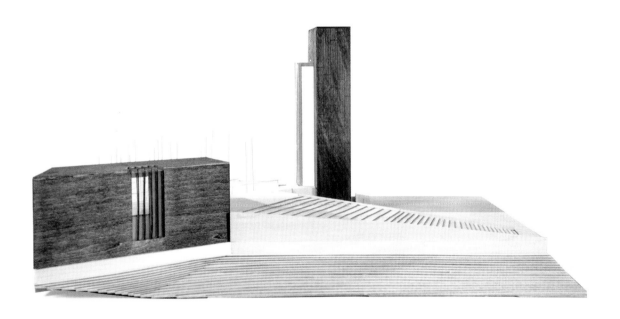

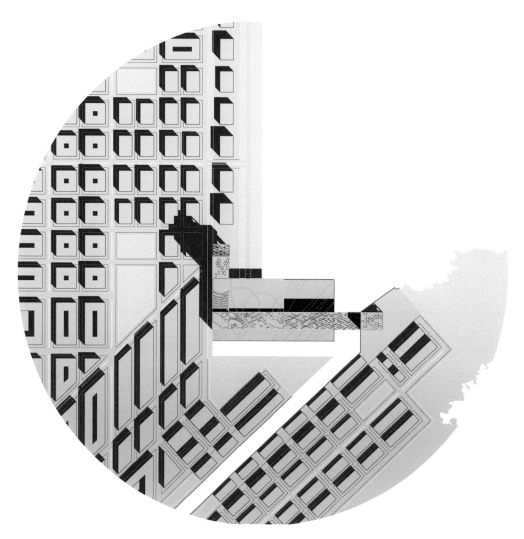

5H Hybrid

Plan view

ALBERTO EMBRIZ DE SALVATIERRA

Västerås, like most cities in Sweden, has a lettuce problem. Providing significant daily values of vitamins A and K, folate and iron, this leafy green is primarily sourced from a number of foreign countries, constituting a 358.6 million SEK import industry per year. Regionally, Northern Europe also has a waste problem, and countries like Sweden are especially well equipped to reduce waste from going to landfills (which would otherwise exacerbate greenhouse gas emissions from released methane in landfills and CO_2 from transport). A powerful syncretism that can address these seemingly disparate market needs is a commercially viable housing project that takes advantage of the material flows of each.

Contemporary society has had a troubled relationship with accepting the dynamics of entropy. Therefore, rather than denying the refuse that consumerism produces, 5H Hybrid proposes to acknowledge these dynamics to create concurrent synergies between a few selected key processes. Situated on the shores of Lake Mälaren, 5H Hybrid is a real estate project that merges a housing tower, hotel tower, WtE power plant, hydroponic lettuce facility, and hedonistic park network for both residents and the local community. Ultimately, 5H Hybrid catalyzes the potential of refuse into a triple revenue stream while proving much needed housing and recreational spaces in a growing industrial city.

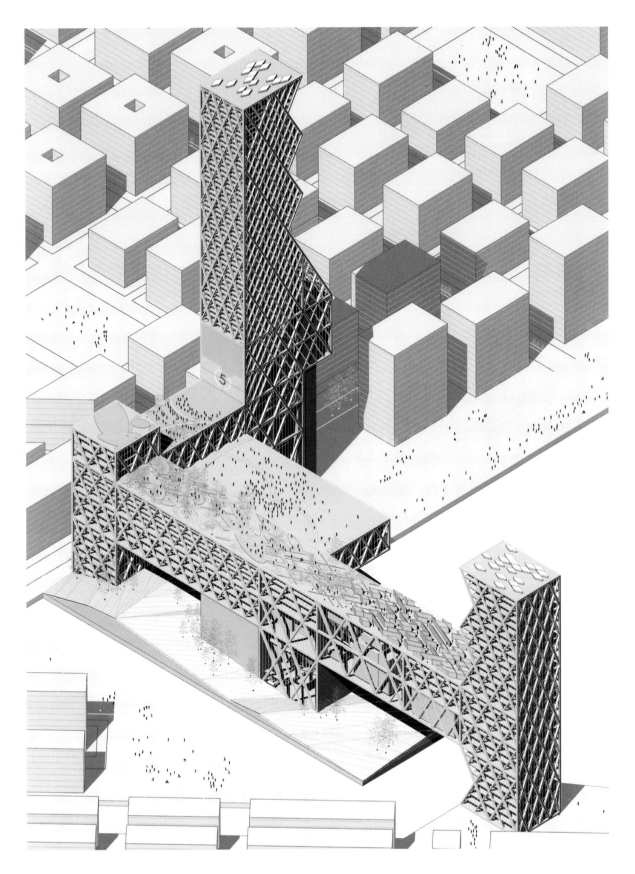

Contextual view

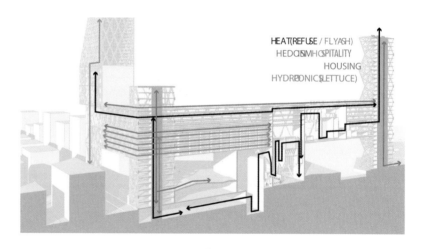

HEAT (REFUSE / FLYASH)
HEDONISM HOSPITALITY
HOUSING
HYDROPONICS (LETTUCE)

Sectional perspective of hybrid relationships

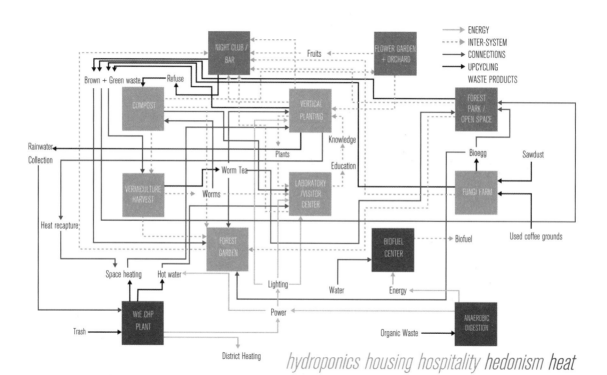

→ ENERGY
⇢ INTER-SYSTEM
→ CONNECTIONS
→ UPCYCLING
WASTE PRODUCTS

NIGHT CLUB / BAR

FLOWER GARDEN + ORCHARD

Fruits

Brown + Green waste

Refuse

COMPOST

VERTICAL PLANTING

FOREST PARK / OPEN SPACE

Rainwater
Collection

Plants

Knowledge

Bioegg

Sawdust

Education

VERMICULTURE HARVEST

Worm Tea

LABORATORY / VISITOR CENTER

FUNGI FARM

Worms

Heat recapture

FOREST GARDEN

BIOFUEL CENTER

Biofuel

Used coffee grounds

Space heating

Hot water

Lighting

Water

Energy

Power

WtE CHP PLANT

ANAEROBIC DIGESTION

Trash

Organic Waste

District Heating

hydroponics housing hospitality hedonism heat

Diagram of hybrid flows

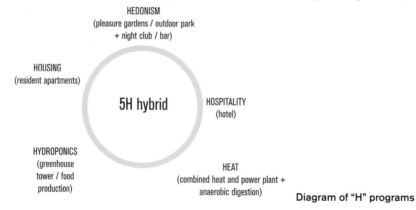

HEDONISM
(pleasure gardens / outdoor park
+ night club / bar)

HOUSING
(resident apartments)

5H hybrid

HOSPITALITY
(hotel)

HYDROPONICS
(greenhouse
tower / food
production)

HEAT
(combined heat and power plant +
anaerobic digestion)

Diagram of "H" programs

342

Perspective of structural system

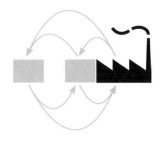

EXPANDED SYSTEMS INTEGRATION

5H Hybrid is a building complex that performs a synergistic choreography between the aforementioned five "H" programs. Waste and water are upcycled into electricity and heat, which subsequently provide energy to the hydroponic laboratories and the hospitality and housing towers.

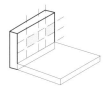

MODULAR CONSTRUCTION METHODS

Structurally, 5H Hybrid was designed with a modular diagrid system with components in 10 m increments, allowing for off-site manufacturing and cost-effective assembly.

VOYEURISM

While plant components can be seen from the exterior, there are various interior moments that provide educational viewing windows into the hydroponic and heat programs.

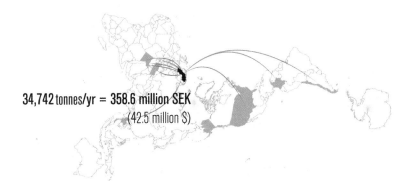

34,742 tonnes/yr = **358.6 million SEK**
(42.5 million $)

Map of Swedish lettuce imports

343

Heat (WtE) program

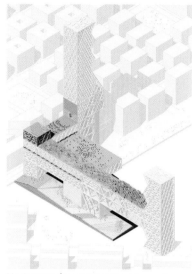

Hedonism (recreational parks and pleasure gardens) program

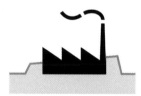

REVEALING FACADE

Furthermore, the entire structural grid is arrested at key moments to highlight and allow a clear view of internal processes, such as the WtE power plant and the hydroponic laboratories.

BERMING

In order to hide the less palatable aspects of waste processing, the loading docks and tipping hall are buried underground and bermed to facilitate an expansive waterfront park.

SHOWCASE THROUGH CIRCULATION / EDUCATIONAL TOOL

The interior circulation from space to space becomes a tool to provide further instruction about WtE processes.

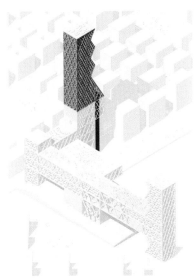

Hospitality program

Housing program

Hydroponics program

ICONIZING

Aiming to rebrand itself as "The City on the Lake," Västerås has a distinct need for buildings that can be seen from a distance and when sailing up to the harbor. Thus, the stacked programs and resulting towers disguise the WtE stacks and iconize them into monuments to ecological industries.

MUTUALISM

The WtE Combined Heat and Power plant can process 800,000 tonnes of refuse a year and convert it into electricity for 68,000 homes and heating (steam) for 12,000 homes, fulfilling the combined waste disposal needs of both Västerås and the immediate region.

COMMENSALISM

The hydroponics laboratories (modeled after existing Japanese technology) is capable of growing 401 million heads of lettuce a year (approximately 173,828 tonnes). This yields 98 times more lettuce per square meter than an ordinary farm—growing 2.5 times faster with just 1 percent of the water and 30 percent more cost effectiveness.

STACKING

Typical WtE power plants are massive and occupy a large area. In order to free valuable waterfront real estate, the WtE plant was stacked vertically into a slim skyscraper, which allows other programs to be placed on top.

The twin housing and hotel towers feature a combined 1,232 units composed of studio, one- and two-bedroom units.

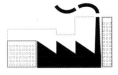

SURROUNDING

While the current site is an industrial area surrounded by a rural setting, the design of the building accommodates a denser urban condition; as Västerås grows from its center toward its periphery surrounding Lake Mälaren, an enveloping city can abut the lakeside towers and its parks.

SOFT BUFFER

A network of parks and plazas intermixed with the rest of the "hard" programs behave as soft buffers between the WtE components, the other programs, and the rest of the city.

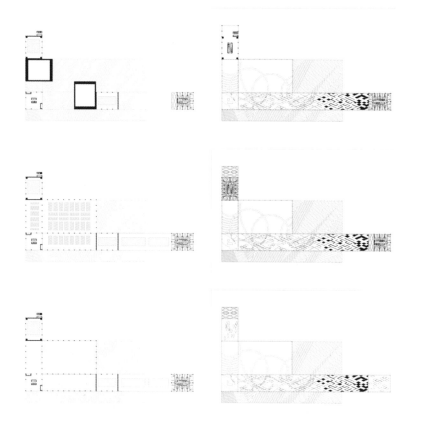

5H Hybrid floor plans

View of hedonistic park

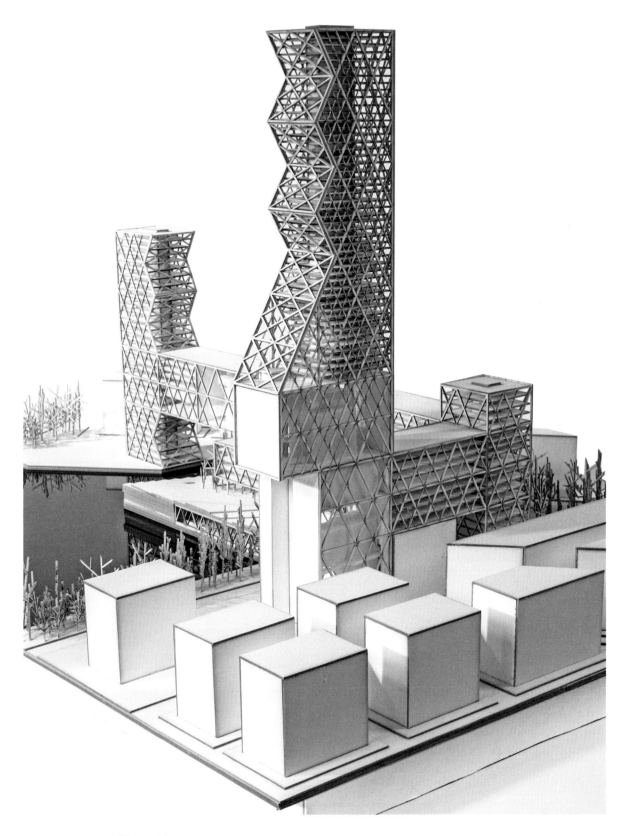

Site model

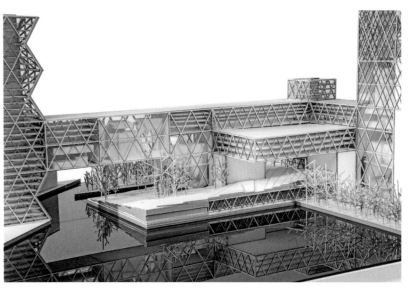

Views of site model

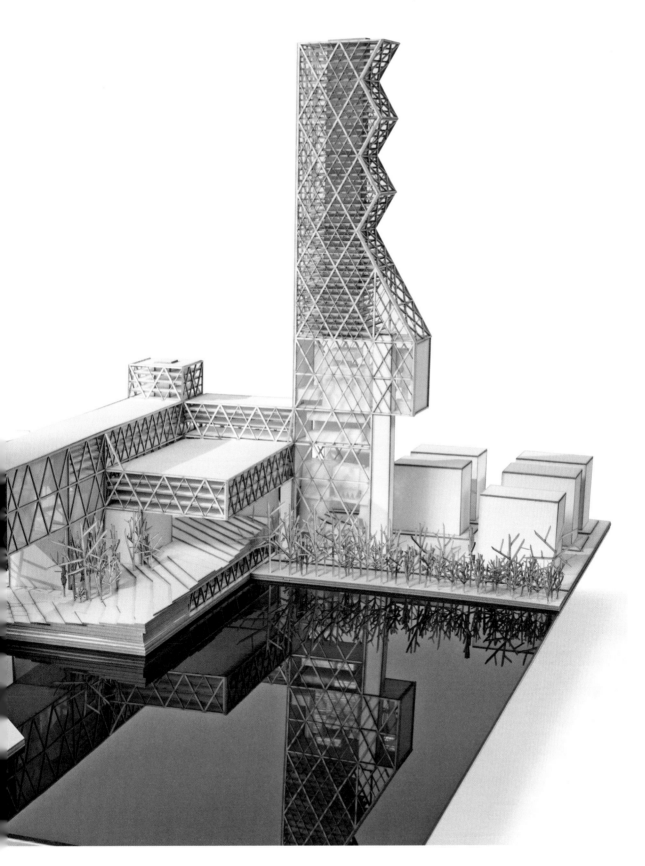

Project Southeastern Connecticut RRF
Date 1992
Owner Covanta Company of Southeastern CT
Operator Covanta Company of Southeastern CT
Status operating
Technology mass burn

Capacity approx. 690 tonnes per day
No. of boilers 2
Gross electric capacity 26 MW (4,264 households)
Full-time employees 43
Customers served 248,233

	20,000	40,000	60,000	80,000	100,000	120,000	140,000	160,000	180,000	200,000
site area (sq. m)							**152,367**			

	5,000	10,000	15,000	20,000	25,000	30,000	35,000	40,000	45,000	50,000
building footprint (sq. m)	**5,181**									

	75,000	150,000	225,000	300,000	375,000	450,000	525,000	600,000	675,000	750,000
waste input (tonnes/year)			**251,850**							

	10,000	20,000	30,000	40,000	50,000	60,000	70,000	80,000	90,000	100,000
electric output (households)	**4,264**									

The area surrounding the Southeastern Connecticut Resource Recovery Facility (SECONN) RRF Waste-to-Energy plant is one of only a handful of areas in Preston zoned for industrial use, which accounts for 1 percent of total land use. It is bordered by undeveloped land to the north, a small commercial area and low-density residential to the east, some low-density residential and undeveloped land to the south, and the Thames River to the east. The SCRRA Facility has approximately 23 acres of undeveloped land outside of it that provides a possible development area. In 2014, the Preston Planning Commission revised the zoning at and surrounding the WtE facility (to the north and west) for the Preston Riverwalk in anticipation of its redevelopment to Thames River District.

As of 2010, Preston is a rural town of 4,700 people. Upwards of 67 percent of Preston's land remains either undeveloped, open space, or agriculture. Of the developed land, most is low-density residential. Of the surrounding towns, the population of Preston has slowed in the last decade, currently claiming the lowest growth rate.

PRESTON, CONNECTICUT

Show/Flow

ANDREW WADE KEATING
SCOTT MARCH SMITH

This project hybridizes an assortment of large public program into an iconic, regional-scale entertainment, leisure, and transportation complex supported by and supporting a WtE facility. The program—a regional transit hub for buses and electric vehicles, sports stadium, amphitheater for music performance, and riverwalk—grows from the relatively open, semirural site, which currently hosts the SCRRA facility. The plant sits on the riverfront between the two largest casinos in the United States—Foxwoods, several kilometers to the east, and Mohegan Sun, just across the Thames River to the west. This intensity of entertainment space and lack of urban density near the site motivated a search for a large-scale program that would capitalize on the draw of the casinos, bringing visitors (and their attendant waste) to the facility, rather than solely relying on trucking in waste.

Site strategy diagram

Waste travels from the stadium and other facilities to the bunker hall via a vacuum system, so on-site collection does not require additional trucking.

The project proposes a new way of thinking about regional-scale buildings and entertainment facilities, one that uses waste generated on site as an energy source, minimizes the carbon impact of waste removal, and reduces the inevitable loss of energy in transport from power plants to the point of use. Further, the WtE processes supports a new kind of regional transit, relying on small electric vehicles, which may soon be able to drive themselves across the southeastern Connecticut region.

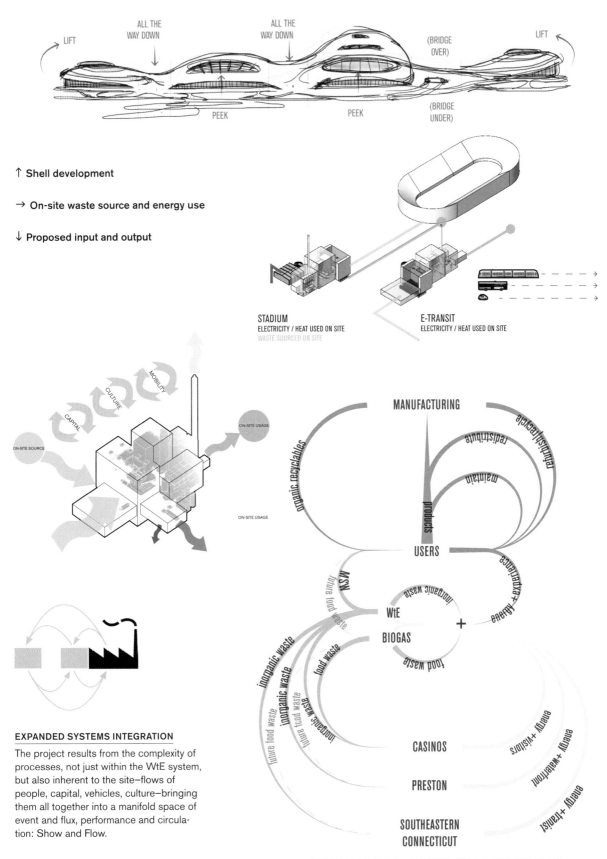

LIFT

ALL THE
WAY DOWN

ALL THE
WAY DOWN

(BRIDGE
OVER)

LIFT

PEEK

PEEK

(BRIDGE
UNDER)

↑ Shell development

→ On-site waste source and energy use

↓ Proposed input and output

STADIUM
ELECTRICITY / HEAT USED ON SITE
WASTE SOURCED ON SITE

E-TRANSIT
ELECTRICITY / HEAT USED ON SITE

MOBILITY

CULTURE

CAPITAL

ON-SITE SOURCE

ON-SITE USAGE

ON-SITE USAGE

EXPANDED SYSTEMS INTEGRATION

The project results from the complexity of
processes, not just within the WtE system,
but also inherent to the site—flows of
people, capital, vehicles, culture—bringing
them all together into a manifold space of
event and flux, performance and circulation: Show and Flow.

MANUFACTURING

organic recyclables

redistribute/recycle

maintain

products

USERS

inorganic waste

redistribute + reuse

MSW

future food waste

WtE

BIOGAS

food waste

inorganic waste

inorganic waste

future food waste

future food waste

food waste

energy + visitors

energy + waterfront

energy + transit

CASINOS

PRESTON

SOUTHEASTERN
CONNECTICUT

EXPANDING THE LOCALIZED CIRCULAR ECONOMY

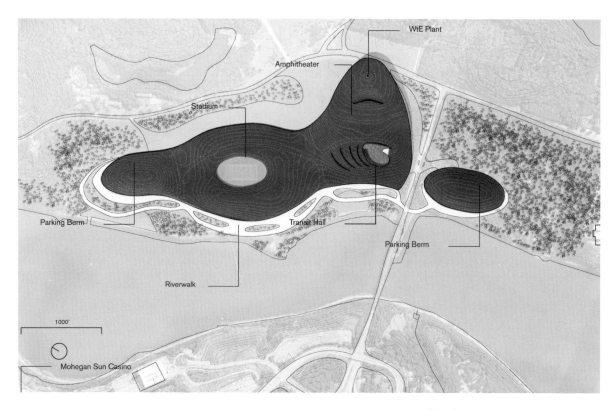

Site plan

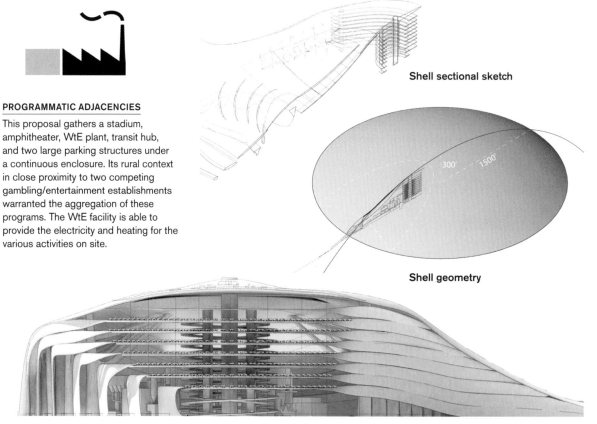

Shell sectional sketch

Shell geometry

PROGRAMMATIC ADJACENCIES

This proposal gathers a stadium, amphitheater, WtE plant, transit hub, and two large parking structures under a continuous enclosure. Its rural context in close proximity to two competing gambling/entertainment establishments warranted the aggregation of these programs. The WtE facility is able to provide the electricity and heating for the various activities on site.

The hub: east elevation

FRAMED APERTURE

Indirect sunlight is channeled into the WtE facility via the ribbonlike striations of the shelled facade enclosure. This provides a consistent amount of filtered daylight illuminating these typically concealed industrial processes.

A large oculus punctures the curved shell exposing the transit hall to direct sunlit conditions for certain hours of the day. The dichotomy of these two conditions is in part informed by their relative position within their respective waste and transportation networks.

ACOUSTICAL BERM

A continuous sinuous shell, which at times rises hundreds of feet above the landscape, functions as a physical acoustical buffer against the periodic boat traffic of the Thames River while also allowing visitors access to its greenscaped surface.

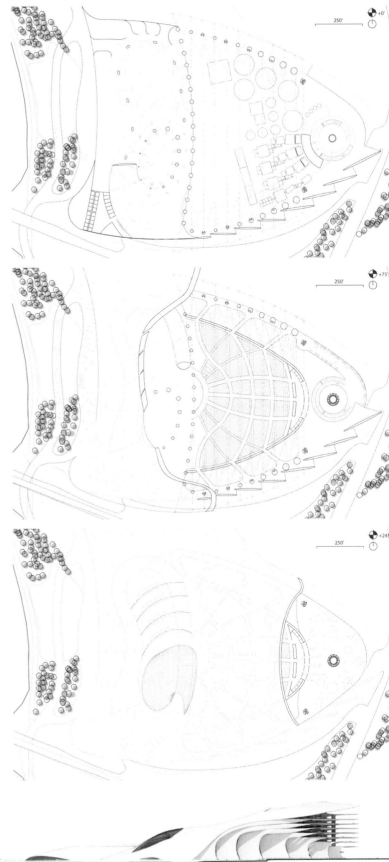

Floor plans: transit hall and WtE plant, theater, lobby

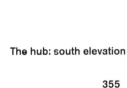

The hub: south elevation

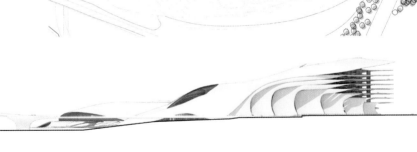

355

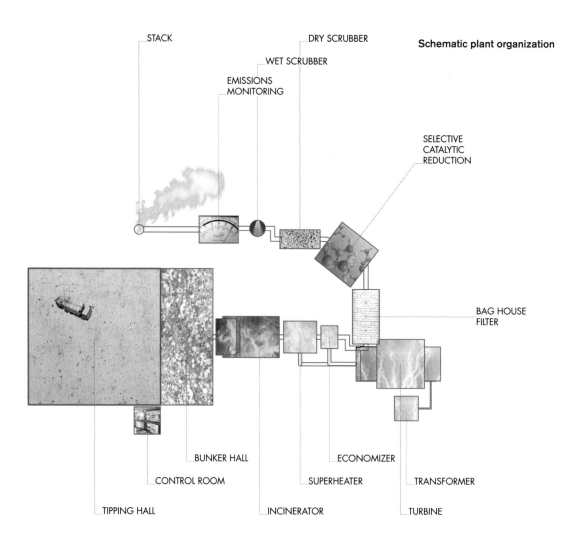

STACK

DRY SCRUBBER

WET SCRUBBER

EMISSIONS MONITORING

Schematic plant organization

SELECTIVE CATALYTIC REDUCTION

BAG HOUSE FILTER

BUNKER HALL

ECONOMIZER

CONTROL ROOM

SUPERHEATER

TRANSFORMER

TIPPING HALL

INCINERATOR

TURBINE

CENTRALIZING

The shell takes part of its form from the spatial requirements of the WtE process, which, while linear, can be reorganized so that the tallest elements (the bunker hall, incinerator, and stack) all collect to one end. This creates the dramatic slope of the hub, the central lobe of the greater shell.

CONCEALING / TRANSFORMING / MINIMIZING THE CHIMMEY

The consolidated and wrapped arrangement of internal components conceals vertical components, most notably the chimney, by allowing them to appear to function as structural elements. In this proposal the chimney is wrapped as if it were a central structural core by a winding path that feeds trash into the tipping hall. Its close proximity to typically unassociated components along their sequence contributes to its perceived hidden effect.

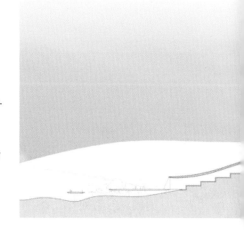

Tipping access ramp

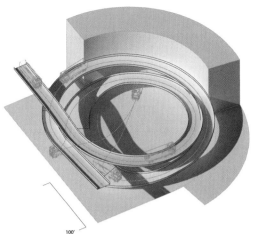

INCINERATION

POWER GENERATION

TRANSMISSION

FLUE GAS CLEANING

EXHAUST

CONCEALED CHIMNEY / TIPPING HALL

The tipping hall sinks below ground, accessible via a spiraling ramp that brings tipping traffic down while sending electric vehicles up to drop visitors at the sky lobby for music and cultural events in the amphitheater. The amphitheater is suspended directly above the waste processing equipment. Bus traffic proceeds below the western portion of the hub, where visitors ascend into the transit hall, and can proceed up a long, sculptural ramp through the oculus overhead and out onto the riverwalk. The WtE facility provides electricity and heating for the activities on site, and also to surrounding communities.

Plant components

The hub: section

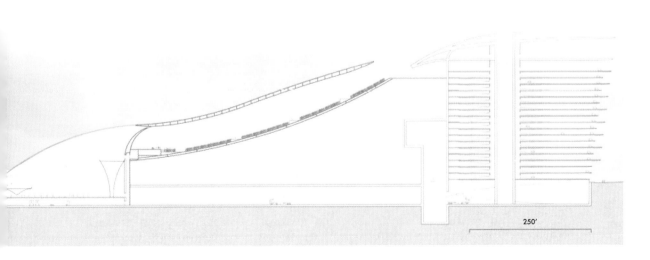

Structural aggregation

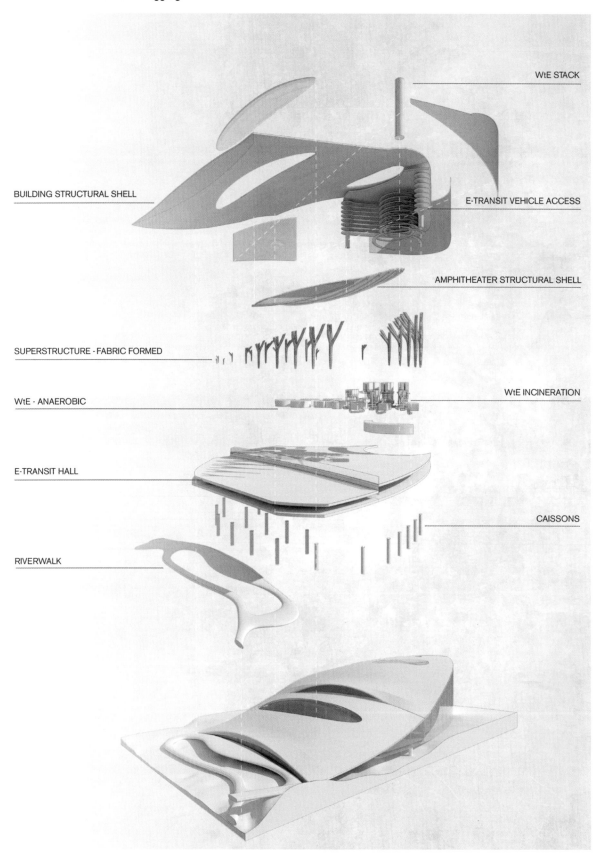

WtE STACK

BUILDING STRUCTURAL SHELL

E-TRANSIT VEHICLE ACCESS

AMPHITHEATER STRUCTURAL SHELL

SUPERSTRUCTURE - FABRIC FORMED

WtE - ANAEROBIC

WtE INCINERATION

E-TRANSIT HALL

CAISSONS

RIVERWALK

View of the oculus that illuminates the transit hall
Besides functioning as a skylight, a swooping walkway grants access to and from the rooftop greenscape of the structural shell

Winter view of riverwalk
The potential for recreational activities such as skiing is activated with the oncoming of seasonal snows

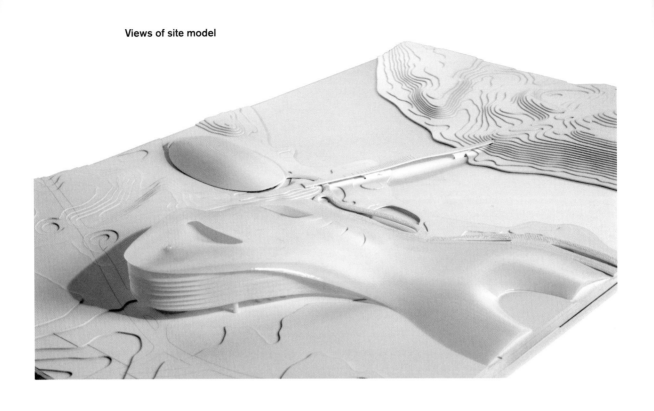

361

More or Less: Concluding Remarks

HANIF KARA AND LEIRE ASENSIO VILLORIA

Managing household waste is not a new problem. What we learned in this research, however, is that the increased amount of waste produced by each citizen (in particular in the United States), and how towns and cities struggle with its disposal—in part due to the closing of landfills caused by capacity constraints or the failure of landfills to meet current health standards—has magnified the problem to crisis levels. While large-scale recycling and waste reduction at the source help deal with household waste, WtE incineration remains a good solution for communities provided we overcome the obscure way in which WtE is currently framed (or contemptuously delivered) as a solution. We hope this manual will dispel some of the unjustified canards that spur lobbies against this type of waste treatment. We chose to counter such myths through the application of design thinking in architecture, where good design coupled with good-quality construction usually triumph through unsolicited sharing of design research.

In the early stages of this investigation we recognized that convenient access to knowledge regarding WtE facilities and processes was not readily available, and in addition to determining what is worthy of study, it became essential to decipher WtE's key aspects, common technologies, and terminologies. This informed how we approached and presented our findings, and also prepared us to undertake focused, in-depth study in an academic environment. The research took us to Sweden, where a mature and globally recognized waste management culture already exists. In poignant comparison to the United States, more than three decades ago Sweden overcame the banal and often misleading dichotomy between "recycling and incineration" or "landfill and incineration," relying on wider state-controlled fiscal and political policies, which dispel the resistance to incineration technologies.

What we observed in our general cases is that layers of policy, ethical, moral, and scientific considerations carry more weight and are viewed as more critical than the design of WtE facilities. This book therefore presents and defends the need to consider the role of design as an equal concern in the broad array of issues that include site selection, community engagement, and education related to public health (air quality, ash toxicity, groundwater contamination) when examining waste incineration and its architecture as a solution.

One goal is to ally design with the WtE industry through igniting a renewed interest among architects to engage with what we have labeled "Architecture and Waste," encouraging an earlier and closer collaboration with those involved in this contemporary building type. We hope to get those directly involved in waste incineration—governments, large specialized private industrial organizations, city authorities, and the public—to see the value of design. One common obstacle we discovered, for instance, is that the lack of awareness of waste disposal costs has detached the industry and citizens, in particular in the United States, from the necessary rethinking of this subject in the context of ecological and economic challenges. Techniques or operations in design that are showcased in this publication have the potential to close the gap between designers, the industry, and the communities these facilities serve and reside in. Ultimately aspiring to change consumer behavior through the greater visibility and improved status of WtE facilities requires the attention of architects, as we see in the rare cases presented in this manual.

It is also clear that, from the beginning, these facilities' substantial capital costs are often misleadingly coupled with a "we do not need to spend more money on design" mentality, which rules out architects' involvement. More significantly, when building these facilities, the lack of design (as can be seen in the case studies) produces uninviting, detached, homogeneous, "siteless" responses time and time again. In formulating our research, we have been careful not to shy away from the premise that waste incineration is not cheap, or from that fact that this method reduces volumes of waste, but does not do away with the existence of waste entirely.

Throughout our research, we have sought to create a framework that cultivates a peda-gogical curiosity about and reconsideration of the role of waste in society. We had to carefully negotiate industry connections, which can be market driven and thus lead to the marginalization of research methods and outputs. Our starting point was that the large degree of abstraction that can mark design research in architecture could only be avoided through the investigation of actual specific design problems that allow the architect to engage in a fully integrative process, which demonstrates the tangible opportunities of our work. The first phases of the framework then included investigations, seminars, interviews, and site visits to create sound knowledge, manifest in a combination of drawn and written outputs, that merges the technological, regulatory, and economic aspects of these facilities. This allowed an informed studio based on the critical framing of a design problem as developed by an interdisciplinary team of researchers—individuals who operate and respond across the boundaries of their discipline, and who are not constrained by the struggle to maintain the identity of their own discipline. This distinction was deliberate given the specific sites and issues we looked to investigate; it also stretched the design speculations and opportunities across the boundaries of the disciplines involved, which was essential to achieve an outcome that can make a difference. To create coherent outcomes that challenge the myth of architects being detached from making of buildings, the research embraced familiar techniques of diagrams and design models and extended them to develop an associative (not performance-based) model as a tool to interrogate and manipulate the designs. This associative model resists employing techniques that use self-generating democratic parameters to create formal designs or, for that matter, aesthetic agendas that control the outcome to an extent that it strays into the defending of styles and form-making for its own sake (a tactic we at times see dominate outputs in academies of design). A particularly important aspect of our research showed that, with few exceptions, most of the stakeholders perceived architecture only from an aesthetic lens, and when this view was challenged, it became alarmingly clear that they possessed a very narrow understanding of aesthetics.

Looking to the horizon, economic models that decouple global economic development and finite consumption, first developed by major schools of thought in the 1990s, have recently gained more traction and hint at recasting the historical principles of obsolescence as we know them today under the rubric of the circular economy. A key principle of this approach is that waste itself is designed to become obsolete. As a society we are some way from this becoming a reality, but as we edge toward that goal there is a demand for many more facilities to be designed and built throughout the world. We hope this manual adds value to and improves the design approach toward these WtE plants.

Sysav WtE plant, Malmö, Sweden, 2016

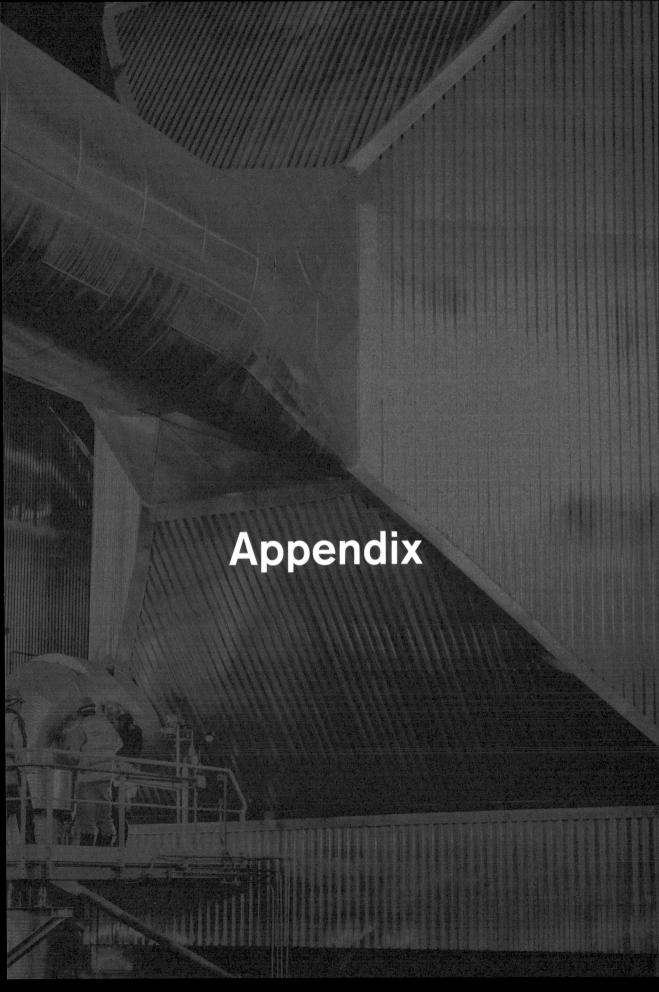

Appendix

Figure Credits

44: ©Martin Falbisoner, Wikimedia Commons, cc by-sa 3.0, https://commons.wikimedia .org/wiki/File:US_Capitol_west_side.JPG.

46: Diagram by Andre Thomsen and Kees van der Flier, "Obsolescence and the End of Life Phase in Buildings" (paper presented at Management and Innovation for a Sustainable Built Environment, Amsterdam, The Netherlands, June 20–23, 2011; and Donald G. Iselin and Andrew C. Lerner, eds., *The Fourth Dimension in Building: Strategies for Avoiding Obsolescence* (Washington, DC: National Academies Press, 1993).

49: Diagram by Iselin and Lerner, eds., *The Fourth Dimension in Building.*

51: WtE Design Lab.

53: Elaine Kwong, WtE Design Lab.

WASTE-TO-ENERGY PRIMER

54: ©Alan Levine, Flickr, color filter applied, cc by 2.0, https://www.flickr.com/photos /cogdog/9090732482.

56: New York City Department of Sanitation.

57, 60: Alberto Embriz de Salvatierra, WtE Design Lab.

64: Laura Smead, WtE Design Lab; data from Daniel Hoornweg and Perinaz Bhada-Tata, *What a Waste: A Global Review of Solid Waste Management,* Urban Development Series, Knowledge Papers no. 15 (Washington DC: World Bank, 2012), Annex J (https://openknowledge.worldbank.org/handle/10986/17388); Eurostat, "Municipal Waste Statistics," Statistics Explained, http://ec.europa.eu/eurostat/statistics-explained/index.php/Municipal_waste_statistics 2015; and US Environmental Protection Agency (US EPA), Municipal Solid *Waste Generation, Recycling, and Disposal in the United States* (US EPA, February 2014), https://www.epa.gov/sites/production/files/201509/documents/2012_msw_dat_tbls.pdf.

65: Smead, WtE Design Lab; data from Hoornweg and Bhada-Tata, *What a Waste*, Annex L; Eurostat, "Municipal Waste Statistics"; and US EPA, *Municipal Solid Waste Generation.*

67: De Salvatierra, WtE Design Lab; data from Confederation of European Waste-to-Energy Plants (CEWEP), "Waste-to-Energy in Europe in 2012," http://www.cewep. eu/information/data/studies/m_1342; and Ted Michaels, *2014 ERC Directory of Waste-to-Energy Facilities* (Energy Recovery Council, 2014), http:// energyrecovery-council.org/wp-content/uploads/2016/01/ERC_2014_Directory.pdf; and US EPA, *Municipal Solid Waste Generation.*

69, 70, 71: Daniel Hemmendinger, WtE Design Lab (Note: in figure on 69 [top], six million tonnes of waste were treated as "other"; in figure on 71, 2008 data was used for some states); data from Eurostat, "Municipal Waste Statistics"; and US EPA, *Municipal Solid Waste Generation*; Dolly Shin, "Generation and Disposition of Municipal Solid Waste (MSW) in the United States—A National Survey" (master's thesis, Earth and Environmental Engineering Department, Columbia University, 2014), 22, http://www.seas.columbia.edu/earth/wtert/sofos/Dolly_Shin_Thesis.pdf.; and Emma

Watkins et al., *Use of Economic Instruments and Waste Management* (Paris: Bio Intelligence Service, 2012), 56, http://ec.europa.eu/environment/waste/ pdf/final_report_10042012.pdf.

74: Klaus Leidorff Photography.

77, 79 (top): Hemmendinger and Nikos Georgoulias, WtE Design Lab; data from Watkins et al., *Use of Economic Instruments and Waste Management*, 55; and Swedish Waste Management, *Assessment of Increased Trade of Combustible Waste in the European Union*, 12, 16.

79 (bottom): WtE Design Lab.

81: Hemmendinger, Georgoulias, and Zach Seibold, WtE Design Lab (Note: 2008 data was used for some states); data from Shin, "Generation and Disposition of MSW in the United States," table 4.

82: Hemmendinger and Georgoulias, WtE Design Lab (Note: average remaining life of landfill calculated as remaining MSW landfill capacity [2010] divided by average MSW landfilled per year from 2000–2010); data from *Waste Business Journal* 2011.

83 (top): Hemmendinger and Georgoulias, WtE Design Lab; data from Ted Michaels, *2014 ERC Directory of Waste-to-Energy Facilities* (Energy Recovery Council, 2014), 6, http://energyrecoverycouncil.org/wp-content/uploads/2016/01/ERC_2014 _ Directory.pdf).

83 (middle, bottom): Hemmendinger and Georgoulias, WtE Design Lab (Note: data from 2003); data from Edward W. Repa, "Interstate Movement of Municipal Solid Waste," *NSWMA Research Bulletin* 05-2, 2005, https://wasterecycling.org/images/documents/ our-work/advocacy-issues/Interstate-Waste-2005.pdf; and James McCarthy, *Interstate Shipment of Municipal Solid Waste*, update, (Congressional Research Service, 2007), table 1, research.policyarchive.org/18953.pdf.

85 (top): Hemmendinger and Georgoulias, WtE Design Lab; data from Avfall Sverige, *Swedish Waste Management 2014*, 4; and Avfall Sverige, *The Swedish Waste Management System* (Malmö, Sweden, 2013), 12, http://www.avfallssverige.se/fileadmin /uploads/ swedish_waste_management_130910.pptx.

85 (bottom): Hemmendinger and Georgoulias, WtE Design Lab; data from US EPA, *Municipal Solid Waste Generation*, table 30.

86: Hemmendinger and Georgoulias, WtE Design Lab; data from US EPA, *Municipal Solid Waste Generation*, table 30; Avfall Sverige, *Swedish Waste Management 2014*, 4; and Avfall Sverige, *The Swedish Waste Management System*, 12.

87: Hemmendinger and Georgoulias, WtE Design Lab; data from Eurostat, "Municipal Waste Statistics"; US EPA, *Municipal Solid Waste Generation,* table 30 (converted to kg per year).

90: Georgios Athanasopoulos, Hemmendinger, Smead, and Seibold, WtE Design Lab; data from Avfall Sverige, *Swedish Waste Management 2014*, 5; Avfall Sverige, *The Swedish Waste Management System*, 9, 29, 31, 38, 39; OECD, *OECD Factbook 2014: Economic, Environmental, and Social Statistics* (OECD Publishing, 2014),

13, http://dx.doi.org/10.1787/factbook-2014-70-en; and International Energy Agency (IEA) Database, http://www.iea.org/statistics/ statisticssearch/.

91: Athanasopoulos, Hemmendinger, Smead, and Seibold, WtE Design Lab; data from US EPA, *Municipal Solid Waste Generation*; OECD, *OECD Factbook 2014*, 3; and Nicholas Themelis and Charles Mussche, *Energy and Economic Value of Municipal Solid Waste (MSW), including Non-Recycled Plastics (NRP), Currently Landfilled in the Fifty States* (New York: Columbia University, 2012), http://www. american-chemistry.com/Policy/Energy/Energy-Recovery/2014-Update-of-Potential-for-En-ergy-Recovery-from-Municipal-Solid-Waste-and-Non-Recycled-Plastics.pdf. (Note: Themelis and Mussche's data from 2011 is higher than that reported by the US EPA; see Shin, "Generation and Disposition of MSW in the United States," for a possible explanation.)

92: Athanasopoulos, Hemmendinger, Smead, and Seibold, WtE Design Lab; data from Eurostat, "Municipal Waste Statistics"; CEWEP, "Waste-to-Energy in Europe in 2012"; and converted from IEA database for energy generated from municipal waste for the EU-27. Note: household heating and electricity rates were proportional to Sweden's energy rates (assumes district heating); waste plant numbers exclude countries not in the EU-27 including Norway, Switzerland, and Croatia; and as of 2013, Europe in total has 456 WtE plants. Conservation data from Themelis and Mussche, *Energy and Economic Value of MSW*, 31. Heat and electricity data is based on gross electric and heat production from municipal waste, with statistics converted to TWh from statistics for the EU-28 in 2012; see IEA database. Extraction data is difficult to estimate accurately; see Themelis and Mussche, *Energy and Economic Value of MSW*, 25; and T. Fruergaard, T. H. Christensen, and T. Astrup, "Energy Recovery from Waste Incineration: Assessing the Importance of District Heating Networks," *Waste Management* vol. 30, no. 7: 1264–72, http://dx.doi. org/10.1016/j. enpol.2014.08.001. For data on reducing CO_2 emissions, see Avfall Sverige, *Assessment of Increased Trade of Combustible Waste in the European Union*, report F2012:04 (Malmö, Sweden, 2012), 16, http://www.av-fallsverige.se/fileadmin/uploads/Rapporter/F%C3%B6rbr%C3%A4nning/F2012-04.pdf; and Themelis and Mussche, *Energy and Economic Value of MSW*, 30. The EU sample is more efficient than the US sample; see OECD, *OECD Factbook 2014*.

93: Smead, WtE Design Lab; data from Hoornweg and Bhada-Tata, *What a Waste*, Annex J; see figures on 90–92.

96, 98, 100–108, 110–113, 115–116, 119–12: WtE Design Lab.

99, 114, 124: Alkistis Mavroeidi, WtE Design Lab.

109: Elaine Kwong, WtE Design Lab.

THE ARCHITECT AND WASTE-TO-ENERGY DESIGN

128: Skitterphoto, Pixelbay, Public Domain.

130: Ábalos, Herreros, and Sentkiewicz.

132: Georgios Athanasopoulos, WtE Design Lab.

135: ©Oran Viriyincy, Flickr, cc by-sa 2.0, https://www.flickr.com/photos/ viriyincy/7004881064.

137: ©Jacco van Giessen, Flickr, cc by nd-2.0, https://www.flickr.com/ photos/45609060@N00/4362403607.

139: WtE Design Lab.

143: Andreas Georgoulias, Ethan Levine, and Aman Singhvi, WtE Design Lab. Plants used for the creation of the charts include facilities in Roskilde, Barcelona, Copenhagen, Begles, Giubiasco, Minneapolis, Leeds, Palm Beach, Hiroshima, Oxfordshire, Buckinghamshire, Cardiff, and Suffolk. Data comes from research encapsulated in the "Waste-To-Energy Primer" section of this text. Further information is available on the individual plants' websites; International Energy Agency and Nuclear Energy Agency, "Projected Costs of Generating Electricity," 2015 ed., August 31, 2015; and Simon Rawlinson and Matthew Hicks, "Cost Model: Energy from Waste," *Building Magazine*, April 23, 2010, 54–59.

146: ©NAC, Wikimedia Commons, cc by-sa 3.0, https://commons.wikimedia.org/wiki /File:Inceneritore_Giubiasco_140314.jpg.

147: Spittelau Waste Incineration Plant: ©Lukas Riebling, Wikimedia Commons, cc by-sa 3.0, https://commons.wikimedia.org/wiki/File:Hunderwasser_Fernheizwerk.JPG.
Chaux-de-Fonds Waste-to-Energy Plant, Calce Incineration Plant, Rouen Waste Processing Plant: WtE Design Lab.
Rotterdam Waste-to-Energy Plant: ©Jacco van Giessen, Flickr, cc by nd-2.0, https: //www.flickr.com/photos/45609060@N00/4362403607.
Marchwood Energy Recovery Facility: ©Peter Facey, Wikimedia Commons, cc by-sa 2.0, https://commons.wikimedia.org/wiki/File:Marchwood_Incinerator_-_geograph .org. uk_-_1072047.jpg.
Northeast Coastal Park Waste Plant: Ábalos, Herreros, and Sentkiewicz.
Uppsala Block 5 CHP: ©Holger Ellgaard, Wikimedia Commons, cc by-sa 3.0, https: //commons.wikimedia.org/wiki/File:Uppsala_Block_5,_2010b.jpg.
Giubiasco Incinerator: ©NAC, Wikimedia Commons, cc by-sa 3.0, https://commons .wikimedia.org/wiki/File:Inceneritore_Giubiasco_140314.jpg.
Kara/Noveren Thermal Power Plant: Erick vanEgeraat.
Veolia Energy Recovery Center: Veolia/Jean Robert Mazaud, S'PACE Architecture.
Amager Bakke Resource Center: Bjarke Ingels Group.

150, 151, 154, 157–158, 160, 161: Ábalos, Herreros, and Sentkiewicz.

152–153: Elaine Kwong and Ethan Levine, WtE Design Lab; Ábalos, Herreros, and Sentkiewicz.

162, 166–167: Studio Vacchini.

164–165: Elaine Kwong and Ethan Levine, WtE Design Lab; Studio Vacchini.

Author Biographies

HANIF KARA

Hanif Kara is a London-based structural engineer and educator. Since cofounding Adams Kara Taylor (1996), his interests in innovative form, material use, and complex analysis methods have allowed him to work on award-winning and unique projects. Between 2008 and 2011 he was professor of architectural technology at KTH in Stockholm, Sweden, and he is currently professor in practice of architectural technology at the Harvard University Graduate School of Design (GSD). Hanif is a fellow of RAE, RIBA, ICE, and IStructE, and he serves on the board of trustees of the Architecture Foundation, as a commissioner for the Commission for Architecture and Built Environment (CABE), and on the steering committee for the Aga Khan Awards for Architecture. Notable publications include *Design Engineering* (2008) and *Interdisciplinary Design: New Lessons from Architecture and Engineering* (with Andreas Georgoulias, 2011).

LEIRE ASENSIO VILLORIA

Leire Asensio Villoria is a registered architect in Spain and studied architecture at the ETSASS and the Architectural Association (AA), where she received her diploma in architecture with honors. She has taught at the Harvard GSD since 2010 and previously at the AA and Cornell University. Since 2002, Leire has collaborated with David Syn Chee Mah as asensio_mah. Together Leire and David were design research coordinators for the prototypes design research team of Harvard University's Health and Places Initiative (a collaboration between the GSD and the TH Chan School of Public Health) from 2014 to 2016. Publications include *Lifestyled: Health and Places* (with Mah, 2015), and *Platform* 7 (2014).

ANDREAS GEORGOULIAS

Andreas Georgoulias works with the private and public sectors worldwide on sustainable urban development and infrastructures. He teaches at the Harvard GSD and is research director of the Zofnass Program for Sustainable Infrastructure. His work focuses on infrastructure and large-scale developments. Current projects include the Infrastructure 360 Awards with the Inter-American Development Bank, and the Zofnass Economic Tool. Andreas previously worked with Obermeyer, Hochtief, and US General Service Administration, and in infrastructure financing with UniCredit Markets and Investment Banking. His books include *Infrastructure Sustainability and Design* (with Spiro Pollalis, Stephen Ramos, and Daniel Schodek, 2010), and *Interdisciplinary Design* (with Hanif Kara, 2011).

LAURE SMEAD

Laura Smead is the town planner for Canton, Massachusetts. After receiving her degree in urban and environmental policy and planning from Tufts University in 2014, she served as a research associate at the Harvard Graduate School of Design's Waste-to-Energy Design Lab and Health and Places Initiative. Her accomplishments include research, writing, and production support for three publications, including coauthoring *Creating Healthy Neighborhoods: Evidence-based Planning and Design Strategies* (2017).

ARCHITECTURE AND WASTE:
A (RE)PLANNED OBSOLESCENCE

By Hanif Kara, Leyre Asensio Villoria, amd Andreas Georgoulias

Published by
Actar Publishers
Harvard University Graduate School of Design

Editor and Project Manager
A. Krista Sykes

Proofreader
Ophelia John

Graphic Design
Ramon Prat Homs

ISBN 978-1-945150-05-0
Library of Congress Control Number: 2016958863

Harvard University
Graduate School of Design

ACTAR